LAURA'S GHOST

Women Speak about Twin Peaks

T0307095

LAURA'S GHOST

Women Speak about Twin Peaks

Courtenay Stallings

Book designed by Scott Ryan
Cover and back cover designed by Natalie Rulon
Front cover photo by permission of ABC Photo Archives © ABC/Getty
Images
Back cover art by Jill Watson
Back cover author's photo by Amy T. Zielinski
Edited by David Bushman, Elizabeth Smith
Photos of each interviewee courtesy of each person

Published in the USA by Fayetteville Mafia Press
Columbus, Ohio

Contact Information
Email: fayettevillemafiapress@gmail.com
Website: fayettevillemafiapress.com

ISBN: 9781949024081
eBook ISBN: 9781949024098

For Laura and Sheryl
and women everywhere

CONTENTS

Art by Geneva Rougier

Foreword
by
Sheryl Lee

<u>Dear Laura</u>

Laura, Laura, Laura
A ghost of me, you are
For one who did not want to live
You are never very far

A soul lost deep in trouble
You gave my art a name
But if I did it all again
I might not do it
quite the same

Pulled down from heavens' ethers
You arrived to share my life
I instilled your death with purpose
you left me with your knife

I take it out from time to time
Run fingers down smooth blade
Is my destiny the same as yours
Or do I
    Just
        Simply
            Fade?

Dear, sweet Laura
My doorway into death
Alive and yet not living
In this play
I am your guest

I offered you myself to use
In expression of your light
And in exchange
Was tricked quite well
When you rewrote my rites

Fair, you say
Do I not agree?
Your fame
After all
Did rub off on me

It isn't what I wanted tho
or wished for
Had I known
I wanted back my freedom

my existence
as my own

but you my friend
had different dreams than mine
and lifetimes later
we are stuck in time

lingering on
in this story of ours
Caught somewhere between
My earth
and your stars

As an image is reflected back to us on the surface of still water, so too is the character of Laura Palmer a reflection of the millions of women and children who have suffered in the hands of abuse . . .
  a collective ocean of suffering.

My hope is that expression of this pain becomes a great river of healing waters with the connecting energy of beautiful streams, branching creaks and winding tributaries reaching out to quench the thirst of those still in need.

Courtenay, the women of this book, and all of those I've met along the path of my life who have so bravely dared to tell their stories
are the ever-flowing droplets that keep these waters flowing.

May Laura's story continue to offer strength to the wounded who witness it.
                                    You are not alone.

Introduction

"It encompasses the all. It is beyond the fire, though few would know that meaning. It is a story of many but begins with one, and I knew her. The one leading to the many is Laura Palmer." - Margaret Lanterman, The Log Lady[1]

"I want to be haunted by the ghost. I want to be haunted by the ghost of your precious love." - The Pogues[2]

This book is a ghost story. Ghost stories by their very nature contain supernatural characters who haunt. In *Twin Peaks*, the character Laura Palmer is dead yet she lives—as some form of her proclaims in the liminal space of the Red Room in *Twin Peaks*. Laura functions as a ghost within the canon of *Twin Peaks* and outside of it. She haunts us, the viewers. Ghost stories help us express our fears, anxieties, and resentments over societal restrictions. The ghost is the ultimate outsider, "an absent presence, all-seeing and yet unable to partake of life in any meaningful way. . . . Whatever women repress, ghost stories suggest, will eventually come back to haunt if not them, then those who colluded in keeping them downtrodden."[3] A ghost story is about exorcising repression. It's allowing what is dead, what is forbidden, to speak. This book is a ghost story. This is *Laura's Ghost*.

---

1   From The Log Lady intros. "Pilot," *Twin Peaks*. Written and directed by David Lynch.

2   The Pogues, "Haunted," track #2 on *Sid & Nancy* Soundtrack, 1986, Vinyl and Cassette.

3   Hephzibah Anderson, "The Secret Meaning of Ghost Stories," BBC, Jan. 22, 2016.

In 1990, the groundbreaking television series *Twin Peaks*, cocreated by David Lynch and Mark Frost, opened with a murder mystery when a beautiful homecoming queen, wrapped in plastic, washed up on a cold and rocky beach. Laura Palmer's death triggers a small town to face its fractured self. David Lynch and Mark Frost pitched the idea for the show, which was originally titled *Northwest Passage*, in 1988. Mark Frost said, "We knew it was going to be some kind of serial about the murder of a homecoming queen, and the first image we had was of a dead body washing up on the shore of a lake."[4] Frost has said he was inspired by the mysterious death of Hazel Drew, a twenty-year-old real-life New Yorker who was murdered more than one hundred years ago.[5] Art imitates life.

Initially, Laura Palmer was a MacGuffin who functioned as an object in the story that would serve to reveal how the small town of Twin Peaks was not so innocent after all. On the surface, *Twin Peaks* appeared to be the new nightly soap opera, a sort of twisted take on the nighttime soap that was so popular in the 1980s. Shows like *Dallas* and *Dynasty* accrued high ratings but were waning in fandom by the time *Twin Peaks* arrived. However, Lynch and Frost were telling a different kind of story here, subverting the usual formulas of television in a way that would inspire other groundbreaking shows in the future, like *Lost*. David Lynch scholar Martha Nochimson argues Lynch did not pursue the "low level of formula mystery stories that close down our perception of the world."[6] Instead, Lynch sought to show the "cosmic ramifications of Laura Palmer's death."[7] *Twin Peaks* is a spiritual story.

Before her tragic death, the homecoming queen spent her days volunteering for Meals on Wheels, tutoring Josie Packard in English, caring for Johnny Horne, and being chased by every teenage boy and

4   David Lynch and Kristine McKenna, *Room to Dream* (New York: Random House, 2018), 247.

5   David Bushman and Mark Givens, "Hazel Drew: The Original Blue Rose Case," *The Blue Rose*, June 2017, 18.

6   Martha Nochimson, "David Lynch: Twin Peaks," *Television Rewired: The Rise of the Auteur Series* (Austin: University of Texas Press, 2019), 33.

7   Ibid.

lecherous old man on the block. On the surface, Laura Palmer had it all: beauty, intelligence, goodwill, adoration. But Laura Palmer was in a dark place well before BOB kidnapped her and carried her off to her death in an abandoned boxcar in the dark woods. In the series, we soon learn she had a cocaine problem, and, eventually, we discover she was sexually abused.

Laura Palmer became instrumental to the series at-large. Her character was developed beyond the MacGuffin. Jennifer Lynch's book, *The Secret Diary of Laura Palmer*, was crucial in defining the character. In my interview with Sheryl Lee, she told me she created a backstory for Laura before Jennifer Lynch wrote the book. After she read Lynch's work, she said, she realized there was quite a bit of overlap. The diary was published in the summer of 1990. Young girls, including myself, devoured its contents. We wanted to know if Laura Palmer was like us. It turns out, in many ways, she was.

When David Lynch approached Jennifer Lynch to write the diary, he asked her if she remembered a conversation they had when Jennifer was only twelve. Jennifer had told her father she really wanted to steal another girl's diary. She said, "I wanted to know if she was scared of the same things I was, if she was yearning for the same things I was."[8] Jennifer Lynch said, "Like all other adolescent girls, I was afraid."[9] Jennifer Lynch said that the story of Laura Palmer is "perhaps the most real story about child abuse ever made."

In Episode 16 of the series, when Sheriff Harry Truman is grappling with the idea of the supernatural killer BOB inhabiting Leland Palmer, Agent Dale Cooper responds, "Harry, is it easier to believe a man would rape and kill his own daughter? Any more comforting?" It is not. That's one of the reasons why many viewers found the 1992 film *Twin Peaks: Fire Walk With Me* so discomforting. The film engages with incest directly. Before *Twin Peaks*, films such as *Chinatown* (1974) and TV movies like *Something about Amelia* (1984) explored incest

---

8   Courtenay Stallings, "USC *Twin Peaks* Series Retrospective, May 5," *Red Room Podcast*, May 7, 2013.

9   Ibid.

between father and daughter, but there is no work that confronts the topic quite like *Fire Walk With Me*.

The Darkest Secret of Twin Peaks

Twin Peaks is a world filled with secrets. But there is one secret at the center of *Twin Peaks* that is its deepest, darkest secret: the sexual abuse and murder of Laura Palmer by her father. When *Fire Walk With Me* premiered, some of the reviews were scathing. *New York Times* critic Vincent Canby wrote, "It's not the worst movie ever made; it just seems to be."[10] Many fans of the TV series had a viscerally unfavorable reaction to the film, which concentrated on the last days of Laura Palmer's troubled life and did not include the quirky, more lighthearted moments—the idiosyncrasies of the TV series that appealed to the cherry-pie-and-doughnut crowd.

Chris Rodley, in his book *Lynch on Lynch*, writes that perhaps so many fans of the series rejected the film because "the movie reminded people that at the center of *Twin Peaks* was a story of incest and filicide."[11] This is why *Fire Walk With Me* was groundbreaking—it revealed both the physical and spiritual trauma of childhood sexual abuse. The realism of Laura's abuse continues to resonate with many, including survivors. The supernatural coding made the sexual abuse easier to talk about without it being stigmatized.

In her book *Twin Peaks: Fire Walk With Me* (part of the Devil's Advocates series on film and television), scholar Lindsay Hallam argues the movie can be experienced in different ways: as a *Twin Peaks* film, as a horror film, as a film about trauma, and as a David Lynch film. In the section on trauma, Hallam points out how the home is often the site of horror where the family unit breaks down. *Fire Walk With Me* in particular stresses this as the camera intrudes on Leland psychologically tormenting his daughter to wash her hands while she sits at the dining room table, and then, in one of the most disturbing scenes in the film, when BOB, as he is raping Laura in her own bedroom, reveals

---

10   Vincent Canby, "Review/Film: One Last Gasp for Laura Palmer," *New York Times*, Aug. 29, 1992.

11   Chris Rodley, *Lynch on Lynch* (London: Faber and Faber, 2005), 185.

to her that he is really Leland, her father. Hallam argues, "Here we are confronted with the central truth that the television series could not quite face, but which the film, through the employment of genre conventions, finally reveals."[12] The reality of the trauma that sexual abuse victims endured is ironically revealed with unprecedented power through the use of supernatural coding and horror tropes.

In *Fire Walk With Me*, Laura Palmer's character fits the profile of a sexual abuse victim. According to the Rape, Abuse & Incest National Network (RAINN), the nation's largest anti-sexual-violence organization, "every 8 minutes, child protective services substantiates, or finds evidence for, a claim of child sexual abuse."[13] Of all victims under the age of eighteen, two out of three are ages twelve to seventeen, and 82 percent of victims under the age of eighteen are female. The effects of child sexual abuse can be long-lasting and affect the victim's mental and physical health. Perpetrators of child sexual abuse are often related to the victim, and 80 percent of perpetrators are a parent, according to RAINN.

Laura was only twelve when the abuse began. In the TV series, the audience discovers it was BOB/her father who was the abuser, although the series never clarifies whether the abuser is actually her father or some supernatural demonic entity that has possessed him, or both. Finally, in *Fire Walk With Me*, the audience actually witnesses Leland Palmer (and not some supernatural metaphoric manifestation of the demon inside him) raping his own daughter when his face is revealed to Laura. The scene is jarring because the supernatural entity of BOB is revealed to be her own father. Sheryl Lee said the scene in the bed was the most challenging scene to shoot because, even though the actors and filmmakers created a safe space for her, it was difficult for her to think about how that same abuse happens every day to young girls. She said that's the part that haunts her.

The viewer sees the abuse through Laura's eyes, which magnifies the horror. Sheryl Lee bares Laura's soul—the pain, the sadness, the

12   Lindsay Hallam, *Twin Peaks: Fire Walk With Me* (Devil's Advocates) (London: Auteur, 2018), 84.

13   Rape, Abuse & Incest National Network, www.rainn.org.

confusion, and the rage. *Fire Walk With Me* re-creates the trauma that sexual abuse victims endure. The father's betrayal of his role as protector manifests itself in the terrifying entity of supernatural BOB. The ceiling fan at the top of the stairs, an iconic symbol borrowed from the TV show, becomes the literal mechanism for silencing Leland's abuse of his daughter but also a sign of the transgression of the spiritual boundary between father and daughter.

Fire Walk With Me forced its audience to confront Laura's abuse by her own father as well as the community's silence and denial. Author and scholar Randi Davenport argues, "By sympathetically focusing its audience's attention on the sexual victimization of women, *Twin Peaks* demands that its audience understand not just that sexual violence occurs, but that our culture tolerates a range of practices that serve to authorize violence against women."[14] In the TV series, during Laura's funeral, Bobby Briggs blames the entire town for her death: "Everybody knew she was in trouble, but we didn't do anything. All you good people. You want to know who killed Laura? You did! We all did." Sheryl Lee said she wondered why no one in the community recognized Laura's desperation. "Why didn't anyone do anything to help? There were signs everywhere. There were symptoms of how much pain this girl was in. And the other thing is, how many men were involved in her destruction?" Lee said.

The Missing Pieces, released on the 2014 Blu-ray *Twin Peaks: The Entire Mystery*, functions on one level as scenes literally deleted from the film *Fire Walk With Me*, but on another level the "missing pieces" are the clues to Laura's abuse that are so evident to the audience but not to those closest to her, or at least that those closest to her choose to ignore. And there are many missed opportunities to help Laura. If Sheriff Truman had not told Andy to stop following Jacques Renault, the deputy might have tailed him to the cabin the night when Leland/BOB kidnaps Laura and murders her. The scene is striking because there is a lingering moment of quiet after the exchange, which seems to suggest something has transpired—the opportunity to save Laura

---

14   Randi Davenport, "The Knowing Spectator of 'Twin Peaks': Culture, Feminism, and Family Violence," *Literature/Film Quarterly*, Vol. 21, no 4 (1993), PP. 255-259.

is gone. The audience knows this, but the men do not, although the silence perhaps indicates that on some deeper level they recognize that there are ramifications beyond the obvious.

Another opportunity to save Laura presents itself in a touching scene where Doc Hayward presents a message to Laura and says, "This isn't a prescription. It's a message. 'The angels will return, and when you see the one that's meant to help you, you will weep with joy.'" This moment is important. But no one in this scene takes the opportunity to confront Laura about the message's meaning. Sheryl Lee said, "I do believe that if a person would have intervened with Laura she would have made it. She wanted to make it . . . she was a survivor." Perhaps that person could have been Doc Hayward, the physician who was there at her birth but could not prevent her death, let alone her abuse. And so, Laura is resigned to keeping her abuse secret.

In *Fire Walk With Me*, the audience witnesses the slow erosion of Laura's "good" side. As *Twin Peaks* scholar John Thorne (*Wrapped in Plastic*) argues, "But this good side is never extinguished; Laura manages to keep the evil forces (led, apparently, by BOB) at bay. She does this by never physically hurting another person. She refuses to allow 'them' to use her as a means of inflicting pain on another. This is crucial."[15] Instead of hurting others, Laura turns the violence on herself through drugs and sex.

Post-traumatic stress as a result of incest can manifest itself through many coping mechanisms, including self-injury, substance abuse, eating disorders, disassociation, and promiscuity.[16] Laura is addicted to cocaine, drinks excessively, and has sex with a lot of men (including some for money). Her drug usage was not usual teenage experimentation, but a means to self-medicate. "The fact that Laura Palmer sought medication, no matter how dubious, was actually a positive sign," the character Dr. Jacoby tells Agent Cooper. Laura Palmer was trying to survive.

Laura Palmer does not survive, but she ultimately prevents BOB

---

15   John Thorne, *The Essential Wrapped in Plastic* (Thorne, 2016), 273.

16   Susanne Babbel, "Trauma: Incest," *Psychology Today*, Feb. 7, 2013.

from possessing her. What is most striking about her resistance to BOB is that she does what her father could not—end the cycle of familial violence. In the television series, the audience learns that Leland Palmer first came into contact with BOB when he was a child visiting his grandfather at Pearl Lakes. Unlike her father, Laura never allows BOB in and breaks the cycle of abuse by sacrificing her own life.

Laura had secrets. And, according to Dr. Jacoby, "around those secrets she built the fortress that, well, in my six months with her, I was not able to penetrate and for which I consider myself an abject failure." Many sexual assaults are not reported to the police. In those not reported to police from 2005-2010, 20 percent of the victims said they feared retaliation, and 13 percent believed the police would not do anything. "The biggest immediate help you can offer to a victim of incest is to listen with respect and compassion . . . and belief. In other words, the first step is always to believe the victim," according to RAINN.[17] Perhaps Laura didn't tell anyone because she didn't think anyone would believe her.

Agent Cooper says, "Secrets are dangerous things." He is correct. It's troubling that Laura Palmer, like so many victims of sexual abuse, felt she could not speak about what was happening to her. But there is hope in Laura's story—her guardian angel, who had vanished earlier in the *Fire Walk With Me* but reappears at the end. Sheryl Lee said, "I always think of that angel at the end. For me that was the peace that needed to happen after that. There needed to be peace after that horror."

Perhaps Laura Palmer's legacy after *Fire Walk With Me* is that her character and Sheryl Lee's performance of that character empowered so many with the ability to speak about their abuse. "I would hope that the legacy is we can finally start talking about this, so that we can do something about sexual abuse," Sheryl Lee said.

Laura's Ghost

A ghost who haunts can mean multiple things. In one sense, it is a literal manifestation of someone who has died but who persists. Figuratively, a

---

17   www.rainn.org.

ghost who haunts stays with us, perpetually in our mind and thoughts. Laura Palmer's ghost wouldn't leave me alone. I couldn't stop thinking about her. And I reckoned I wasn't the only woman who couldn't get her out of her mind. So I wrote this book, in which women, and only women, speak about Laura, *Twin Peaks*, and how it all connects to themselves. At the heart of ghost stories is the desire to confront our greatest fears and repressions and, in doing so, exorcise those fears and repressions. Laura Palmer haunts so many of us because we see ourselves in her story. By acknowledging the parts of ourselves in her story, we free the ghost. We help others by freeing ourselves. I am a survivor of childhood sexual abuse. I bear witness to Laura's story because in it I see my own, and I know I am not alone.

Laura Palmer is a fictional character, but she is still very real to many. For the cover of this book, I did not want to use an image of Laura Palmer dead, wrapped in plastic. Nor did I want to use the iconic image of Laura as the homecoming queen that ends up becoming smeared with blood after her parents, Leland and Sarah Palmer, wrestle over it. I didn't want an image of Laura associated with blood or death. Instead, I chose the image of Laura Palmer in happier days, dancing with her best friend on the crest of a pine-lined hill, a great picnic feast spread out at their feet, while her lover gazes at their shared joy. This was Laura Palmer alive. This is how we wish we could keep her—free of dark forces and death in a boxcar, with a reassuring angel appearing in Red Room liminality.

I interviewed several women crucial to the story of *Twin Peaks* and Laura Palmer, including Sheryl Lee, who performed the characters of Laura Palmer, Maddy Ferguson, Carrie Page, and the mysterious entity in the Red Room. It was important to me for readers to hear from Sheryl Lee herself about how this role inspired her and haunts her still in good ways and bad. Grace Zabriskie, who portrayed Sarah Palmer, spent hours with me providing such incredible insight into her career as an actor, poet, and artist. In this book, we engage in a contretemps about Sarah Palmer's complicity in the abuse of her daughter. And Jennifer Lynch discusses writing the character of Laura Palmer in *The Secret Diary of Laura Palmer*, which became foundational for Lee's interpretation of the character and, of course, *Twin Peaks: Fire Walk*

With Me. I also interviewed executive producer Sabrina S. Sutherland, who has been with *Twin Peaks* since the original series and was crucial in the production of Season 3. Sutherland has been the voice for Lynch to the *Twin Peaks* fan community at festivals and events.

In exploring Laura Palmer's legacy, I also spoke with twenty-six women from the *Twin Peaks* fan community. These women represent a cross section of *Twin Peaks* fans. I chose to focus on women because women seem to uniquely understand Laura Palmer. Not every woman endures sexual or physical abuse, but women know what it's like not to be believed simply because of their experience being women. Many of the women I interviewed talked about Laura's agency and whether she had any at all or had it in the moment she chose to die rather than give her body and soul to BOB. Women know what it's like to endure the threat of danger from men every single day. Women know what it's like to see your potential cut down, in large ways and in small ways. Laura Palmer was one of the first complex women I saw on screen. Women are complex, creative, and fascinating people. Let's hear them speak about themselves and Laura Palmer.

In the following pages I invite you in to confront Laura's ghost and to bear witness. See you on the other side.

Part I:
Women Speak

Women Speak

"She's dead, wrapped in plastic."[1] - Pete Martell

When Phoebe Augustine recalled the scene in the *Twin Peaks* pilot where her character, Ronette Pulaski, walks across the bridge after emerging from a train car having just witnessed the death throes of Laura Palmer, she said the whole crew was standing at the end of the bridge as she walked toward them. Her body tensed up when she saw, among the crew, at the end of the track, a man in denim with long gray hair and a beard. She told Lynch there was one guy in the crew who was making her afraid, but she wasn't sure why. It turns out it was Frank Silva—the man who would eventually be plucked from the crew to play BOB, after an on-set happy accident. When she asked Lynch who the longhaired man was, Lynch said, "He's the bad guy, but don't tell anyone."[2] BOB was present at the very beginning of *Twin Peaks* even if he wasn't on paper or on film. There's a strange thing about *Twin Peaks*: art gets entangled with life. Augustine recognized BOB before anyone really knew who BOB was. My favorite part about this story is how David Lynch didn't dismiss her intuition. He listened. He confirmed. He *believed*. *Twin Peaks* is more than just a television show and film. It's cosmic. It's spiritual. It inspires. It haunts.

The image of Ronette, bloody and in torn clothes, stumbling across the train tracks in the brutal cold is haunting. Some have accused

---

1   David Lynch and Mark Frost, "Pilot," *Twin Peaks*, directed by David Lynch, April 8, 1990.

2   Courtenay Stallings, "USC Twin Peaks Series Retrospective, May 5," *Red Room Podcast*, May 7, 2013.

David Lynch of misogyny over the years because of his stark and brutal portrayal of violence against women. But this frank and aesthetic portrayal is the reason why many women are his biggest fans. Often, violence against women becomes fetishized. The horror becomes lost in the obsessive cinematic portrayal of women in pain. But many women respond positively to Lynch's portrayal of violence and women because the characters' humanity is never eclipsed by the violence that happens to them.

Mark Frost and David Lynch created a number of powerful and complex women for *Twin Peaks*, including Catherine Martell, Josie Packard, The Log Lady, Audrey Horne, and, of course, Laura Palmer. The representation of women is not perfect, particularly when it comes to women of color, but, especially in the original series, produced in the early 1990s, the women are fascinating and more layered than other female TV characters of the time.

David Lynch doesn't just write complex women, he employs them—and not simply in front of the camera, but behind the scenes as well. Sabrina S. Sutherland has served as Lynch's producer and right-hand woman for many years. Cori Glazer has been the script supervisor on many of Lynch's works. Noriko Miyakawa has edited Lynch's works for years. These women are in powerful positions usually held by men, but Lynch trusts them, listens to them, and allows them a seat at the table.

In this part of the book, women speak about themselves. Sheryl Lee, Grace Zabriskie, Sabrina S. Sutherland, and Jennifer Lynch, all women who have worked with Lynch closely, discuss their careers and their experiences working on *Twin Peaks*. Then, women from the fan community talk about their connection to *Twin Peaks* as well as their own unique experiences as women in this world, which are wonderful and strange.

'Haunts'

Sheryl Lee

S heryl Lee is not Laura Palmer, but she is haunted by her.
Lee, an accomplished theater, film, and television actor, was thrust into fame at a young age when David Lynch and Mark Frost cast her in the role of the dead homecoming queen in the *Twin Peaks* series pilot, which premiered on April 8, 1990. Lee's first performance as Laura Palmer began with her having to lie perfectly still, barely clothed, and wrapped in plastic for hours on a cold and rocky beach off the Puget Sound, surrounded by a mostly male crew.

Lee, hired for only one day, thought her role in *Twin Peaks* was over and done, but she was called to return as Laura Palmer, alive and on videotape—an analogue ghost frolicking at a picnic with her best friend, Donna Hayward, while her boyfriend James Hurley watches. Sheryl Lee could not escape *Twin Peaks*. She was called back again to play Laura's cousin, Maddy Ferguson, raven-haired and nearsighted.

But what Lee is most remembered for is her portrayal of Laura Palmer during the last days of Laura's tragic life in the 1992 film *Fire Walk With Me*. This is the role that would make her career and nearly break her at the same time. *Twin Peaks* made Lee famous, but she's had a remarkable career as an actor, writer, and teacher outside of the franchise. She's performed in numerous television shows, with recurring roles in *Kingpin*, *L.A. Doctors*, *One Tree Hill*, and *Dirty Sexy Money*. She's appeared in many films aside from *Fire Walk With Me*, including *Wild at Heart*, *Backbeat*, *Vampires*, and the award-winning and critically acclaimed *Winter's Bone*. Despite a long and multifaceted career, Sheryl Lee will forever be known for her connection to *Twin Peaks* as the tragic character Laura Palmer.

How did you get cast as Laura Palmer?

Sheryl Lee: I got cast while I was living in Seattle. I didn't grow up there, but I moved there to study theater. There was a director there who I wanted to work with who was training actors to start a theater company. I also had an agent for commercials or videos or anything that came to town. My understanding is that David saw an eight-by-ten headshot in the agent's office through the casting director. I got a phone call to come in and meet him. It was all very secretive. I was probably only nineteen or twenty at that time. I knew who he was. I was familiar with his work. I was intimidated and nervous to meet him, but he was so kind—immediately just warm and funny. He's such an interesting artist, because he has a way of exploring the darkest parts of our shadow selves, and yet he is so light as a human . . . a true gentleman. He makes everyone around him smile.

Your character is initially cast as this woman who is dead and wrapped in plastic. Then you play Laura Palmer who is alive and on videotape from the picnic. And, there are moments of the show

where Laura Palmer is in the Red Room. When you played Laura Palmer in the Red Room or other scenes in the original series, what guided you as an actor when you didn't have a lot of context?

Sheryl Lee: I was in really good hands. Anything that was a flashback was guided by David. I knew the essence of her and what David wanted in those scenes. This was my first television role, so I was new to all of it. I relied on those who were more experienced than I was, like Lara Flynn Boyle in those flashback scenes in the pilot. She was so experienced by that time already. She was great with me and just funny. Immediately I connected with her and felt comfortable, and out of that could come this backstory.

The Red Room, in a way, is like a different aspect of Laura. It's a different aspect of life, right? It's not reality as we know it on this plane of existence. It has different rules, or no rules. In order to enter the Red Room (or any time I work with David), I have to take a logical part of my brain and surrender it and set it aside so that I can walk into this world of his. It's an incredible experience creatively. Every single time I went into that Red Room, I did not know what was going to happen there. But I know that I am going to stretch and grow and creatively get to do things I would never get to do anywhere else.

Before you got to really dig into playing Laura Palmer, you were cast as Maddy Ferguson. How did you prepare to play her character?

Sheryl Lee: For Maddy, I had to find the difference in them, because that was the only way I could separate them. Laura already had multiple sides to her. She was already complex. So to add another character into it, she had to be so clearly defined to me that I could distinguish between the two. Physically, she had different hair color, the glasses, the clothes. I had to alter her voice enough and change her body language so that I felt inside her—the way she moved, the way she sat.

It is so apparent in watching it that this is a different character, but they are related. It's not just the physical appearance, of course, because it's the same actor, but there are traits that make them

relatable to each other. How much of you is in Maddy?

Sheryl Lee: The biggest thing about Maddy is that she still had hope, whereas that was different than Laura. I knew Laura's end before I started. I didn't know Maddy's end until the day I was shooting it. So even though there was stuff going on, it was very very different not to know the end. I guess one of the biggest differences between TV and film is you never know the ending in TV. But in this TV, as Laura, I did know the end . . . or the beginning.

The scene where BOB/Leland murders Maddy is one of the most intense moments in TV. *Twin Peaks* confronts trauma so directly, and specifically trauma with women. How did you manage/survive those takes—especially having to shoot them over and over again with different actors?

Sheryl Lee: We shot the scene with three different actors—the whole thing—over and over and over, because we had to have a smoke screen so that the crew didn't know who really did it. Working with Frank Silva [BOB], Ray Wise [Leland Palmer], and Richard Beymer [Ben Horne]—they were so kind and professional. They are letting pure evil express itself through them, but they are the kindest and sweetest gentlemen. I knew they had my back. I was in good hands, and they kept checking in with me. It was all safely done. There were stunt coordinators. Physically, I'll never forget it. When you are in it, your adrenaline is going, so you don't realize how sore you are or where you're going to be bruised until the next day. I had a doctor once say to me, "The only part of you that knows you are acting is your mind." So if you are acting in a state of fear, your body is still releasing the chemicals that it does when you are afraid. You go through a day like that, which is an intensely long day, and emotionally your body keeps going through all of these chemical changes. I was crying real tears. It's still just acting, but there is an experience my own system, or an actor's system, goes through that they have to recover from. You have to know what your limit is, when it's too much, and when you need a break—when the emotion is getting to be more than you are able to handle. And you need to slow it down. But they can be awful days because the thing that haunts me always is that I was just acting. This happens every day to our girls. Every day. When I'm doing scenes like that, it never leaves my thoughts.

When BOB is revealed to be Leland, what was your reaction? Here you are playing the character of both Maddy Ferguson and Laura Palmer, and you find out this evil entity is inside the father of Laura Palmer and the uncle of Maddy Ferguson.

Sheryl Lee: I didn't find out until either the day we shot Maddy's death or the day before. David took Ray and I and Richard Beymer aside. I think Frank Silva was there as well. It was so surreal because David did not have furniture in his office or whatever room we were in at the time. I just remember these small details like a dark room, and I think I was sitting on the floor on this brown carpet, and there was a clock that had a waterfall. I think I remember so many details because it was a strange moment. For so long, everyone thought that we knew who did it and we were just keeping it a secret. We had no idea. We had our own guesses and suspicions. David looked at me and said something along the lines of "Well, Ray/Leland, you killed your daughter, Laura. Maddy, now you're going to get killed." Not only was I dealing with the fact that it was Laura's dad, but now I was dealing with the idea he was going to kill Maddy. And then we shot it either that day or the next day. There was no time. We found out who did it, and then we kept going. We didn't hold that secret for long at all. My head was spinning. It made sense that it was Leland, because of the behavior.

Do you think it affected the performance to know so soon before you shot that scene because you didn't have a lot of time to process it?

Sheryl Lee: If I would have been given a choice of knowing a long time ahead or not, I would have said, "I don't want to know a long time ahead," just like it happened.

You've said publicly how when you approach a character you're playing, you try not to judge them and the choices they make. I wonder how that carries over into life for you and your interaction with others. Do you apply that in how you approach people?

Sheryl Lee: I do. That's one of the gifts that comes from acting. You can let it teach you how to be a better human. For my characters, my goal is to embody the spirit, the heart, the emotion, the mind, and the story of that character, and I can't do that if I'm judging them, or making assumptions about them, or projecting my own stuff onto them. I have to be in a space of receptivity and openness to the depth of who they are and the truth of who they are. That's where I'll find them. That is a skill you don't get overnight. You have to keep working at it. Certain characters I've played have challenged me with this. When I won't understand why she does something, I have to get in there and do that archaeological soul digging. I try to apply that process that I've learned through working on characters. It's always a work in progress, but really trusting that what we see is just a small percentage of who someone is. I love studying all different kinds of religions and human behavior, what makes people tick, nonviolent communication. I study them for acting, but I also study them to try to be a better human.

After *Twin Peaks*, you went on to have a long career in film, television, and theater. It's difficult to be a woman in the world, especially in the entertainment industry, a male-dominated industry. What has your experience been as a woman working in the creative field?

[*In answer to this question, Sheryl Lee shared a poem she wrote in 2011.*]

<u>actress</u>

i have been taught self judgment
by a culture that doesn't see the beauty of my lines

i have been taught self repulsion
by those who want the power hidden in my fertile hips

shaved down to meek and slender thighs

i have been taught loss of respect
for the woman that i am
by a city that sells us ladies for the fantasy of our sex
in a town where only youth is met

who are we becoming
us women of today
morphed into still images
as the girls of yesterday

passive expressions
sewn into our face
hidden poison
injected as paste

so that no sign of wisdom is present
nor age
no assertion left
in the reflection of our gaze

just a mask of the former
selves we used to be.......
                         were our feelings really
                                 SO DEEPLY THREATENING

that you've created a look
in which they can't even be seen

sculpted and cut
perfectly manicured we are
silent virgin........
                     as slut.....
                                 and we think we've come so far

'Wabi'

Grace Zabriskie

Grace Zabriskie is a prolific artist. She played the tormented, drugged, prophetic, and despairing Sarah Palmer, Laura Palmer's mother, in the television series *Twin Peaks* and the film *Twin Peaks: Fire Walk With Me*. Zabriskie has had a storied acting career, playing quirky, crazy, and downright fascinating characters from Sarah Palmer to Juana Durango (*Wild at Heart*) to Lois Henrickson (*Big Love*), just to name a few. But Zabriskie is more than an actor; she's an artist and poet as well. Her woodworking shop in her home is filled with all kinds of fancy plywood and scavenged wooden scraps. Zabriskie's woodwork art is present throughout her home. The detail she incorporates, such as textured and colorful frames and wooden circular grooves for knuckles on handles, proves her time spent in the shop is not wasted. She's a true artist. And, she's an accomplished poet. She's written a book titled *Poems* that reads like bright lightning—it's jarring, illuminating, and an electric charge of language.

When I interviewed Grace Zabriskie, she was grieving over the death of her second daughter, the painter Marion Lane, who died in 2019. Her first daughter, Helen, died in the early 1990s. I found myself in a situation where I was speaking with Zabriskie, who had lost both of her children, about Sarah Palmer's relationship with her deceased daughter, Laura Palmer. Speaking about mothers and daughters in the middle of the sacred space of Zabriskie's home felt like a loaded conversation. Not surprisingly, my mother, who passed away several years ago, seemed to nestle into this weighted space between us. Subtext was everywhere. Since I was acutely aware of Zabriskie's grief and the fact that she was an artist, I felt compelled to bring her a piece of obsidian—a starkly black ragged volcanic rock that is supposed to promote healing, advocate truth, and absorb negative energy. The space in this interview required healing energy for all involved. Zabriskie was grieving, but she was also working—on her woodworking, a script, and a music video for the song "Youth" by Grouplove.

After spending hours with her, I got the sense that Zabriskie could exist just fine without *Twin Peaks*, without Hollywood—not that she's not grateful for all of it—but it seems like she's much more interested in the next thing she can create. Her pursuit of wabi-sabi—a Japanese art form in which a flawed detail creates an elegant whole—becomes a perfect metaphor for so many things. Don't pursue perfection, but allow the flawed detail in all of us, whether it be literal or figurative, to just exist, because the whole will render itself beautifully elegant.

You lived in Atlanta for a while, and you are originally from New Orleans. Atlanta has a character to it. New Orleans the city is a character. It has a distinct culture and history—there's no place like it. For myself, I bring aspects of the South—where I've lived—with me. Is there a part of you in your daily life or performances that derives from New Orleans or Atlanta?

Grace Zabriskie: What I am aware of is that whatever character I am doing, there's nothing about me that isn't the result of how I grew up. Now, exactly what those things are—I don't know that that's my business, but I do know that it is, every last bit.

You come from a family of teachers, and you have been a teacher yourself of K-12 students as well as high school dropouts. And you've written a poem about teaching. How do you view yourself as a teacher?

Grace Zabriskie: I used to say, when I was extremely young, that I wanted to be an actor, a writer, and a visual artist. I wanted to do these things as a passionate amateur. To make a living, I would be a teacher, because I did come from all those teachers. But I also knew all those other things were hugely interesting to me. Before long, I realized people could do a lot of things that they were afraid to try. I saw myself as someone who would always say as part of my work, "You can do that," and encourage people to find parts of themselves that they thought were out of the question because they were doing something else. There's a degree of satisfaction that comes with allowing that in yourself. I think it's kept me this version of sane to be able to do all of those things. And not that it's that many, but it's enough to keep me going, rather than not have something that I'd care to do a lot.

You have said that when you were young you "read inappropriately." What a fantastic phrase. What did it mean for you to read inappropriately?

Grace Zabriskie: First of all, no one ever dreamed of telling me what I could read. It wasn't other people telling me what was inappropriate; it was me as an adult looking back and imagining there was wit there somewhere. I said, "Well, I read widely and inappropriately as a very young child." I was reading at a ridiculously young age, and I read everything. My father used to wake me up and bring me downstairs to read T. S. Eliot and Shakespeare for guests he would bring home from the café. I actually did a show for Joe Frank [French-born American writer and performer]. He died recently, and I'm still grieving. He had a radio show. I did a show for him called "Home" where I talked about growing up in New Orleans with my dad and Café Lafitte, and when he lost that, Café Lafitte in Exile, which became a famous gay bar after he died. I told the story of when I was very little. My father had me reading for some lady that he brought home from the café. I just figured her out [snaps fingers] like that. I read some of these things so often that I knew them by heart. So I would take my eye from the page just long enough so that I would see her face change. She said, "Oh, Tom, she's not reading! You've taught it to her!" Then I would prove her wrong. To shame her, because how dare she? I'm four years old. So I was a nasty little bitch way back.

Do you think your experience growing up in New Orleans and your early exposure to all these books influenced your acting and art? Actors can be incredible at observation and picking up the physicality of emotions and expressions.

Grace Zabriskie: When I moved to Georgia, I began learning dialects consciously as opposed to, pretty much up until then, unconsciously. For a few years, I was on the way to being an academic and a collector of dialects. An expert. Then I realized I didn't want to do that. When I did *Inland Empire*, David told me at the last freaking minute that my character had an Eastern European dialect. That was the first I'd heard of it. I'd had my part of the script for over a year. Now, four days before shooting, he tells me, "Oh, by the way, I want you to do it in this dialect." So I decided that there were certain words that I knew would be fun to say a certain way. She was a trickster as well. So I hopped around among dialects, creating a whole new one, so that I could say "mari-atch" for "marriage," or anything that struck me as either horrifying or funny. But then, of course, you have to sell it as an actual dialect. That's just basically conviction. If you are good enough at it—speak with conviction—someone might not recognize the dialect, but they won't call you on it.

The scene when Laura Dern's character invites you into her home

is the one I remember the most. It stays with me. One time I was watching *Inland Empire* with my cat, who was sleeping on the sofa. The scene when you enter the home and begin talking to Dern appeared. My cat, who was sleeping, heard your voice, and he stood up. He looked at the TV and slowly climbed onto the coffee table without taking his eyes off the television. His hair was raised, and he looked right at you. Then I looked at him, and I thought, "Oh my gosh." It's an intense scene. For my cat to take notice was a big deal.

Grace Zabriskie: Thank you. Now, other times I've been more strict with the dialect. In *Ray Donovan*, I did a dialect and I found something I wanted to do and did it. For *Inland Empire*, it was fun to construct something.

There is a subtle dialect with the character Lois Henrickson in *Big Love* too. There's an element of a Southern accent, but it seems like it's something else altogether.

Grace Zabriskie: There were a few days when that dialect was in jeopardy, because when I read the script for the first time, that's how the character came out. I did it for Will Scheffer and Mark Olsen. They said, "We love the performance, but what's with the dialect? No one else is doing that." I said, "I'll try to do it without it." And they hated it. They didn't like it. I didn't either. Maybe I made sure they wouldn't like it. I knew that it should be that way. I said, "Just write a scene that explains why I talk this way. That's all. How hard is that?" I also had short hair when they [everyone else on the polygamist compound] all had long hair.

I appreciated the explanation for your short hair. Lois Henrickson cuts her hair short after her daughter, Margaret, drowns. You had such chemistry with Bruce Dern, who played Lois's husband, Frank. Was there chemistry off-screen as well as on?

Grace Zabriskie: Off-screen involved me trying to get him to set, because he's a storyteller. It seemed like every day that we were working, half the contingent of staff were trying to get his ass to set. They'd interrupt him right in the middle of a story and tell him to go to set. I was the only one who wasn't afraid to grab him by something. He is nothing if not good-humored. He's a trip. He's a very interesting man.

You've worked with so many great directors. What's it like working with David Lynch as a director as opposed to working with other directors? What makes Lynch unique?

Grace Zabriskie: For me, I did feel our communication was subliminal. He virtually never said anything to me besides "slow down," which is funny because it's normally "speed up" when a director says anything. "Faster! Faster!" I did talk once about him wanting to give me some direction in, I believe, *Inland Empire*, but he didn't want to let go of any information, for whatever reason. I would say something, and he would say, "OK now, you see, when you say this word here you're referring to, you know, so say that with more 'significance.'" I would get to that word and somehow say it with a little more "significance." Then we'd go on and he'd stop me again wanting me to say something else with a little more "significance." I cannot think of another director in the world where I would put up with that. But it was just fun.

Regarding this subliminal communication between you and Lynch—you both seem like intelligent people with keen senses of observation. Do you think that's why you have this sort of shorthand form of communication? Is it that you are both highly observant and in tune with each other? What do you think that is?

Grace Zabriskie: I don't know. I think there have been times in my life where I might have imagined that I had something special with him, but I don't think any longer that that's possibly true. What I do know is he respects what I do. He knows that I will not only give him what he wants but sometimes show him what he wants. I don't imagine I am the only one who does that with him. Everyone likes to feel special. I think I do feel that I'm special to him on some level, but I can't say how. I also figure a lot of other people feel the same way. Not everybody. But a lot of other actors do.

Your character Juana Durango in the film *Wild at Heart* is really intense and unforgettable. It seems like she would be a challenging but fun character to play. She's not on screen a lot, but there's so much there. Even if Lynch doesn't provide a lot of backstory, the viewers can begin imagining what a character's backstory might be. Who is this woman? Where did she come from? Why is she the way she is? As an actor, it would be interesting to figure out Juana's backstory and fill in those gaps. Tell me about playing Juana.

Grace Zabriskie: I read something the other day that was about Juana that said a big part of the scene had been cut because it just got too brutal physically. Well, that is not the case. A big part got cut, but what got cut was psychological torture, not physical torture. The little bit of physical torture was still in. Lynch had me—it took me forever to learn these lines, because I would say the exact same thing over and over and over again with <u>tiny</u> little differences. That's the hardest kind of thing to learn. So I'd . . .

Grace Zabriskie in Lynch's *Wild at Heart* (1990) *Photo courtesy of Propaganda Films*

[Zabriskie stands up during the interview, and her body and face transform into Juana Durango. She motions as if she has a cane and lumbers across the

room. She is Juana Durango standing in front of Johnnie Farragut (Harry Dean Stanton), who is tied up in a chair, utterly defenseless and vulnerable. At this moment, I am thrilled and terrified. She is primal and powerful. In Juana's best Cajun accent:]

"So I go over here, and I go over there. Then I'm going to walk over here."

I'm trying to make him piss his pants, you know? When they saw a test screening, people were leaving. Someone claimed he had heart palpitations. But the scene is lost. After the scene was cut, sooner or later they got rid of the footage. I would give anything to have seen it. It might have gone into the director's cut, but it's long gone.

Aside from David Lynch's work, is there a role that you played that you enjoyed or felt a connection to?

Grace Zabriskie: I've never sat and waited for the phone to ring for a role. And I don't think I ever will. It doesn't mean that I don't love the part of me that is an actor. I just like going into something and using every corpuscle as best I can, and then that's over. I learned the hard way to make sure that it is over, because I have to allow myself to get fucked up from some situation that I was in emotionally as a character. I have to be careful about that.

How do you take on an intense role, perform it, and put everything physically and emotionally into it and then walk away and not have that stay with you? How do you take care of yourself?

Grace Zabriskie: There are a lot of different answers. Some people think, "Oh, I know how to do that." For years, they do know how to do it, and then something comes along, and they think, "Oh no, you don't know how to do it now, do you?" Or you forgot how to do it. Or you learn the hard way. Or some combination of all of that. I thought I knew how to do that. When I was dying in *Big Love* and losing my mind and all of that, I got a frozen shoulder. It was unbelievable.

It affected you physically?

Grace Zabriskie: Yes, and that is one of the conditions that are psychogenic.

What was your favorite role you played in a David Lynch project?

Grace Zabriskie: All in all, I would have to say *Twin Peaks*, including *The Return.*

This year marks the thirtieth anniversary of the airing of the pilot. When I think about the pilot, what stands out is Sarah Palmer's reaction when Leland Palmer is speaking to her over the phone after Sheriff Truman shows up to tell Leland that Laura died. What makes David Lynch's work art is every time I come to it, I get a different experience. Sometimes I get to this scene and I laugh. Sometimes I'm horrified, or I cry. Your reaction when you are talking to Leland and you drop the phone gives me that same experience. Every time I watch it, I experience it differently. Sarah Palmer's reaction during that phone call is anguished, over-the-top, intense, and this is only the pilot.

Grace Zabriskie: My reaction happens before Leland tells me, and that is the key. I start freaking before he tells me. Lynch pushed me to be over-the-top in that scene. That was the beginning of him knowing he could make me go so far it could be funny. I did it for him a number of times, freaking out until it crossed the line.

Do you recall if that was in the script or the direction you got or something you decided?

Grace Zabriskie: Well, I had a sense that Sarah had the ability to foresee a little bit. One got that aspect from the script. It looked like it was going into that in greater depth. I remember having a long talk with Mark Frost. Let's say that Sarah's background comes into this and her heritage—showing all of this in just the right way so people are figuring

The famous phone scene in *Twin Peaks* (1990) *Photo courtesy of CBS*

it out as opposed to being knocked over the head with it. Because of course it points to Laura as well. As it is, there's just enough so that all of that can happen.

Twin Peaks, on the surface, is a traditional murder mystery, but then the audience begins to see supernatural elements, like Sarah Palmer's prophetic ability and the evil entity of BOB. How did you negotiate playing Sarah with what was in the script as well as creating a backstory for her?

Grace Zabriskie: No one but a fool expects to be told her backstory. It is your job to understand every word that you say and what you are actually thinking while you say it. The minute you don't know what you're thinking when you say that line, I will know. Other people watching may not not know why, but they won't be gripped. When people speak, they can't help the fact that they are thinking whatever they are thinking. As humans, we have learned to clock that in other humans. You don't even know what you're really thinking when you're talking, because you can't do two things at once, but subconsciously you do. That actually has a result out in the world for anyone who is talking to you.

Sheryl Lee teaches an acting class for actors, directors, and writers. One of the things she tells her students is acting is reacting to the person in front of you. It's a simple idea, but it's a difficult thing to actually do—to truly be in that moment. You, Ray Wise [Leland Palmer], and Sheryl Lee have this incredible chemistry. As actors, you seem to be really present and trusting of one another. What was it like to act with Ray Wise and Sheryl Lee?

Grace Zabriskie: I suppose I have worked with people at times when I couldn't make anything like that happen at all. Sometimes people ask, "How can you write poems that are so personal about yourself?" And I say, "Because I know that there is nothing that I have felt that someone else has not felt." Am I going to walk around all my life imagining that something has happened to me that has never happened to anyone else? It's the same thing with so-called chemistry: if you open yourself to the other person and allow all of those amazing transformations that have to go on—to happen—no one will ever figure out how to put all of that into words. So many synapses are involved in so many ways. We don't know half of them, but it's what makes a performance. All I know is it's opening yourself up. I do know this: I've been told a number of times over the years that the scene that I did with the lead was his best scene or her best scene in the movie or episode. That is an incredible compliment to me, because it means that they felt completely met and able to do their best. And then they just did their best.

In *Twin Peaks*, you/Sarah Palmer and Ray Wise/Leland Palmer/ BOB and Sheryl Lee/Laura Palmer are all in this intense setting together. What was it like playing Sarah Palmer?

Grace Zabriskie: First I want to say that when we did *The Return*, I privately decided that this is what happened after Sarah had to understand, after all these years, how she had let this happen. It wasn't just losing her daughter that destroyed her life. It was the guilt of knowing that perhaps she could have stopped it. I didn't discuss that with David, because if it had caused me to do anything that he wasn't happy with he would have told me.

Originally, you spent so much time with this character, and with *The Return* you had to go back to being this character. What did you think when you found out you were going to be Sarah Palmer again?

Grace Zabriskie: Beyond thrilled. I couldn't wait to see what it was going to be. It was beyond my dreams. People still haven't figured it out. People still don't get it. I couldn't wait to see what it was going to be and to figure out how I was going to play it. There was never any worry. I always know how I'm going to play something pretty soon, depending on if I know the director well. And I keep it open even after I figure out what I want to do. When I worked with Gus Van Sant [on *My Own Private Idaho*], I remember—the third time I had worked with Gus—I remember him coming to the trailer and saying, "So what are you going to do? What are you going to do for us this time?" He just wanted to let me at it. That's the best—when you get hired because somebody knows you're going to figure it out.

For some characters, they seem so real to people that they confuse the actor for the character. Sheryl Lee said that often when people see her, they are not looking at Sheryl Lee, they are looking at Laura Palmer. Have you ever had an experience where people see you as Sarah Palmer or Lois Henrickson or any other character?

Grace Zabriskie: I would say there's been a lot of assumptions about Lois that I've had to field, and with all kinds of characters. It seems like I've played really evil people. That would sometimes scare people. They would tell me that they're scared of me. Lois had things about her that weren't too attractive. I think people said they were scared of me as Lois too.

I don't know what it says about me, but I love Lois.

Grace Zabriskie: The right stuff—that's what it says about you!

I'm also not sure what this says about me, but I saw a lot of my own

family in the compound family even though I'm not a polygamist or from Utah. But I recognized the dysfunction. And a lot of my family lives in a rural area on a farm in different houses. Even Bill and his immediate family, far from the compound, had that dysfunction, even though they tried to seem normal on the surface.

Grace Zabriskie: He tried so hard.

In 2010, you released your book *Poems*, published by NYQ Books. What inspires you to write poetry?

Grace Zabriskie: Just about anything. To me a perfect example is "National Geographic Poem #3." Something from the *National Geographic* has inspired me. Love, but more likely misery from love. Words. I'm really into words.

Writers, especially poets, love language and playing with language. In poetry, one can say the thing without saying the thing, or the thing can have multiple meanings. With biographical pieces, the writer is inserting herself, but the reader might see aspects of her own story in there. Poetry allows that room to read into things.

Grace Zabriskie: For me, I would never say I write biographical pieces. I am inspired in some way by things that have biographical origin, but it's different from using them that way. I once was asked to write an erotic story. The woman who wanted to put together these erotic stories sent invitations to all kinds of women writers. Most of them gave it to someone else to see if they wanted to do it, because they certainly couldn't risk their reputation. A friend of mine received one. She said to me, "Let's write one. Let's both write one." So, mine got in. It was supposed to be a true erotic story, but I didn't pay any attention to that at all. It was a mixture of things that had happened and fiction. Then the next one she wrote was supposed to be real life, which, again, I paid no attention to. It was a mixture of fiction and based on something in real life. I say all that because everything that I write is a combination of biography and fiction. I'll probably never write anything else that isn't more or less that combination. To me, that's the way to be the most truthful.

Are you writing anything now?

Grace Zabriskie: I'm working on poems. I haven't forced myself to finish one in a while. I think all my work in the woodshop is partly going to be in aid of reading scripts and looking at different versions of a poem all at once. [*Zabriskie showed me a wooden piece she was working on that holds up multiple scripts/papers to read and review.*]

How long have you been doing woodworking?

Grace Zabriskie: When the kids were about two and three, I had like two tools to my name. I made a little table and little chairs with a heart back. In some ways, I've been doing it a long time, but it was after the Northridge earthquake in 1994 that I got my workshop downstairs. Prior to that, I was a silk screen printmaker, but I left it all in Atlanta. I listened to some idiots who said, "Oh, but your acting career—you need to not spread yourself so thin. What if you were trying to get parts instead of just not caring? You could be doing more if you stopped doing all these other things." So, I thought, "I'll move to LA, and then I'll get serious." Well, that did not last. I couldn't survive without other things to do. I just cannot stand not being able to work with my hands. One thing I look forward to getting back into the shop is bumbling. You just walk around down there and you don't know what you are going to do. You just think, "Well, let me clean up this little part. Well, this hasn't been dusted in a long time." Before long, you see a piece of wood and you remember when you first found that piece of wood. And you get an idea. You know, you can bumble your way into things. I suppose it's possible to bumble your way into writing things as well. And maybe that's what some people do, but I'm not familiar with it. I don't quite know how you would think of bumbling into something as a way to write. But that could be my lack of imagination. There's something very nice about it. First of all, it means that your time is stretching out in front of you—or what's left of it is. I don't go into the woodshop when I know I've got a role coming up. When I go into the shop, I like to not have a clue whether I will ever work again. So, time to bumble. Freedom to bumble. Then slowly work your way into some sense of knowing what you want to do. On the other hand, writing doesn't tend to make me bleed, whereas in the shop . . . .

Where do you find your pieces of wood?

Grace Zabriskie: People will bring me stuff that they have in their garage. Or I would get it when I was going to studios for auditions. I haven't in many years. I would go to a studio for an audition and often I would have to be in heels. Studios are famous for their waste. So I would get some guy to jump into a dumpster on the lot and get me stuff I'd see poking out, and then they would get me off the lot without me getting arrested. I will go down into my shop and look for a piece of wood for a specific thing and not until I find something that will have no more than a tiny amount left over will I stop looking. The only wood that I tend to buy is plywood. I buy really good plywood. You don't find that on the street. You do find furniture on the street, and you can bust that up for really good wood.

Do you ever see a piece of wood and envision something from the piece of wood?

Grace Zabriskie: I have a piece upstairs. [*She presents a photo of an intricate bedside table with drawers and nooks.*]

What is on the top?

Grace Zabriskie: That is a technique that is invented. Read what I wrote. [*She hands me a piece of paper.*]

[*I read the writing aloud*] "I needed a multi-functional piece of furniture next to my bed. It had to include a pull-out slab to write on, a lazy Susan to hold vitamins and herbs, a pull-out tray for lotions, a pull-out for carded medications, a pull-out drawer for

ideas I get right after waking up, drawers for journals and shelves for books and magazines. The writing slab height was a given. Overall height had to be right for my reading lamp. Width was dictated by the distance between my bed and the wall. Depth was dictated by how wide I wanted the writing slab to be. All materials had to resonate and be in my shop already—scrap, basically (my favorite). A few years ago, neighbors gave me a walnut board found in their garage. When I knew that board would be the critical part of the table, the writing slab, I knew also that it could serve for the length of the slab but would require biscuited augmentation for the width I wanted it to be."

What is biscuited augmentation?

Grace Zabriskie: Do you see the walnut there? Here's the augmentation using a different color wood. You can hollow out a place there in both pieces of wood. Then you put glue on these little things and stick them in. It causes them to be very trustworthy together as opposed to just butt-joining them. The little things are called biscuits.

[*I continue reading aloud*] "Somehow much about the design of the table has been implied. Parameters are fundamental to creation, I suspect. Even some of those that appear given have actually been chosen. The Japanese concept of wabi was newly part of my consciousness when I began this project. Wabi is defined as a flawed detail that creates an elegant whole. As I was cutting the maple stock that would be the ebonized sections of leg for the piece, I sawed out the knothole section and placed it in the cubby hole of my shop that contains interesting natural phenomena and tantalizing scraps in general, and forgot it until the widths of the drawers became clear due to the requirements of other elements. I had a space between the other drawers to fill and the knothole piece had by then been varnished, and, after a week or so, framed in walnut. During times when I should have been working through problems of the table instead of playing with interesting scraps, it was now the perfect width for between the drawers and the same height as

the drawers once it had been shaved a tiny bit. It struck me as a humorously Western version of wabi—look, here's the flaw framed so you don't miss it. For the top, I found a piece of veneer plywood with cathedral grain. I painted irregular stripes of melted wax on it, cross hatched the dry wax and then flooded the top with black sumi ink. Mineral spirits removed the wax and left the dried ink. I painted most of the bare areas with a red oak stain. I added and removed ink, wax and stains for days and got thoroughly disgusted and gouged crude furious diagonal troughs in the wood with a variety of sharp instruments. I vacuumed up the mess and put on a coat of polycrylic and then a fairly thick coat of clear, two-part epoxy resin. The beautiful distinctive aesthetic flaw that distinguishes the spirit of the moment in which the object was created from all other moments in eternity is further explanation of wabi in a small book called *They Have a Word for It: A Lighthearted Lexicon of Untranslatable Words and Phrases* by Howard Rheingold, published by Tarcher St. Martin's Press. The top, in other words, does not have wabi. The top is wabi. 1950s American wabi, framed and plastic-coated."

This is gorgeous. So you designed this. You said, "This is what I need. These are the aspects I need." And you designed it for your bedside table with the idea of wabi in mind.

Grace Zabriskie: Yes! This concept of some small imperfection in the finish of a clay vessel, say, being appreciated as a source of aesthetic pleasure—not as a flaw to be corrected, but as the very element of the piece that completes the perfection of the whole . . . that knocked me out! I still love the idea of wabi. It was new to me then, and I was struck by it—even though I had grown up in the French Quarter, old buildings, the variegated colors of old brick, old wooden fences, missing stucco, I didn't grow up in an American city. So the Japanese concept was bound to attract me—and of course I was not slow to extrapolate; to come to see the implications for the world, for my fellow humans, For myself.

'Juggling'

Sabrina S. Sutherland

Sabrina S. Sutherland is David Lynch's right-hand woman. She has worked with Lynch full time since 2008 and has been a part of *Twin Peaks* since the original series aired in the early 1990s. She even had a role in Season 3 as Floor Attendant Jackie at the Silver Mustang Casino. She's more than a producer. She's a doer. The late, great Catherine E. Coulson, who famously played The Log Lady in *Twin Peaks*, tirelessly worked with David Lynch to produce his first feature film, *Eraserhead*, in 1977, said she was a "handmaiden to genius."[1] Coulson operated a

---

1   Courtenay Stallings, "USC Screens David Lynch's Eraserhead," *Red Room Podcast*, Nov. 22, 2013.

camera, cooked for the crew, styled Jack Nance's hair, pushed the dolly, operated boom mics, and did just about everything else she could to help Lynch reach his goal. Like Coulson, Sutherland is a "handmaiden to genius" and so much more. Sutherland's credits include producer, production manager, artist, set decorator, and actor.

How did you get involved with *Twin Peaks* originally?

Sabrina S. Sutherland: At first, I watched the show. I loved the show. I was working on another show at the time, and we were shooting nights. I was in the office [during the broadcast]. My mom would record it on VHS tapes. I would sneak the tapes, and we would watch them in the office. There were three of us who watched it, and we loved it. I looked up the production company and saw they were in preproduction for Season 2. I called, and the producer Gregg Fienberg answered the phone. They hadn't started yet. They were just coming back. So he answered the phone, and I said who I was and how I wanted to work on it. He said they needed a production coordinator. He said, "Come down next week." So I met with him, talked with him, and then he was like, "OK, start tomorrow." That was the one show that really meant a lot to me to get.

It's one thing when you're a fan and you get to enjoy something and another when you get to be deeply involved in it and see how the sausage is made. What was that experience like?

Sabrina S. Sutherland: There was always an excitement around the show. The people who had worked on the first season were elated because it was such a success. There was a whole new crew that came on for the second season. And we were all excited to be there. It was this feeling of joy and excitement. I've worked on so many shows, or been around that, so it wasn't like I was in awe of anything, but I was just excited. You were happy to go to work every day, you know? David wasn't around that much during the second season, but when he was there it was like a different thing. It went from excitement to nth-degree excitement. It was very special.

Season 2 gets some criticism, but some of my favorite episodes are in that season. And so many great directors directed Season 2 episodes. I mean, of course, David Lynch was the best, in my opinion.

Sabrina S. Sutherland: It was great to have so many different people in there, and it was just fun, and we were happy. The second season has deep sentimental value for me. I was, at that time, even a little disappointed by it, honestly. But I didn't care, because I was just so happy to be there. But it went in a direction that was more silly than what I had hoped. When I watched the first season, it was so different and exciting. The second season was kind of like that, but toward the end for me it wasn't as powerful. But I loved everybody there and had the best time. I didn't care about the storyline as much as just working and still being happy. So I could separate the actual show from working on the show.

From my standpoint, and I've talked to some people about this, it looks like during the second season other people who were working on it besides David Lynch were trying to capture that magic that he has of using a tricky combination of terror and humor. But it didn't always work. They didn't quite capture how he was able to do humor.

Sabrina S. Sutherland: When you have David Lynch and Mark Frost writing together, that's one thing. The second season was different because there were different people working on the scripts. Mark wasn't even that much involved, but he was more involved than David. He was there. But David wasn't even there. So it was a different thing. I think Harley Peyton was the showrunner. It was that collective. Prior to that I'd worked on other TV shows. You have that writers' room. They all bring something, and it's a collective thing—not that it waters things down—but you get this patter that these are the points that have to be hit, and it becomes rote. And that's the difference when David and Mark were writing. It wasn't so much hitting points, it was where their imagination took them. They were writing in a different way. I think it's the same with the directors who came in. Each director wants to put their own spin on stuff and make it interesting. And that's why I think Season 3 was so different from Season 2. Because the directors coming in wanted to make it "*Twin Peaks*-y," and they would do almost wall-to-wall music. They would get all the music cues and think, "Oh, yeah, let's put this in, and put that in." And then when you see what David did with Season 3, you see that it wasn't all music cues. But David's not about doing that same thing. He's always going in a different way. He's not copying somebody. They were trying to copy what that show is, and that's really what their job is, right? As they come in, they have to maintain that look. That's what you do in television. That's the unfortunate thing. You want it to be that planned thing, and there you go. And everybody coming in doesn't mix with it. You don't make something not *Twin Peaks*; you make something that fits that mold. But I think it's like playing telephone, where as it goes down it alters as it goes. They're still trying to say the same thing, but it's not quite there.

I appreciate television or art when you don't know where it's going. You watch those network TV shows, and they're hitting the points, like you said, but that's boring for a lot of us. It's why we appreciate people like David Lynch and Mark Frost, because we don't know where they're going to take us, and it's a fun ride. And then after we're there, we don't always know what happened. So we get to spend all this time theorizing and talking about it and arguing about it, which is fun.

Sabrina S. Sutherland: That's what makes it entertaining to me. I like things even if it's something badly made. I don't mind seeing it if it's something I can talk about, and it stays with me. So much TV I forget watching because it's just so predictable, so nothing, so bland. They're escapism. It's fun. But I do like to talk about stuff and think about things. Films used to be like that more so than television. Now television is getting that way because you do often have one creator doing the series.

Working on the original *Twin Peaks* and Season 3, what do you take away from that experience? Season 3 was essentially nine two-

hour movies. You had such a hand in it, particularly as executive producer. How has *Twin Peaks* changed you?

Sabrina S. Sutherland: *Twin Peaks* definitely changed me. I met David Lynch and worked with him subsequently over the years, and now I'm more heavily involved, obviously, which is huge. I met Deepak Nayar, who became a producer, and I worked with him for many years. He was a big influence on my early producing career. Then, other people I've met on that show have become friends. I don't even know how to explain it, but the same people I've worked with on *Twin Peaks* I've worked with on all different sorts of shows, not even David's shows. I call in the same people. Working with Deepak, we call in the same people. And we start getting this melting pot of friends over thirty years. We've worked with so many of the same people for so long, it's like a family. Working on Season 3 was a huge endeavor. It was wonderful. I'm just very grateful that David had such faith in me. He put faith in me to do what I do. I think Hollywood is a very difficult place, and it's kind of cliquey. If you haven't done this or if you aren't a "name" kind of person, they don't really trust that. And so you have to prove yourself over and over again. I'm just very grateful that David just said, "Yeah, I've worked with you forever, and so, no problem." I'm like, "Really? OK, all right!" And my job is to make him happy.

If you're going to go into a project like Season 3, where there is a specific vision, a limited budget, and a very short timeline to do it all, it seems like there's got to be a very deep trust between the creators Lynch and Frost and someone like you who is very hands-on as a producer.

Sabrina S. Sutherland: Yes, absolutely. The thing with David and Mark on producing Season 3, they're not really involved in the producing side of it. I mean, they are producers, executive producers and the creators and that kind of element, of course. I'm talking about the nuts and bolts of the actual filmmaking: budget, schedule, crew, day-to-day things. That's certainly not in the realm of what they're doing. They're concentrating on the creative aspects. And my job is to make those creative aspects happen. So, I've been working with David since the end of 2008 exclusively. Before that, I was freelance and I'd come back and forth. But since then I've been with him. I work in his company. I do all these other things in his company besides the film work. So there is that trust that's there from just knowing what he wants, what I can deliver, and how to approach that. My job is something that they're not really involved with. And in fact, with David directing, he can't be involved. He has to concentrate on his job of directing, which is a huge task. And he just needs to have all those things there available to him. It's Michael Horse who always says, "David is an artist, and I'm like his paintbrush. I'm just a tool there basically to put out on canvas." And my job is to make sure all of those elements—the paint, the water, the brushes, and the canvas—all that stuff is there ready for whatever he wants to do. And that's kind of a hard job. But I know him well enough to know certain things to expect, like special effects.

On most shows they want to have a special effects team only on the days where effects are being shot. For example, in the script it calls for smoke coming out of an exploding car, so you need to have an explosion. In the schedule, the effects team would be there on those days for that work, and they'd have some prep to fix it. Every day David needs special effects. For example, going in to see Showtime and saying, "Hey, here's my budget," and they ask, "Why is there a special effects person every day?" "Well, because that's how David works. He needs somebody there every day. They need to be there. This is how it has to be." And it's true. We had a truck and a special effects crew there, and every day they were working on new things. And David would say, "OK, get Phil [Bartko] here. OK, Phil, I'm thinking, can we do this?" And he'd be like, "Yeah, OK." And he'd go back to his truck and try to figure out how to make things happen. So there were things scripted, but then there's so much not scripted. And that's just how David works, and then you have to be prepared for anything. And it's hard, especially when you have a budget and you have a schedule.

It sounds like you, in your multiple roles, are a huge problem solver. You're always thinking ahead of time, but when something comes up you are trying to solve that problem.

Sabrina S. Sutherland: One of my main functions is to solve problems, to be detail oriented, make sure everything is accounted for. I always have to be thinking ahead. David is not predictable in any way, but there are things I know that he likes, like I said, with the special effects, lighting, or smoke. So there's that whole little kit in the back of my head, that I know these things always have to be around. There are a lot of problems that have to be solved, and you just deal with them. But I've found in production, it works. You can always find a way of doing something. And if you can't do this thing, you can do something else instead. But there's never a "No, you can't absolutely do this," or nothing is going to get done. You work out something. And there's a line. There's a crew, and I'm responsible for them. There are always personality issues, interdepartment things that are happening that I have to help with, because I am the person that can come in and say, "OK, let's resolve this problem that you have. You're having these issues. How can we resolve it?" I am that person. I am the person who is probably the most disliked on the set. Because I am a person who will say, "No, you can't do that." I'm always setting all the rules. "You can't talk about that. You can't take pictures on the set." I'm a naysayer, right? And that's not a happy position to be in. A lot of the crew and cast have certain ideas in their head about things, and a way they like to work, which is totally realistic. But in my world it's not realistic. It's trying to maintain everybody collectively. It's a juggling job, but that's what a producer does.

It is admirable to see a woman such as yourself in that position having a long career and being able to be a naysayer, being able to tell people, "Yes, you can do this" or "No, you can't." There are so few women in those roles historically.

Sabrina S. Sutherland: Very much so. There are a lot of women, actually, who are in that same position, and they've been able to be much more aggressive. I'm not aggressive. I'm very passive in many ways and very quiet. And there are times people do try to take advantage of that, and I know that's how it comes across as being. I don't need to fight those small things. It's the big stuff that I worry about. I don't like to scream.

I don't like to say, "It's my way or the highway." I'm compassionate, and I do try to negotiate and figure out ways to make people happy. But my main goal is getting David what he wants, and if it's going to conflict with that, that's where I draw the line: "OK, you can say anything you want to say about me, but when it comes to this, this is where it stops." So there are a lot of women producers who are probably better in their way of working, where they're intimidating and much more of an authority figure, but I don't work that way. And I'm happy not to work that way. I can get what I need done being the way I am. And I think that's a challenge for women. I'm not saying these other women are bitchy, because that's the word you use for a woman. Because you don't call men bitchy, right? You don't even call them aggressive. You just say that they're doing their job. And that's what the women are doing. I've never been the kind of person to go out there and say, "This is how we're doing it." That's not my personality, but I love the job I do. I'm more of a quiet producer.

There's been a lot more books and studies about how introverts/quiet people make great leaders of organizations. I think it's important you're sharing that aspect of yourself.

Sabrina S. Sutherland: I will say there are a lot of men who are not very happy that I'm in a position that I'm in. And David says this all the time, "I'd hate to be a woman, knowing what you go through, because they just don't like to take anything from you." And it's true. Sometimes they don't give me the proper respect I'm owed. It doesn't bother me, because I don't care, honestly. You know, I think it bothers David more so than it bothers me. I just want to get the work done.

You've not only worked with David Lynch over the years, but you've worked with Sheryl Lee as well. What are your thoughts on Sheryl Lee?

Sabrina S. Sutherland: Sheryl Lee is a special person. When David cast her in the role, there was something there. And David sees the inner soul of a person—that she was Laura Palmer, in a way—that she could become that character and be that person in real life. And I just love her, and I think the character is such an indelible character that won't ever fade away. It's that important. Sheryl is just so good, vulnerable, authentic. It's not like an actor portraying a role—she is that person, and that's what makes her noticeably special. In real life, as a person, she's that genuine kind of person. She's not a phony person. Even when she's listening to people it's not an act; she's truly listening. She's very special.

'Energy'

Jennifer Lynch

Jennifer Lynch is not a female filmmaker. She is a *filmmaker*. Lynch is a director, writer, and artist. Her first feature film was *Boxing Helena*, about a surgeon whose obsession with a beautiful woman leads him to do terrible things. The film, told through a female gaze, is a fairy tale in the sense that the story is fantastical and has a happy ending. When the film was released in 1993, many labeled it misogynistic in the way Helena is objectified and her body, an object of a man's possession, is literally dismantled. But Lynch was interrogating this idea of obsession and possession in a creative, albeit horrific, way. Lynch went on to direct *Surveillance* and *Chained* as well as countless television shows, such as *The Walking Dead*, *American Horror Story*, and *Quantico*. In the *Twin Peaks* community, Lynch is most famous for being the author of *The Secret Diary of Laura Palmer*, a novel in diary format from the point of view of Laura Palmer. It was published in 1990, between *Twin Peaks* Season 1 and Season 2. The diary fleshed out Laura's character in a much deeper way than the television series, as the protagonist invited readers inside her head. We discuss her book in Part II. Lynch is the daughter of two artists, David Lynch and Peggy Reavey. She was the last person I interviewed for this book, and it just so happened to be in the middle of the COVID-19 pandemic, which couldn't help but invade our conversation. After dyeing an elongated earth-green doll while singing Alice Merton's "No Roots" and shaking her platinum dreadlocks loose for the camera in a post she labeled "Undone" on Instagram, Lynch spoke to me via Facetime while we both sheltered in place during the worst pandemic of our lifetime.

I saw *Boxing Helena* on VHS when I was quite young, not too long after I saw *Twin Peaks*. I was fascinated by the way obsession and control are explored in this film, where a surgeon [Julian Sands] captures a beautiful woman [Sherilyn Fenn].

Jennifer Lynch: *Boxing Helena* was so misunderstood and so mispromoted. *Boxing Helena* was never about "This is women's fault." It's not about fault—"Someone did this, and of course there are repercussions. It wouldn't have happened if somebody hadn't done it, so that's where the issue is." Stop going over here to what happened. None of that would've happened if what? This. Start talking about that instead of the women who get raped.

I wonder if that movie came out today, if it would've had a different reception. Not everyone interpreted it as a misogynistic story. You describe it as a fairy tale. It was delightful and mind-bending and sexy. I'm curious about women's response to that movie versus men's response. Do they differ, in your experience?

Jennifer Lynch: It tends to be women who like it more. I've been given a great gift over the past ten years where people have actually started to say, "I loved that movie" or "I really enjoyed it." For a lot of different reasons, people were not able to ever see the movie. For me, it was very clear I was making this over-the-top film with every bit of dialogue, every action, frame—a hypersurreal fairy tale that you knew was going to end a certain way because it was a fairy tale. But due to the things that accompanied that movie, it had its own struggles, but I'm pleased to have gotten people talking about that issue of control—that issue of who's in charge and how long it took people to realize he innately didn't want that kind of love from her, that "OK, you're the only one who's gonna do it." If a man made the movie, the question would've never come up to begin with. Ever.

I remember the scene where Sherilyn Fenn's character emerges from the fountain, and I fell in love with her in that moment!

Jennifer Lynch: What I wanted to do was hyperchew and ingest all of those moments that you replay, and how long that goes on and what you're willing to do and what it looks like from the outside when you're that obsessed with someone. And to do it as joyfully as possible and to make him as bumbling as possible so it wasn't a horror film in a bloody way but in a we-really-want-to-possess-each-other way.

That goes back to why it's important to have a woman tell certain stories. That would have been a very different movie if a man had directed it. You've directed so many things in your career—TV and film. I was there when you screened *Chained* at the 2013 Twin Peaks Festival, and you made *Surveillance* a few years before that. You've done a lot of TV—*The Walking Dead, American Horror Story*. What's been your experience being a filmmaker and navigating that as a woman?

Jennifer Lynch: I don't wake up in the morning and think, "I have a uterus," you know? I don't even think about it halfway through the day. It's usually someone else who brings it up. My experience when I first started working was "You're a girl, and you're someone's daughter, and you're nineteen." Those were really good things—things that brought attention and things I had to surpass, which was a shame. I'm a woman, but I can still go do the job, so go fuck yourself. There was a lot of "Aren't you amazing! God, for being a woman—and your age!" But it is still, to me, a tremendous issue.

TV in particular is hiring women sometimes just because they're women, not because they're the best director for the job but because they get bonus points. It helps them. Diversity is now a thing required of the studios. And I think that's lovely—just pick the best ones, you know? Do us all a favor and don't hire a mechanic because they're female if they're not the best mechanic for your car. Don't hire a male mechanic who's not the best mechanic for your car. We need to start talking about directors and not male or female or lesbian or trans, just directors—not anything else about them. It's been used against us, in a lot of ways, and it's another way to remove the skillset. It's a way for them to say, "It's great to have a female director!" and not to have you and what you do. And the less they have to acknowledge that, most of them, the more comfortable they seem to be. It's new to them. I think it's intimidating. A lot of women feel they need to act like men to do the job. And that is devastating in my opinion. The whole point of directing is you are offering people a story through your eyes, your voice. Don't be a different voice. It's just like lying in images—don't do it. And it hurts me. It really does.

When you're just reduced to your gender by how people approach you, it hurts. You just want to be seen for who you are or what you do and not, like you said, your uterus—what's between your thighs or what's not between your thighs.

Jennifer Lynch: It's just so unnecessary and so divisive. It's clearly about fear and intimidation. Nobody happy and confident or brave enough to say they lack confidence would ever treat people that way. It is only because they feel threatened that anything is done the way it's done, so I'm sad for them. These are not happy people. I just don't want to have to talk about it anymore. Unless it's relevant, you know? I've often said, "If I held a camera with my vagina, let's talk about it." But I don't.

I want to see that!

Jennifer Lynch: Right? And I don't walk up to an actor and say, "Hey. Because I'm a woman, I was thinking, maybe you could do it like this." So it's this weird thing where they're celebrating it because it benefits them—and there are a lot of wonderful directors out there who happen to be women, so that's spectacular!

I hope it's changing. I hope, past this pandemic, there is a greater focus on "Who do you want to spend time with? Who do you respect? Who's going to enrich you in ways you realize are now most important?" We had been, but we lost sight of it. It would be really nice if out of this pandemic we were able to realize our universal vulnerabilities and needs and that the fear we have of each other is really something that is being fed to us by the people who are now failing us.

Women—and not just women, none of us—are in competition with each other. We all have our own thing. If I don't get a job, it wasn't supposed to be my job. All you're doing is going around to find out what your thing is, and if you're not willing to hear "no," then that's not living. "No" can be a great thing. It's not that I don't love being a woman! I just don't think of it that way, and I'm not angry about it. It's about acknowledging that we got here because people who were afraid have the control, and they're not always men, but they're mostly. I find in the business that it has taken years, but people talk about me directing more than they talk about me as a woman.

Directing horror, people would tell me, "Wow, for a woman, that's a dark piece!" Are you fucking kidding me? We women are actually so dangerous. Men will punch each other and fucking blow shit up, but we play the long game. We play dark. Did you ever go to high school? Men are so busy wanting to have sex with people they're not realizing what we're up to. Hollywood is missing an incredible series of terrifying things. It shows me they're not paying attention to the same things, because I far more feared the women in my junior high and high school than any of the men.

The men—you knew exactly what they were going to do, how long it was going to last, this, this, and this. So easy to see. The women? Nuh-uh. And I love women. I'm not against anybody. But I think in this business, a lot of women feel they have to act like men and that we need to compete with each other. Sometimes, I come home, and I'll talk about that with [my husband] James [Robbins]: "I had another experience with a director today who seemingly could not get close to me or be friendly because we were in competition."

A lot of times, you'll share a set for a little while because you'll finish your day, and the last third of the day will be dedicated to another director who has scenes with those actors for another episode. So there's always this moment of shift where it goes from being one person's set to another person's set. You feel the different energy in different directors, and it can be a beautiful thing or it can be this weird thing. I know that's about fear because I'm scared when it's happening. I try to just walk up and say, "Hey, have a great day." But sometimes I just can't because I'm too afraid, so I'm a part of that. I know it's wrong, but it is a thing that I think is done to women. Making things OK is done to women, which goes back to Laura. It's not like BOB or Dad were doing any work to pretend things were OK. She had to do it all. That was all on her. And not just because she was a victim, but because she was a girl. And then they were going to judge it—"Wash your hands" and "Come on, sing!" And it serves this weird setup.

I was talking to my friend the other day, and we were talking about how normal sexual harassment was in the eighties and nineties. There were behaviors where, if it had happened to my daughter, I'd say, "You called the police, right?" There was a part of Laura [Palmer] that would speak up for Donna [Hayward] but could not speak up for herself. And I relate to that so deeply.

I am very clear with my daughter. You would've had to have stopped me from going over and hurting who did it. About myself, I don't want to think beyond five incidents that right now I think of when I think, "Why didn't you tell somebody about that?" At one point I told and had that go so badly. So it's this strange thing where, for me, because it was a real wish my twelve-year-old self had, I wanted to ask and play with these thoughts and questions and fantasies. Allow certain moments of the scary things to be arousing and not know why, because of the hormones going on in her. And to show that she had to do and make it something else. She had to make it OK. And the best version of that was someone coming from the outside in. Someone out there—it's not Leland. But he smells like him, and he always gets in. That works for any situation where we make excuses for the behavior of other people. We fabricate entire worlds around it.

That's come up in my book, too, with other survivors. I'm a survivor myself of childhood sexual abuse. I think sometimes when you do tell—whether it's just an assault or something bigger—like you said, it goes badly. You're not believed. You're the problem. I've heard this again and again. I think it's changing, but slowly.

So I decided to talk about my experience of abuse in the book. I want to mention my own story because it's my book on my own terms, and I thought it might be healing for me, but even my husband asked, "Are you sure you want to put that in there?" I have really thought through it, and I do want to tell my story. I'm in my forties now. What do I have to lose, you know?

Jennifer Lynch made her directorial debut with *Boxing Helena* (1993).
Photo courtesy of Orion Classics

Jennifer Lynch: I love that. I also understand your husband's question, because he loves you.

Yeah. He's trying to protect me.

Jennifer Lynch: Right. But isn't it that idea that you would need protection?

Yeah.

Jennifer Lynch: You're shining a light on a survivor, and our terror prevents us from putting the light on abusers. We are living among each other. I do not know many women who have not been assaulted or abused. That means I know a lot of men who are assaulters and are abusers. And we're only talking about one end of that. That's where the problem is. Years ago, I was in a foreign country, was assaulted, found the group I was with, and said, "We have to go," and was able to point out the person as we drove away. The people I was with had some friends with the police department. About forty-five minutes later I got a phone call saying it's been handled. The man was killed. He had done this in front of his wife and son to me. I had now done this thing wherein a boy and a woman were now alone, where it was very important to have a man with you. That's not what I would've had happen to him. It's not that I told the men to kill him, but it's how those guys handled it. None of it was about me. And none of it was about any of the energy that was there.

I love your husband for asking, and I know mine would too. I also think the new response should be not "Why are you talking about that?" That whole process is wrong. It's like trying to drive a car from the trunk. I really hope that that changes. I think being female and working in this business has become more familiar, and I am grateful for the directors who happen to be female who I think are handling it truly as themselves and not as women or women trying to be men or compete with men. And to the ones who are, I beg you to realize you're the storyteller, and I'm not asking about your physical genitals when I listen to your story unless it's about that.

The director should disappear anyway. It's one of the few times I want to not be called out. I don't want my shot to be so much about my shot that you're not in the moment. For me, I should vanish until it ends and you realize that was a moment; you were involved. A lot of people feel differently about that. I don't know how people enjoy the job if they're acting like someone else or something else to do it. How do you have any ideas? How do you have any joy in it? That's the mystery for me, and hopefully this pandemic gets us talking about being humans rather than any gender. Any surgeon or serial killer will tell you we look the same inside.

What's your advice for young female filmmakers who are just starting out?

Jennifer Lynch: You're going to see everyone again. Everyone matters. Everybody you encounter you are likely to see again, and they're all going through something, and they're all making choices based on what happened last night, this week, whatever. We're all in the same boat, but we have amnesia about it. Don't buy into the competition. There are going to be—minimum—thirty people up for any job. Sometimes thousands. Have a plan. Be yourself.

When you are up for a job, It's not about you interviewing them or them interviewing you. These are all people who will have a memory of you. Go in there, read the room. If you're actually listening to understand and not just watching their lips and then saying your part, if you're really being in there, you will have a good conversation, and then they will think of you. But enjoy the moment. That gets stolen all the time because we think we're in competition and we have to say something a certain way. What people are looking for are people they can work with because they are interested in them or it's nice to talk to them or they really listen. And that's where you want to be, in any life situation. Making the best of it. It's not about taking some kind of class, or understanding whatever. I make little films all the time on my phone. Know the equipment, play with the equipment, fail, stumble, whatever. There's no one way to do it.

Tell your story your way. Listen to people. You'll see them again.

And just being thought of is the magical thing. People are afraid to take risks on new people because their name is on the line, their job is on the line. They are less afraid to take risks on people who they feel will make anybody appreciative, and someone who's gonna really do the job—that's what people need. So whoever you are, that's who should walk into the room. Listen. Watch. You know if the person in the room is terrified of losing their job and a little bit intimidated and is judging you like, "Will I be fucked if I . . . ?" So talk to that. We all know what that's like.

Be the person you are. Technical, shmechnical. There's a way to do it, yes, but that's so simple. And it's common sense. It's what my father told me, I remember, right before *Boxing Helena*. He says, "You want to talk about anything?" I said, "I think I'm good. Is there anything you want to say to me?" He says, "You know. It's all common sense." And it's true. And all of us have common sense if we've been listening.

A smile is universally a good thing, and listening is always a benefit. Women are made to think that we aren't going to be able to do it and don't be emotional and don't do this. Imagine if we had a list of what men should not do before going into a meeting. It's all they would think about. They would instantly fart or burp or say something inappropriate about their mother or who knows what. We only do that to women. It's ridiculous.

The secret is keep going and talk to each other. We should have a once-a-month thing where we call in and go, "This happened." "Really? Fucker." It's not about us against us. But there is no secret. My advice is remember that. Be kind, be teachable, and remember, a "no" can feel like shit, but ultimately it's a gift. Gifts come looking like disasters sometimes.

With all this horseshit, there must be a pony. There is a pony somewhere. It's not about denying the bummers and the sexism, but we should just let that stop working. It's like, "Aren't you tired of talking about that?" I don't go around going, "You know, for a man, you did a good job on that scene. It was funny and cute and had women in it! And they weren't being, like, penetrated from behind! Good job!"

I try to enter a space and have as productive of a time in it as I can regardless of what it is. Often, with a scene I don't love or believe in, it is my job to say, "Well, I need to find a way to believe in it. So what can I do to make this the best scene I can?" It's not always easy, but it's always as simple as that. I don't have to do this; I get to do this. This is the next thing I get to do. And when it's over, I will have done it. So let's have a positive experience—how can I make this better instead of arguing it, because you can't have good ideas from that. Just by doing that it takes the weird gender-panic thing out of it.

The pandemic has gotten me thinking about the world before and what the world is going to be after. Speaking to that and Laura, all of these increased cases of domestic violence and abuse are happening because people are forced to be at home with their abusers. There's tension—we're going to learn a lot. And we are reaping what we have sowed in terms of letting go of certain regulations and not listening to certain things.

Men are not innately bad. They are being taught to behave a certain way, and that's where BOB is born. Part of me believes in the supernatural element of it, but *FWWM* is about what the diary is about. It's so absolutely difficult to see your father's face do that that you will make it become another face or you will die. It is the only way. It's like multiple personalities or hiding it, blocking it out, calling it something else. That's what we do.

I hope we don't go back after this pandemic. I don't think we can truly go back to normal, but I hope it changes everything. I hope it changes who we have in power, how we allocate money, how we protect people. I hope it changes the empathy we have for people, the compassion. If anything good can come from all this, I hope it changes things for the better.

Jennifer Lynch: Absolutely. That is ultimately what I believe. I want to be on the other side of it and be grateful that we were able to lose as few lives as we did. I feel like there will be a greater global consciousness about what's important and where the flaws were in how it was handled. And how do we protect each other? Because we all affect each other. And that's a beautiful thing! And we should start talking more and supporting each other more and not making it about, "Oh, now you fucked it up.

You had to go and say something." I say I completely understand what your husband said, and I think what you're doing is great.

Thank you. I appreciate your support. It means a lot.

Jennifer Lynch: Congratulations. It's a really big deal. It's a nice superhero cape you have on!

Women in the Fan Community Speak

There is no fan community quite like the *Twin Peaks* fan community. It comprises some of the most creative, caring, and compassionate people I know. They accept the eccentric, the vulnerable, the weird. It is safe to be all of these things in their company. *Twin Peaks* has inspired many of us to share our stories of trauma and survival. It's also given so many women, including myself, an opportunity to explore their own complex and creative nature. The following is a celebration of women, their love of the show, their creativity, their vulnerability, their survival—their love of *Twin Peaks*. These are their stories.

Mary Czerwinski
Writer & Actor

"People are intimidated by female characters who are sexually self-possessed. They don't know what to make of women who have sexual licenses, who don't need a man, who don't need a relationship to define their existence."

Mary Czerwinski is a poet, an actor, and a writer. She is also uncompromisingly beautiful and intimidatingly intelligent. Czerwinski grew up in Chicago working in theater—writing and producing plays. A journalism graduate, she started a TV show reviewing DVDs. This is where she earned her alternative name, Televixen. Czerwinski eventually moved to Los Angeles, where she lives now, to act. She's published a book of poems titled *Elements of Change: A Collection of Poetry*. There is, of course, a *Twin Peaks*-inspired poem: "Sparkwood and 21." She also does an uncanny cosplay of Teresa Banks.

Excerpt from "Sparkwood and 21":

"Nature's electricity illuminates the view,
Chemicals commingle consciences,
Hope flickers through trees,
Souls separated for centuries
balance with perfect symmetry,
Fear no longer dictates where
secrets are stored."[1]

When did you first watch *Twin Peaks?*

Mary Czerwinski: My mom and I used to watch a lot of TV together. She was into soap operas. She watched *Knots Landing, Falcon Crest, Dallas,* all the big ones of the eighties. And we watched *Beverly Hills, 90210* together. Occasionally I would watch something I shouldn't have watched. She watched bits and pieces of *Twin Peaks,* and so I would catch it every now and then. But she didn't want me to watch it, and I didn't understand why she didn't want me to watch that one particular show. I actually got a TV in my room in the mid-1990s right after *FWWM* was on cable. I caught that on cable late at night. So I'm the rare case where I saw *FWWM* before the series, and a lot of people feel sorry for me. Or they say, "I can't believe you experienced it that way." I

---

1   Mary Czerwinski, *Elements of Change: A Collection of Poetry* (Scotts Valley: CreateSpace, 2015), 13

think of it as a great gift, because I always identified the series with Laura even if her presence wasn't there physically. To me, it started with her and always ended with her. It was this full circle, and circles are a huge theme in Lynch's work. To me, it never seemed odd. As an actor and a writer, I'm always looking for depth of character in the pieces I create, and so to look at Ray Wise's work and know what journey he had been through, to know the revelation before, it didn't hurt me. It's like seeing *Psycho*. Everybody knows the twist now. Unless you watched it in the theater in 1960, you wouldn't have been brought up without knowing that. So it doesn't really kill the story, because the writing is still there, and the characters are still there, the depth is still there. Because then I could appreciate the backstory that all these people referred to and have it have a profound impact on me the way it did the characters of this town. I felt I got to know Laura first and foremost, and put myself in her shoes, and then be carried through this Cooper journey of discovering the mystery. So it didn't ruin the mystery; it enhanced the mystery.

When you were a teenager, did you feel you had someone you could truly confide in or did you keep parts of yourself kind of hidden from everyone?

Mary Czerwinski: I mean, yes and no. I always had a side to myself that was very secret and very hidden. But I was closest to my grandmother. She was somebody I felt like I could tell a lot of things to. In fact, we had a correspondence. I think of my letters to my grandmother as more of a diary, in a way, than my real diary, so maybe I did have a secret diary.

We would physically correspond through handwritten letters—this was before e-mail—and she kept them, and I kept hers. One of the things she absolutely said in her handwritten will is she wanted to be buried with those letters. Some of them she still kept off to the side, but the very, very secret ones that talk about my personal feelings, my sadness, she wanted it to go to the grave with her, which is interesting, because in essence she was keeping my secrets.

One of her last letters to me was one where she told me she always wanted to fire walk. Which I thought, "Gosh, of all phrases." She had no idea I was a fan of *Twin Peaks*. She didn't even know what *Twin Peaks* was. But she used that phrase. She was a Polynesian dancer. For her, that meant the physical act of walking on fire, dancing on fire, which typically men do in Fiji. I guess it's a Tibetan thing too in the *Twin Peaks* world. But her dance teacher at the time, a woman, told her, "Only the men do that. Why would you want to do that? You're just going to get hurt." And I think, secretly, she was always implying to me that maybe her dance teacher was not willing to teach her that or show her that or give her an apprenticeship doing that because she thought, "Oh, maybe she'll outshine me." Because she was getting a lot of solos and a lot of attention—she was a very beautiful woman. And so she wrote to me in this letter and said, "Don't let anyone ever tell you you can't fire walk." And I thought, "Wow, that's saying a mouthful." It was her last letter to me. So when I got a *Twin Peaks: Fire Walk With Me* tattoo it wasn't just about my love of the show.

I never had another friend growing up who watched it. So I didn't have anyone to discuss the show with for years. And then around 2009 or so I started to get more and more interested in wanting to go to the festival in Washington. Then around 2013, I went to the USC [University of Southern California] *Twin Peaks* retrospective events. And so I started to mobilize and meet other fans, which I think sharing our love for it makes it less this dirty little secret or a guilty pleasure or whatever. It legitimizes what you liked as art is powerful and on a level that's bigger than all of us.

Twin Peaks, I think, will transcend space and time, much like the Black Lodge or the White Lodge, because it resonates with the core of what it means to be human. That we have this dichotomy, that we have this capacity to be the brightest light but also sink to the deepest, darkest depths, and not one person on this earth is the perfect balance of just one. It's always both; it has to be a balance of both. Even Laura, you know? I think, for me, my grandmother was probably my real diary. I think she understood a lot more than what I said. She could read between the lines, and it meant something to me to get that on paper and to give it to someone who I knew would never share that with anyone. And she never did. Maybe a lot of it had to do with her education, which was only an eighth-grade education, even though she was very street-smart and savvy.

Sheryl Lee was very brave to take on the character of Laura Palmer, because whenever you embody a character there are pieces of you in it. And even if you try to say, oh, you're just playing a role, you have to tap into something that is deep inside yourself that maybe you wouldn't outwardly admit is there. But as a kid, I think I was a loner in a lot of ways. I felt like I was always the queen of popularity, but no one really knew me. And I think that's the heart of why I relate to Laura. She meant something to everyone, but she had no idea how much she meant to everyone. When I go to *Star Trek* conventions, young girls come up and say how inspiring it is that I'm onstage. There are times where I just want to give it all up and say, "I'm a private person. I'm not really in the public eye. Why does it matter?" But it does matter, because you don't realize sometimes how much your presence can be an inspiration to someone else. I don't have the ego that most actors have. You have to have a certain level of ego to be an actor. Acting for me is so emotional and so personal. That's why I didn't go to the Twin Peaks Fest for many, many years, and even my first Twin Peaks Fest I didn't enjoy it in the way I did later. Because I always thought of this as such a personal journey and something I wanted to protect and not share with anyone. Being a fan of *Star Trek*, there's this one-upmanship in fandom. Like, "I have the most action figures" and "I know the most stuff about trivia" and this and that. At first, on the surface level, I thought, "Gosh, that's what this fest is about. It's like everyone who has all the T-shirts, and it's no longer this weird quirky thing that only I know what it is." And I didn't want to share that. But now I take it back. I've met so many incredible people that I connect with on a soul level that *Twin Peaks* also resonates with. I don't mind sharing it with them. It actually brings out something in me. It makes me feel like you're not alone. It makes me feel like maybe others had that same kind of feelings I did about Laura I did growing up.

What role does trauma play in *Twin Peaks?*

Mary Czerwinski: I think it was incredibly powerful to use the symbolism of masks or disassociation by using the BOB character. It could have gone two ways. It could have literally been Leland creating this alter ego to be able to deal with (or not deal with) what he did to his own daughter. That in itself is incredibly powerful. It's like the Norman Bates character [in *Psycho*]. He's so innocent. He doesn't realize that he's killing people. With *Twin Peaks*, here's this guy who can't deal with this horrible thing he's been doing to his daughter, which has been done to him, so there is this legacy of that. The thing that is powerful about Laura is she actually has the power to stop the pattern, the pattern of abuse that is happening. Finally Laura's the one who puts her foot down and says, "No, this is not OK, and it ends here. I'm not going to pass this on to anyone else." I think it's incredibly powerful material—Leland not being able to come to terms with what's happened. So when Leland is having his death scene and he's coming to terms with what he did, but also feeling tremendous remorse, what happens to him? All of the sprinklers go off in the jail, and he's doused with water. What is water? Water is the one thing that can fight oil and fire. It can put out a fire. It's like The Log Lady says: "Once the tender boughs of innocence burn, it's hard to put out." So in some ways, he's redeemed at that moment. Laura's redeemed in her death.

But what is the one through line? It's this feminine energy; it's the water. And oil and water are diametrically opposed—you can't mix them. There's no coincidence in the Lynch world. There's definite symbolism at play here. The fact that both Teresa and Laura were put in water after their deaths is interesting. I look at Teresa as the cautionary tale now. If you look at Laura and Teresa, Teresa's the dark Laura, in a lot of ways, or the dream Laura. If you look at the whole thing, there are some people who think that is the dream side. I don't know if I buy that opinion, but it is interesting to entertain, because there's so many parallels there. But the thing that Laura had going for her is that she was so beloved, she had so many things going on in her life, whether she realized it or not, that it meant something to all these people, and she meant something, which is why the town is such a mess when she dies. Teresa didn't have that. Teresa had no next of kin, she was a drifter, she lived in a trailer, she didn't have love and family. Clearly, she was a young woman, but we don't know anything about her family life. Where are these people who were supposed to protect her from this evil? So she did not have the support system Laura had. If you look at even the diners and you look at the Deer Meadow and Twin Peaks sheriffs' stations. In Laura's world you have Norma, who is sort of the mother character who is taking care of all these people in this place, and it's this tremendous diner of warmth and positive energy. And then you've got Irene at Hap's diner, who couldn't be anything further from that. And then the Deer Meadow Sheriff Station is like anti-Twin Peaks Sheriff Station. They're the evil twins of each other. Lynch likes to play with those opposites.

But I feel like Teresa as a loss is incredibly sad. Because to me, she's the true mystery, and she's still a mystery you could tell a whole backstory about. How did she get to where she is? Teresa got to be a mystery, and that's why I'm fascinated with her as a character. That's why I cosplayed her. I don't think people think about her as much as they do Laura. But to me, that was the first imagery I ever saw of *Twin Peaks* that stuck with me. It was her body floating and her backstory, which is how he starts with the whole *FWWM* movie . . . and it's an ax going through a TV screen I think there's a huge message to the networks of what he wanted to do, and he finally gets to do it . . . tell this mystery. So, she's a compelling character to me because we don't get it all out there.

But the reason why I like *FWWM* is it's such an unapologetically dark movie, but that's just on the surface. If you look at it, and inspect that last scene, there's so much hope and so much happiness that Laura has that people dismiss. People don't like to be faced with things that are hard to watch, and because *Twin Peaks* tends to be irreverent at times and have all these joyful characters, *FWWM* is on the opposite end of that spectrum for some people. So there are fans of one who aren't fans of the other. The reason why there is that divide is because it is unapologetically Lynch. It's like Lynch didn't get to do what he wanted with the series, so he was going to do it and then some with this movie as a big "F" you to critics. And people didn't get it at the time, but I love it, because it is such a tour de force, and Sheryl Lee's performance— there's so much going on behind her eyes in every scene. There's just something haunting about her.

You've worked as a journalist, a writer, and a performer. Women face so many obstacles when they put themselves out there creatively. How do you deal with that?

Mary Czerwinski: My work is always perceived as dark, but I don't intend it to be that way. It's OK to laugh. Laughing breaks up the tension of something that is heavy. So it's funny that the takeaway is "Oh, but she's so dark and kind of sad. She goes to these pathetic places. What a sad existence." I'm like: "I don't think of her that way, I don't think she thinks of herself as that way." People are intimidated by female characters that are sexually self-possessed. They don't know what to make of women who have sexual licenses, who don't need a man, who don't need a relationship to define their existence.

What are you working on now?

Mary Czerwinski: I am writing a new poetry book, and it's going to incorporate my grandmother's artwork and perhaps some of her journal entries. In a way, her ghost is a light that always shines upon me in all creative aspects of my life, from the first shell I glued to the first stage I stepped on. My grandmother, a feminine hero, was the reason I found courage to express myself. Just like my grandma, Laura gave acceptance of the dark and light sides of myself at a time when I needed understanding the most. Her ghost lives on as a beacon of hope. Laura showed me that even through the roughest life there's still goodness that never goes away. If you love yourself and forgive yourself, that light will be your salvation from the darker forces that seek to destroy you. Self-love is a weapon. Laura's light was the ultimate weapon against her descent into complete darkness. Her light transferred to all of us at a crucial age when we needed to know we weren't alone. Laura, thank you for haunting me. Thank you for being an angel to a girl you never met.

Milly Moo
Artist

"It takes a lot of bravery to say you're an artist."

Milly Moo says, "'Artist' is not a dirty word, just a messy job." She recently gave up many years of working with challenged youth to commit herself to her art full time. Her art involves many things, but in particular the surreal and yet lifelike dolls she creates based on *Twin Peaks* and Lynchian characters. There's Red Room Laura Palmer, a big-haired blonde donned in black, stretching her palms into that classic "meanwhile" gesture. Her work is iconic and has grabbed the attention of many in the community—even David Lynch himself.

What was your journey as an artist, and how does *Twin Peaks* factor in?

Milly Moo: I live in a small town in the country in Victoria, Australia. I think it's technically a city—but it's a town. It's very football [soccer]/sports oriented. So when I started watching *Twin Peaks* as an adolescent—and I think I was barely thirteen—I didn't have anybody to talk to about how I loved this show and ask, "Who do you think killed Laura Palmer?" There was none of that. It was a secret obsession. I was a young mom. I've got two sons. For most of my professional life I've worked with adolescents who have experienced significant trauma and abuse and have been cared for by the Department of Health and Human Services. I worked in both residential care and as a case manager until recently. Now I'm going to have a fair crack at doing this artist thing because I think it's been a long time coming. It takes a lot

71

of bravery to say you're an artist. I've always dabbled in things; I like sewing and obviously dolls and painting. That's the sort of stuff that I love—this bizarre moonlighting thing where during the day I would go to work with teenagers and people would say, "How do you cope with the stress of doing that?" And I'd come home and make dolls and watch *Twin Peaks*, which I do religiously.

Working with children in the system, what made you choose that profession and what effect did it have on you?

Milly Moo: I was pretty young when I had my first son, and I remember feeding him one day while watching a Bob Geldof interview. He was talking about children in Africa and starvation and how awful it was. Some footage came across of this mother trying to breastfeed her child, but she couldn't provide much milk. I just felt so awful. I had to do something. Initially, I volunteered with an agency that provides some support to families going through difficulties. Through them I connected mostly with adolescents. So I went to work in a residential-care setting for kids who have been removed from their parents and just aren't suited for foster care due to their extreme behaviors. The majority of the kids I worked with had experienced significant trauma—abuse mostly. One thing I noticed through the character of Laura is how over-the-top the scene is where she's screaming at James on the motorbike in *FWWM*. But over the last couple of years, I've witnessed young women doing just that. Sheryl Lee's ability to capture that trauma—having seen it firsthand and worked with it over the last fifteen years—it's just astounding. Really astounding—almost like a mirror image of watching Laura Palmer. Just bizarre.

I connected well with those kids, and at the end of the day they just want to be heard and be with someone who's consistent. You almost become a sort of faux parent to them. I think I've always been able to see the good in these kids; society's really against them a lot of the time. So I followed that career path for a long time. It's becoming more difficult with the kids becoming quite materialistic. Back in the day when I worked in residential care, I would say to the kids that if we all have a good night and nobody fights, then I'd take them to

McDonald's, and we'd have a fantastic night. Nowadays if you say, "Yes, I will buy you those Nike Air Maxes," then there's just no negotiating with them; they don't see the value in it for them—plus they don't have respect for themselves, so they don't have respect for anybody else. It is getting more challenging working with kids. Hence why I'm stepping away from it for a bit.

You have created some incredible art based on David Lynch, Mark Frost, and _Twin Peaks._ Can you talk about that journey and why you create this particular type of art?

Milly Moo: About seven or eight years ago, at a thrift store, I ended up with a bag of dolls, and I thought, "I wonder what can I do with these." One of them was a Barbie doll, so of course one of the first things I did was to paint her face a little bit corpselike, add some blue, wrap her in some plastic, and pop her in a fish tank. And I remember looking at that and wondering if I could expand on that. The second doll I made was actually Lil, the dancer from _FWWM._ I decided that I needed dolls with more articulation, so I moved on to Monster High dolls. I don't actually sculpt the entire doll; I repaint it.

So I made Lil the dancer and found this wonderful thing called Instagram that would be a good platform to share artwork. It gave me a little bit of traction. After Lil the dancer, I made Shelly Johnson in her Double R uniform. I made Bobby Briggs as well. Then it just kept building and building. The first response I got from a member of the cast was Mädchen Amick [Shelly] sharing the doll on her Facebook profile for International Pie Day. I didn't know there were other fans out there until I started sharing on Instagram and realizing there was a community and it was alive and well—T-shirts, artists, a community of _Twin Peaks_ merch.

I just kept building on it from there, and I thought maybe I could make the Palmer house. Certainly if you were to go on to my Instagram and see the dolls I was making seven or eight years ago, they're getting better, and that's just through practice. When people contact me and say, "Oh, I could never do what you do," that's not true. I've spent a lot of time refining what I do and figuring things out. It is a lot about experimenting, and over time I became known as the Doll Lady, and I kind of like that!

When did you first watch *Twin Peaks* and what was your reaction?

Milly Moo: I watched it as soon as it aired in Australia; I believe I was thirteen. I had never seen anything like it before. I think I've always lived as an introverted young person. I always lived in a fantasyland and never connected to anything except my own head. I loved everything about it—the town was mysterious even before you knew there was a BOB and a Red Room and all this other mystical-type stuff. It was magical from the moment I saw it. I recorded every episode on VHS, and if I was lucky enough to be there I would pause out the ad breaks. I think I missed one episode. I'm not much of a crier, but I do remember crying when I asked my mum to record it for me and she didn't understand the high level of importance of that matter and she missed it. I can't even remember what episode it was.

Then I purchased the entire collection on VHS and eventually the Gold Box set [*Twin Peaks: The Definitive Gold Box Edition*]. I reckon I watch it three times a year, at least. One of the reasons I like it is I can put it on and instantly get that homely feel. I'm from a broken family, so that sense of going home to the family home doesn't exist for me. We moved around a lot, had lots of houses, so there is no family home to me. *Twin Peaks* was always like that feeling of coming home.

You had the opportunity to meet some of the cast in Australia. What was it like to meet the actors who played these iconic characters?

Milly Moo: It was overwhelming for me to have the cast in this country, because I thought I would never get that opportunity. I'd have to save my pennies and fly over to a *Twin Peaks* fest and get to meet some of the cast over there with any luck. So when they came to Australia, it felt like that year was for me! It was such a special event. I got to talk to David Lynch that night as well. In the e-mail they sent out to members with VIP and platinum passes they asked us to send in questions for Lynch and told us he would be Skyping in. My question was selected. I asked him, "You're an artist who works in a lot of different mediums—is there something you haven't tried yet that you'd like to try?" So I got to the theater. I sit down. I hadn't eaten, so I had this bag of salted caramel popcorn. And I was feeding my face and listening to Electric Moon, the *Twin Peaks*-inspired band that was playing—they were really great. And Ben Jackson, the event organizer, comes up and says, "Now Milly, you're talking to David Lynch tonight." And I was like, "OK. I wish I'd dressed a bit better." Lynch Skypes in at the very start, before any of the cast came out. We were taken to a little room, and Sabrina [Sutherland] was sitting at the end of a long table, and she had a laptop in front of her, and that's where David Lynch was appearing. There was a little "X" on the side of the stage where you had to stand to ask your question, and his answer to my question was that it was a good question and he's very interested in learning how to sew. David's a man of few words, so it was sharp and to the point, and then he let somebody else have their moment with him. But I would not have thought in a million years I would be even over the Internet face-to-face with David Lynch.

I interviewed Sabrina Sutherland a while ago, and I asked what she and David Lynch are working on now, and she said, "He's learning to sew." He's actually learning to sew on an industrial sewing machine! He wants to take his art and embroider it into certain designs. I wonder if your question got him thinking about that again or if he was already planning to learn anyway.

Milly Moo: I really wanted to say, "David, I'd be super happy to come over and teach you a French seam." The other great thing that happened from the *Twin Peaks* Australia event is I'd made a Sabrina doll, and she had seen it on social media and had commented on it. I told Sabrina, "Hey, at the event in Australia can I give it to you?" And she said, "Yes, of course!" So Sabrina was the third person I met, after Sheryl Lee and Dana Ashbrook. So I gave her the doll, and she said, "Milly, I was showing David—he just can't believe it." And I said, "You know, I've made David." She said, "Have you?" I'd been trying to organize getting it through Debbie Zoller, the makeup artist on Season 3, because I think she wanted Diane. So when Sabrina got home and settled, I messaged her and organized sending her the David doll. Another cool thing that happened was meeting Michael Horse. I told him I make dolls, and he was intrigued. When we were lining up to do the Skype thing, they had to drag Michael onto the stage because he saw me and went, "You! These dolls—how do I get one? How long does it take? How would you get it to me?" And they were dragging him like, come on, time to get up on to the stage! And he just wanted a doll. So I ended up sending Hawk, Gordon Cole, and Richard Horne to Sabrina. I believe all of them got their dolls at the Festival of Disruption.

It's taken me a long time to just say the word "artist." I don't know if other people experience that as well, but for a long time people would ask, "What are you in your spare time?" and I'd say, "I'm a crafter." But the more people started calling me an artist, the more I thought, "OK, I just have to go along with this artist thing." I don't necessarily want to be a millionaire, but I do want to support myself to continue making my art and give back to the community. When I posted Pete [Martell], knowing Jack Nance is no longer with us and how treasured he was as a character, Jennifer Lynch commented on Instagram that she was crying when she saw him. It's just beautiful. I love being able to bring parts of *Twin Peaks* back to life in doll form.

Mya McBriar
Writer

"I decided to revisit the series in my own way."

In her *Twin Peaks Fanatic* blog, Mya McBriar wrote, "*Twin Peaks* was a private obsession that haunted me but challenged me to think outside the box. *Twin Peaks* was my domain, and I never wanted to share it with anyone. I liked getting lost in it alone, particularly with *FWWM*, because alone I felt free to feel everything without concern for how others might perceive the film or my reaction to it. I suppose I took a part of it with me as I entered my teenage years and got into high school. I had *TP* on the brain. I had Laura's tragedy stuck in my own vernacular and parts of it began to bleed into my real life. I ran a bit wild for a time."[1] This blog post of McBriar's seems more personal than her others—a hint at what connects her to *Twin Peaks* and Laura's story. Mya McBriar was the first woman I interviewed. I admired her gumption in creating this platform to share her thoughts on *Twin Peaks* and David Lynch's work. She's been a vocal voice in the community for some years now. She's also written consistently for *The Blue Rose* magazine and published a chapter that directly confronts violence against women in *The Women of David Lynch: A Collection of Essays*. Her work resonates.

Your *Twin Peaks* blog has been a staple of the fan community for years now. You are known throughout the Internet as *Twin Peaks Fanatic*. Tell me about starting your blog.

Mya McBriar: I started it a day or two after they first announced the show was coming back in 2014. I really had no plan for it. It was spontaneous. When *The Missing Pieces* came out and there was suddenly talk of *Twin Peaks* again, it was getting exciting, and I thought, "Maybe I should do something with *Twin Peaks*." But once it was announced I thought, "Ugh, I have to do something with *Twin Peaks*." I decided to revisit the series in my own way. I try to be creative. I'm always looking for new things to do with it. But I'm glad I did it. It's been so much fun.

When did you first watch *Twin Peaks*?

---

1   Mya McBriar, "Laura Walked With Me," *Twin Peaks Fanatic*, May 10, 2016.

Mya McBriar: I watched it live pretty much from the pilot episode to episode fourteen when—spoiler alert—Maddy gets killed. I remember seeing pretty much every episode up until that point. And then I fell in love with *FWWM*. When I finally acquired the whole set, including the pilot, which I had to buy separately, I finally got to see the whole thing. Because of the way that I watched it originally, leaving off when Maddy got killed and then going into *FWWM* a year and a half later, it made *FWWM* better for me. Because I wasn't going into it looking for answers from the finale or looking to find out what happened to Dale. I didn't know anything about that. I was more fascinated with Laura's story. And I think the movie really delivered on that.

Do you feel as a woman writer that you're under more scrutiny or less? Do you feel you're treated in a different way, publishing your thoughts out there on the Internet?

Mya McBriar: Mostly I think it's been very, very positive. I don't know what some other women in the community have experienced or not. I know most of the men have been wonderful. There is a male-dominated feel to who is publishing and who is putting things out especially related to the show. There's not as many women doing it. When I started it, it certainly wasn't a thought. It was more like, "I love *Twin Peaks*, and I want to write something." Along the way I think I have learned that you are opening yourself to people being curious about you. But most of the time I think people have been really wonderful. The more I do it the more comfortable I am. I'm just going to keep going, you know? Writing something like my piece "Laura Walked With Me" will just keep me doing it. If it turns out it's also good for women, then I'm honored.

You've written about the music from *Twin Peaks*, and David Lynch's music. Is there a particular song that you enjoy listening to?

Mya McBriar: I like the *FWWM* soundtrack a little bit better than the series. I like the "Montage from Twin Peaks" song a lot, and I've always liked that song "A Real Indication." I think the *FWWM* soundtrack is my favorite. I like David Lynch's music in general. It took me a while, but after a few listens to "Crazy Clown Time" I fell in love with it. People don't feel that way, but I did. The *FWWM* soundtrack brings me back to that time of my childhood when I first saw the movie and I was first

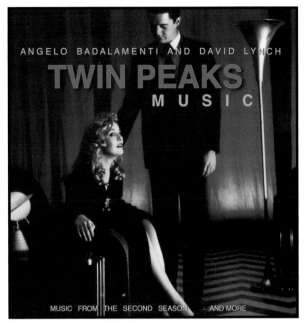

Photo courtesy of Rhino

falling in love with all that stuff, and I like that a lot. The soundtrack for the movie does that more for me than the series soundtrack. There's a sadness to it. Sometimes that sadness isn't necessarily something that's comfortable to feel, but in a way I still like it. The sad elements of it bring out creativity and get you thinking. The Pink Room music is like when you want to go get drunk and have a cigarette, you know? And the other music makes you cry. You're sad for Laura. It takes you through this range of emotion.

You wrote a fiction piece for a chapter in *The Women of David Lynch* book that creatively addresses violence against women. What inspired you to write the piece?

Mya McBriar: I wanted to do something stylistic and creative that would encompass important elements of Lynch's work through expression, not analysis. I wanted it to seem a little funny at first, maybe even uncomfortable, but as the reader continues a mystery unfolds, and I hoped that would be intriguing. What was important to me to express was that the lead character was not a good man. He, like many Lynchian characters, was struggling with his dark side. The female presence in the story I kept nameless on purpose, because to me she was sort of a composite of all the "women in trouble" from Lynch's films. Violence against women in Lynch's work is inescapable, in my opinion, so I didn't see a way around that in my own story. Whether the viewer sees Lynch's work as exploitive or insightful probably depends on their perspective. I often viewed it as insightful, but in a raw way, and through a masculine lens. I suppose I wanted to create something similar, but with my own, feminine perspective.

Rosie Stewart
Scholar & Podcaster

"It's good to have films that represent everyday life for women, but it's also great to have films that represent women as dreaming creatures, as people who have fantasies and nightmares and who can be really weird."

Rosie Stewart and her brothers and friends get together in their town of Brighton in the United Kingdom a few times a month, drink a beer, talk about *Twin Peaks*, and record it for their *Diane* podcast. Stewart's background as a scholar makes this podcast a deeper dive than most, but all of the participants make it fun. The podcast is named after Agent Dale Cooper's assistant, Diane, to whom he religiously dictates all of his taped recordings in Seasons 1 and 2, including important FBI crime info and what he had for lunch. In Season 3, we finally see the real Diane, portrayed by Laura Dern. The podcast touts itself as being about "art, storytelling, and the magical lodge-ics of Frost and Lynch." It certainly is all of these things, and more.

Tell me about your journey as a scholar and a podcaster.

Rosie Stewart: I'm currently making a podcast about *Twin Peaks* with my brothers and friends here in Brighton. I've previously worked in the anthropology of religion. I thought it might be a way that I can go out into the world and find out interesting things and meet interesting people. Then I completely fell in love with the subject and the discipline. I did my own research with evangelical and Pentecostal Christians, which was a huge culture shock for me, but just so fascinating to be able to go into a world like that. I was able to go somewhere that was very close by for an anthropologist. Most anthropologists would be halfway around the world. So it felt very familiar and strange at the same time, one of the main things I love about *Twin Peaks*. When all of the academic stuff didn't work out long term, I was able to get bits and bumps of funding and bits and bumps of work, but I wasn't able to continue the career the way I thought I would eventually. When that ended up not panning out, it did inform what I wanted to do with *Diane*, because I didn't want to stop using the knowledge about how we can approach the world through strange eyes, or how we can approach things that aren't familiar to us and come to an understanding but retain that strangeness. That's a good way to read *Twin Peaks*. You are visiting this world, and it is foreign to you, and some things about it will be very, very familiar to you and some things about it will be terrifyingly strange, and you just have to get on with it. That's certainly what I like about *Twin Peaks*. I hope I'm able to bring that onto the podcast without boring on too much about academic theory. People want to hear stuff about a TV show that engages with the text in a way they haven't heard before. But what you don't want to do is alienate people using this incredibly arcane language and being a sort of stuffy academic about it. I try and avoid that.

Why did you create the *Diane* podcast?

Rosie Stewart: When I stopped doing stuff in academia, I applied for a big funding award in 2015. I didn't get it. At that stage I was like, "OK, I'm done. This is too hard, I've got no money, absolutely none. I'll go full time with my office job." Around the same time, my older brother Adam reached out to me and said, "I'm thinking about doing a podcast about *Twin Peaks*. You are, obviously, very obsessed with *Twin Peaks*. Would you like to come on board?" So we started recording a couple of months later. Our first attempts at recording went so badly they had to be scrapped, and we had to start again. But we were lucky enough that our other brother, Mark, and our friend Bob were able to come and share the load with us hosting it. We record every week or whenever we can—twice or three times a month—in my living room in my flat in Brighton. The guys come around, we have a beer, and then, afterwards, I do the editing, and I'm very lucky that my boyfriend has taken over all the sound duties. He makes us all sound good afterwards. I'm not sure what the technical term for it is, the mastering, making the levels work and bringing in all the sound effects. So that's how the sausage gets made.

Since you've worked in academia and on a podcast, what has been your experience working as a woman in these worlds?

Rosie Stewart: My own experience back in academia was enormously positive. I was working on broadly feminist projects, work that was to do with gender, a lot of the time, and working particularly with women as research participants. I had a positive experience with my particular supervisors and my peers that I had around me. I would say a big difference that I noticed coming into podcasting and also just into a sphere that is slightly more creative is that in academia it feels like a lot of the ways you would build networks as women can feel quite established and codified. There are particular groups that you would reach out to—there are particular journals you publish within, for instance—whereas I've found in doing this podcast that everything is so organic and it still feels quite fresh and new, so it's up to us to build the kind of networks we want to see in the world. It's so exciting, and this is why I think your book sounds so wonderful. It's wonderful you get to speak to all these women and find out what they're up to.

When did you first watch *Twin Peaks*?

Rosie Stewart: So I first watched *Twin Peaks* when I accidentally caught a glimpse of it when I was about five. My parents were watching it while it was on TV, and I saw one of their old VHS tapes of it. Basically, it was very, very frightening, and my mum was like: "You're not supposed to watch that show." And I got it in my head that I wanted to watch it. I was reminded of it again when I was about thirteen. Suddenly I thought, "I absolutely must see *Twin Peaks*. I really want to see it." So I got the VHS set for my birthday and watched it all. And since then I've been just completely obsessed.

What are your thoughts on David Lynch? Are you a David Lynch fan? Do you have a favorite David Lynch movie?

Rosie Stewart: I definitely enjoy Lynch's work a lot. My favorite Lynch film is *The Straight Story*, which I think is not the most usual choice. It's not incredibly representative of his style, I don't think. But I absolutely love it. I love the pace of it. I love that there's a sort of sweetness about it. I think Angelo Badalamenti's score is one of his best pieces of work ever. So that's actually my favorite one. The thing I like about David Lynch's work so much is how it feels like you're engaging with a community. You're engaging with so many writers and collaborators and actors, and you get the feeling he gives them a lot of space to work, and that thought is enormously pleasurable. And I like his depictions of women. Again, it's about opening up this space where you can be weird. Women are allowed to be weird in David Lynch films. They're not just attractive. And we're not just seeing their daily lives. It's good to have films that represent everyday life for women, but it's also great to have films that represent women as dreaming creatures, as people who have fantasies and nightmares and who can be really weird. I love that in David Lynch's work. I think it gives you so much that you don't get elsewhere.

Maja Ljunggren
Artist

"I usually start with a setting—I create the place. I look at all the pictures and go back and watch an episode to see what it actually looks like in this place. Sometimes the idea of what's going to be in the image comes first, but mostly it's the setting."

Maddy Ferguson pauses before the Palmer house. She's wearing a sweater, a pleated skirt, and those signature Maddy glasses. She's carrying a suitcase while a taxi whizzes away. There's a foreboding owl statue perched in the window of the Palmer house. Maddy is home. Home is where the heart is and where death finds Maddy Ferguson. This is *Twin Peaks*, but more specifically this is Maja Ljunggren. Ljunggren creates a mood when she designs her *Twin Peaks*-inspired art. She invites you in to stay a while. To look at the details. To pause. To be taken by the visual juxtaposition of objects and people set in familiar themes. Ljunggren is an artist. She's worked in several media, including 3D and gaming. Her art has caught the attention of the *Twin Peaks* community and beyond.

You grew up in a small town in Sweden similar to Twin Peaks and are now creating art inspired by the show. How did that come about?

Maja Ljunggren: I am forty-five years old, and I live in Gothenburg, Sweden. I was born in a town that is very much like Twin Peaks. It's a small town dead set in the middle of the forest. And of course forestry and the wooding industry is the main part of town—that's what the

Art by Maja Ljunggren

town was living for, and still is. I lived there when the first season of *Twin Peaks* started. It hooked me because it felt like this could be my life. There's also a lot of weird, inbred people as well and it was very much like Twin Peaks in many ways. These days, I'm a 3D graphic artist, but I don't do the same thing every time. I mostly do drawings of things going to be built; I make it look like it already has been built so they can see what it's going to be like. They also call them "visualizers" these days. So that's my main job, more or less. I just started making the art that I'm making because I was bored and was trying to learn a new tool. With that tool, I needed something to practice on, so I started making an image, and thought, "I can do this or this or I'll do something *Twin Peaks*—for fun." So I started making one image. Later I thought I should share it online. I shared it in one of the *Twin Peaks* groups and decided to make another one because I needed to practice more! So I made another one and then another one.

What's your favorite *Twin Peaks* art that you've done so far?

Maja Ljunggren: I think I like woodworks most—the one with the mill and Josie coming out of the wood, probably because it kind of reminds me of home. We have a lot of mills. I think that was my favorite.

Your art is so surreal, with lots going on in the background; how do you come up with the ideas for what to put in visually?

Maja Ljunggren: I usually start with a setting—I create the place. I look at all the pictures and go back and watch an episode to see what it actually looks like in this place. Sometimes the idea of what's going to be in the image comes first, but mostly it's the setting. So I create the setting and think, "Hmm, what should happen here?" So I figure out what's going to be in it and, you know, things just fall into place after a while.

Your work was exhibited at the Twin Peaks UK Fest, and people were excited about it and talking about it online. What was it like to have your work displayed and people come up to you to talk to you about it?

Maja Ljunggren: Extremely fun and very surreal. I've been doing images for most of my life, but I never, ever thought I'd have an exhibition of any kind—and definitely not with my people, who actually get what I mean about the images. It is so much fun to start a discussion about it: the images, all the details I put in. I love when they actually see you and comment on it. I have a lot of fun reading the comments for my images online. I even collected some of them!

You're a woman working in the world in the creative arena—what's been your experience as a woman trying to create a voice and vision for yourself?

Maja Ljunggren: 3D graphics is a very young profession. When I started out I was almost always the only woman. I was working in gaming before—made video games. The company was ten years old, and I was the first woman employed. When I started, there were about thirty-four people, I think—all men. Four years later, when I left the gaming industry, we were five women and about five hundred men. It's kind of been like that most of my life. I'm very used to working with a lot of men, because that's how it still is. These days I have a few more women around me at work, but very few are doing the things I do. It's been good, it's been bad. Sometimes I know I didn't get a job because I'm a woman. I had a colleague get an interview and he had twenty years less experience, but he was a guy, so he got asked and I wasn't even considered. The good part about it is that people put you at the forefront—"Look, see, we actually have a woman employed!" I'm like, "Yep, that's me!" So in some ways I can actually get a job because I am a woman, and in others I didn't get a job because of that. I realized, though, that I probably didn't want to work there anyway if that's how they were looking at it.

When did you first watch *Twin Peaks*?

I think it was o n the air during the fall in Sweden the first time I watched it, and I was lucky that my mother pushed me to watch the pilot. I remember her saying sometime in the morning, "I know there's a new show coming on tonight—are we going to watch it?" And I was like, "OK, whatever makes me not have to do my homework." And right before the show started, she thought to pop in a video kit to tape it. She thought it might be good, something we might want to rewatch. I was so hooked. I think I watched the pilot at least five times that week, and that continued for every episode—it was, I think, Mondays at eight when it aired in Sweden, and that was my sacred moment, for me, to watch *Twin Peaks*. I think both my parents have a lot of artistry in them. They hated if I watched a show like *Dallas*. They usually thought that was just a stupid waste of time. She was right. That was the hottest show in Sweden at that point. So you can imagine what a contrast it was, watching *Twin Peaks*! I started making these artworks for fun—and I still just do it for fun; if I didn't think it was fun, I would stop. But it has led to so many things I had no idea would happen.

Amy T. Zielinski
Photographer

"There's certainly much more of an ability for women to work, but if you open up pages of The New York Times or LA Times, it's still disproportionate on the number of pictures that you see, whether or not the byline's going to be a man or woman, it's generally going to be 90 percent men."

David Lynch walks the red carpet with his wife, Emily Stofle. This is Cannes—not the 1992 Cannes, where *Fire Walk With Me* screened to mixed reviews. This is Cannes 2017, where, twenty-five years later, Season 3 is screened. Lynch pauses and looks toward the gallery of photographers, who are snapping away. He spies a female photographer who is also pausing and offering a thumbs-up. He smiles largely and lifts his single thumb as well. This is a knowing exchange—one that *Twin Peaks* fans understand. Amy Zielinski, a professional photographer and longtime fan of David Lynch, had a dream come true when she worked the red carpet during the Cannes Film Festival and got to photograph Lynch himself. Raised in Indiana, Zielinski eventually moved to New York City to pursue photography. She made her bones photographing musicians and "sitting in places down on the Lower East Side where Norah Jones used to hang out." Zielinski then relocated to London for some years before recently moving to Los Angeles, where she works as a photographer and photo editor. She is trying to avoid the monsters who hide behind diner dumpsters in the City of Light.

You're a photographer and editor who has worked internationally. Tell me about your career as a photographer.

Amy Zielinski: I studied photography in undergrad and grad school. I then moved to New York City, where I struggled to become a photographer using film. But as digital was coming in, I realized that was the way of the future and hurriedly got myself a digital camera and started photographing everything all day long. Then I met singer-songwriter Nellie McKay, and that changed my life. I took a chance on photographing her. She was starting to get noticed by record labels, and she brought me into the fold and made Sony Music take me on as her photographer for her album that she got signed for. Eventually I got hired by Getty Images as an editor, and through Getty I moved abroad. And once I moved abroad, to London, I started photographing classical music, and that was basically my beat, and I was photographing three, four gigs a week, getting published in *The Guardian* and The (*London*) *Times* and lots of little publications that are music specific.

You were a photographer at the Twin Peaks UK Fest. What was it like, as a fan of the show yourself, to photograph the fans and celebrities?

Amy Zielinski: I can think of different friends throughout my lifetime who I introduced Lynch's work to. It's always been a common thread, where people know me as the woman who likes his work. In fact, when I was an undergrad, I had a *Blue Velvet* night and had twenty people crammed into my dorm room to watch *Blue Velvet*—mostly women, in an all-women's dorm. And nobody had seen it before, and it was a revelation to people seeing that piece of art. When I saw the festival being advertised, my curiosity was piqued. I was like, "Well, I have all these press credentials, so I'll contact the festival and see if I could cover it." And the response was yes. I think Lindsey Bowden, the director, looked at the Getty clout behind it and was like, "Yep, that looks pretty good for publicity's sake." I went to the first festival in 2015, which was the twenty-fifth anniversary of *Twin Peaks*. I remember when I was in the signing session with Mädchen Amick and Sherilyn Fenn that had this 300 mm lens, and I was fairly close, and I was trying to get this nice portrait of her [Fenn], with the light shining on her—and she looked up! The eye contact right through my lens—I just felt this shiver down my spine. Audrey! That whole weekend, I felt like time was spinning backward. Things that I hadn't thought about in years were right in front of me, and all these people were dressed up as characters. It was a surreal hoot to me to see people walking around as BOB, and the dwarf was walking around. And the music playing from the soundtrack in the background just took me to a different place and a different time. It was such a special experience.

By the end of the festival, I shot two days' worth of content, and I was happy with the product that I got. I decided that I wanted to cross over that lawn and get a picture with Sherilyn Fenn. So I walked up to her—she's talking to people right after the Q&A—and I talked to a security guard, and I was like, "I'm going to ask her for a picture," and he said, "OK, I'll help you with that." I was feeling very shy, so he nudged her and said, "The photographer would like a picture with you." She had that look of, like, "Oh! Really?" And he said, "She likes your character." She said, "Sure!" She was absolutely and positively warm and held me close with her arm around me to take some nice pictures. I forget what I said to her, but I wanted to tell her thank you for her work. She ended up giving me this massive hug and didn't let me go. She said, "I know you've been going through so much. I've been there too. It's going to be OK. Everything's going to be all right." And I remember leaving that embrace and that moment shell-shocked, thinking, "What was that about?" I was going through something at that time, and I felt she somehow zoned into that. A lot of Lynch's stuff and *Twin Peaks* stuff is very mystical—things you can't explain—but you try to find these connections.

For that experience, your primary role was not a fan at the festival— you were the photographer. And yet you can't help having those lines blurred in the moment because you are looking at Audrey Horne and remembering you're a fan of hers. It's interesting, the crossover that happened in that moment with her.

Amy Zielinski: I had a similar experience a couple of years later where I was working in France at the Cannes Film Festival covering amfAR Cap d'Antibes. That particular night, *Twin Peaks* was showing the first two episodes of Season 3. I stayed on to cover the regular editorial movie premieres at the festival red carpet. Our assignment editor was like, "Amy, you got your camera? Would you like to go on the red carpet to cover *Twin Peaks*?" And I said, "Yes, I would!" I had never covered a red carpet event—it wasn't my thing. So not only was it my first red carpet event I photographed, but it was *Twin Peaks* at the Cannes Film Festival! So here I was, getting the opportunity to photograph this. Just being on that red carpet, hearing the *Twin Peaks* theme song come over the PA, and seeing down the line, here walks teenage crush Kyle MacLachlan—Dale Cooper—walking in front of me with David Lynch, arm in arm with their significant others. It was just a really surreal thing to capture them on the red carpet. Then they walked up the stairs, and right as David was turning around before he went into the movie theater, I stretched out my arm and I gave him a thumbs-up. Nobody else was doing this, but I knew that was his signature thing to do with Dale Cooper [as Gordon Cole]. Lynch of course gave a thumbs-up. I thought, "Oh my God, he gave the thumbs-up back!" I wasn't hitting my camera shutter as quickly as I should, so our German photographer got that shot. I got it too—it just wasn't as good. That moment felt like life came full circle.

When did you first watch *Twin Peaks*?

Amy Zielinski: I didn't watch the first premiere of the pilot. I think I watched it the second time around, because my mother was a very conservative woman, but she loved soap operas. And she checked it out, and she said, "You need to check this one out." So we watched the second airing. I was just absolutely captivated by it. So by the time the second season premiered, I couldn't wait to see the two-hour premiere. I was hooked, line and sinker. I still have scrapbooks back at my parents' house where I would put sticky, laminated things—not the actual magazines but my carbon copies. I was just like, "This is so special; I have to hoard it!"

What drew you in? It's a soap opera, but it's strange, it's Lynchian, unique for its time. What made you keep watching?

Amy Zielinski: Well, Dale Cooper was hot. I loved him. He made me happy. He just seemed like the good guy. He reeked of goodness and intrigue—he was smart—everything you want in a man today. And then I liked Audrey, this little-bit-cheeky woman who you'd think was maybe a whore, but at the end of the day she ended up being a virgin. She was very innocent yet very clever. She was somebody I liked and wanted to be. I could relate to her. She wore the plaid skirts, and I went to Catholic school. She wanted something more out of her life, and she was aiming higher. She liked the older guy.

Photography is a male-dominated field, so what has been your experience as a woman in your industry? What are the challenges?

Amy Zielinski: In some avenues of my company they are making considerable efforts to right the wrongs and things that were going on when I started and prior to when I started. They are definitely hiring more women as photographers. If I had been younger and getting into this, I would have had different opportunities. The problem is a lot of the women starting out in photography now will have more opportunities, but with opportunities as a whole in photography how much will there be because of the way the industry has changed? There's certainly much more of an ability for women to work, but if you open up pages of *The New York Times* or *LA Times*, it's still disproportionate on the number of pictures that you see, whether or not the byline's gonna be a man or woman, it's generally going to be 90 percent men.

What was your reaction to Laura Palmer?

Amy Zielinski: I don't think I would have been friends with her in high school. When I was in high school I didn't belong to any group—ever. I weaved around and kept to myself. I remember anyone who was ever popular, they would always talk to me one-on-one. But when the group was around, there was no connection there. So the homecoming queen I knew from grade school, and we grew up together, and I knew from day one going into freshman year that she would be the homecoming queen.

I don't think she was troubled like Laura was—but that's the thing with Laura: we didn't know much about her. I wonder about anybody who wasn't in the main cast, like how did they view her? That pilot set the tone that everybody was devastated, but are they devastated because they knew her or just because a student died? And like the guy who announces it—he breaks down, and he's crying, and it's like, did he know her that well?

That's a good question. What is the grief for? Was it because it was someone young, because it was a student there?

Amy Zielinski: Did anybody die at your school?

Gosh, several died after high school. Suicides and car crashes. Did anyone die when you were in high school?

Amy Zielinski: When I was fourteen, before *Twin Peaks* was around, we had one girl who was crossing the railroad tracks when she shouldn't have and got killed by the train hitting her. I do specifically remember how the vibe was in the school. You could hear that screaming and the crying and the people in huddles. So I guess when I saw *Twin Peaks* at fifteen, that was relatable. I don't think TV had portrayed that kind of grief before. *Twin Peaks* got the deranged looks people get on their faces. I think Lynch is so good about distorting people's faces. Laura Dern has taken that in every character she's been through from learning from Lynch. It served her well. There is that level of humor in grief. Sometimes, when I'm in serious situations, I get the giggles. I can't help it. You start to see how ridiculous something serious can be. Lynch does that so well.

In the pilot, when Sarah Palmer gets the phone call from Leland, she starts crying, and it's so over-the-top. Sometimes I watch it and it's funny, and other times it's tragic. Each time, I bring something different to my viewing experience.

Amy Zielinski: I went to a screening of *Blue Velvet* for their twentieth anniversary in New York City, and Isabella Rossellini showed up in the Q&A afterward. That was my very first experience of being in a room with other people in which I wasn't introducing someone to Lynch or *Twin Peaks*. These were people just like me who'd been along for the ride. I couldn't get over how everybody was laughing at the same parts I did. Everything I found ridiculous that maybe somebody else wouldn't everybody was laughing at. And then Isabella gets up and does the Q&A, and she said the first time she went to a screening with another audience she didn't understand why some people were laughing at certain moments, like, "We're being very serious here—and they're laughing!" I thought that was fantastic to hear. I think Lynch does well at tapping into that. Maybe he can't even explain it himself, but he knows it, that gut feeling—the absurdity of the experience. I just wonder, in all those years of living here, before he found fame, the things that informed him on a lot of different levels, like the homeless people in *Mulholland Dr.* coming out from behind the dumpster—I've had that experience!

Marya E. Gates
Editor & Film Critic

"I wish that more films by women made it to the mainstream, because it is such a different feeling. I don't know if there is something intrinsic in women or if it is just an inherent bias against women. It feels different."

I met Marya E. Gates outside of a Los Angeles Whole Foods in 2013. We were both in line to meet David Lynch for the first time. He was hosting a small event highlighting his latest album and celebrating the sale of his David Lynch Signature Cup Coffee at Whole Foods. She was first in line. I was second. We bonded over our love of Lynch and film. A few years back, when Gates opened up a dialogue about women filmmakers on Twitter, she sparked an important conversation about elevating female directors and encouraging people to watch their films. She inspired people to start watching films made by women with her articles and social media events, "A Year with Women" and "Female Filmmaker Friday." When I initially interviewed Marya, she was living in Atlanta and working as the social media manager for Turner Classic Movies and FilmStruck. As of the publication of this book, she's working in editorial for Netflix. In all of this time, she's continued the conversation about women filmmakers and inspired me and others to support them.

You have had quite the journey—from a small town to Los Angeles to Atlanta. Tell me about your original hometown.

Marya E. Gates: I come from the middle of nowhere. It's very similar to *Twin Peaks*, actually. It seems smaller than my hometown, and my hometown has 2,800 people in it. Every time I watch *Twin Peaks*, I'm thinking, "Your population is too high." So I come from a small town. It is literally one hundred miles from everywhere. It's in Northern California right below the California/Oregon border. I mostly spent my youth reading books and watching movies. I lived at the library and at the video rental store. I've always had websites. I think I built my first website when I was twelve, so I was always an early adopter to the web. Facebook was invented when I was a freshman in college, so I had The Facebook when it was still The Facebook. I always expressed my love of film on the Internet with my website and other groups, and then I had about eight million Tumblr pages. Then I wanted to start doing more long-form, so in 2009 I started *Cinema Fanatic,* so I would have some more long-form.

That was the same year I started watching *Twin Peaks*. I had heard of it when I was in college because I had a friend who rented every single one on VHS before we met and he was telling me that I would love it because I liked *Blue Velvet*. In 2009 I moved home because it was the recession and I didn't have a job and I had dropped out of grad school, and I was living in the back of my parents' house and catching up on a lot of movies. That's when I got obsessed with TCM and *Twin Peaks*. So I decided I should watch all of David Lynch's films in chronological order. I watched them all and then watched *Twin Peaks*. I watched all of *Twin Peaks* a disk at a time—this was before it was streaming on Netflix. At the same time, that's when I started to build my online presence and tweeting and blogging about *Twin Peaks* and classic film and film in general. All of that snowballed into where I am now.

I went back to grad school for film production. I have a master of fine arts in screenwriting from the Academy of Art in San Francisco. Then I got hired at Warner Bros. to work at Warner Archive Collection doing their social media, and then there was some shifting in departments so I ended up over at Rotten Tomatoes, which at the time was still owned by Warner Bros. I worked at Rotten Tomatoes for two years building their social media. Then TCM, which was very much my love, contacted me and said they had a position and they wanted me to apply.

You've been vocal about bringing attention to women in film and particularly women filmmakers with "A Year with Women" and "Female Filmmaker Friday." Can you talk about how these projects came about?

Marya E. Gates: It started when I was living in Los Angeles. I had discovered Susan Seidelman because I was watching a movie starring Aidan Quinn called *Reckless*, from 1984. A friend of mine from Twitter asked, "Have you seen *Desperately Seeking Susan*? He's superhot in that." I was like, "Oh my gosh, what?!" So I decided to finally watch *Desperately Seeking Susan*. I watched it and thought it was so good. And then I was watching all these other Susan Seidelman films. I'm a superfan of the eighties, and I had never heard of her. I hadn't seen any of her films. She had five really great films in the eighties. I thought, "If I haven't heard of her, and I'm a huge cinephile, how many people who are casual eighties fans haven't heard of her?" And that made me think of how many women filmmakers are out there that I've not heard of or that others have not heard of because they have not made it to the canon. That was the origin of the original "Female Filmmaker Friday," where every Friday I would write about a film directed by a woman. I started with looking at all of Susan Seidelman's eighties films. While I was in the middle of doing that I decided to spend a whole year only watching films by women because I bet it was possible. I know in LA I can see them in theaters and streaming. I thought it might be difficult to seek them out. I tested it by going to Netflix and found one hundred films, all directed by women. I thought, "If there are one hundred films on Netflix, there's definitely others I can find elsewhere." That's when I decided to launch "A Year with Women" filmmakers. I didn't quite do a film a day, but I got close. I think I got a little over three hundred films directed by women. It was great because it was a whole point-of-view shift that I can't explain. People ask, "Does it feel different?" and I respond yes, but I can't put it into words. It is hard to say why it is different, but it just is. I wish that more films by women made it to the mainstream, because it is such a different feeling. I don't know if there is something intrinsic in women or if it is just an inherent bias against women. It feels different. I enjoyed being able to spotlight so many different filmmakers and get so many eyes on so many films and get so many thinking, "Wow, maybe I should just try watching more women filmmakers." So many people have tried watching more women filmmakers, and I am so glad, because there are a lot of great films that just don't surface for one reason or another.

There seemed to be such an outpouring from the film community to you. People were grateful for what you were doing and bringing attention to it. Can you talk about your interaction with other people on social media and your reaction from women about what you were doing?

Marya E. Gates: It was actually positive for the most part. I got more hate when I would do video reviews of male filmmakers who I felt were really sexist. When I did this whole year of films by women I would check Twitter to see if people were sharing it, and I saw this one guy who wrote, "Wow, I had never thought about who was directing films and what that meant. I don't even know if I have seen films by women." It hadn't occurred to him that maybe he hadn't seen any films by women, because he just assumed there was equality. I think most people assume there is equality unless told otherwise. That's why I think it's so important to point out biases and to point out lists, like when *The A. V. Club*, or someone else, does a list of fifty great films of the year and only three of them are by women. This is fantastic, but you need to have more than three films even if that means throwing out the other films. People won't notice if there are only three films by women unless someone points it out. I went through the American Film Institute's greatest one hundred films of all time—two different lists—and I think neither list had a film by a woman on it. It's just frustrating, because once it gets canonized people won't even realize they are not watching films made by women. What I have found is people are grateful for pointing it out, because they hadn't realized. You have to be conscious, and you have to make an effort. The other thing that's great is you'll have things like statistics lists that are depressing, and a lot of the reporting on them makes it sound like consumers can't do anything about it—by pointing out the fact that all of these films were released last year and if you actually went and saw them, you as the consumer could change this. Being able to talk about this on social media and see people actually take my suggestions to go see films by women was really great, because you get more and more people thinking, "I should put my money toward the film that was directed by a woman this week because if I don't, then who is going to?"

You have a high profile on social media, and you are a woman working in the entertainment industry. As you've said, as a film critic you've gotten some pushback by calling out sexism. What has been your experience as a woman working in this industry and having a voice out there? Has it been positive or negative?

Marya E. Gates: It's a little of both. There's less of us women out there who are talking about our love of cinema on Twitter because we know that we'll get yelled at by men. I don't see the negativity as much as other people, and I think that's because I try hard not to interact with men I know I can't trust. When I first started out on Twitter, I definitely followed a lot more of the high-profile film Twitter guys—those dudes who have been tweeting for years and years and years and reviewing films for years and years and years. A lot of them are toxic and not respectful to women and women's opinions. I have unfollowed and blocked a lot of them because they will not listen to an outsider's perspective, especially if that outsider is a woman. I am not paid to work in a critics' sphere, so I've had a lot of time to speak my mind. I know a lot of female critics who don't speak up because they have to work with these guys and they have to interact with them at events. I don't have to do that, and I'm grateful that I don't have to do that. I'm grateful that I do social media instead of criticism, because my paid work is not interacting with people, so I can put myself out there in a way that if I were paid to do this it would not be the same. I've been doing a lot of podcasts the last few years, and a lot of them are very male centric. For the most part I get great feedback, where people tell me they would not have thought about the film a certain way after learning my perspective. I did a few episodes on an *Alien* podcast, which is a podcast where they break down the filming of *Alien* every minute. I did the episodes covering where Ripley is in her underwear—the worst part of the movie. For the most part, the comments from men have been, "Wow, I would not have thought of it this way." But there were a handful of comments where the guys would not come out of their own perspective. That's the most difficult aspect of trying to convey, as a woman, "I feel this way," and then men will react, "Well, I don't feel that way." Well, no, because you are not a woman. Try to listen to women's opinions without thinking about yourself, because as a man you cannot automatically feel the same way. Even if you don't agree, you have to understand that at least some women feel this way. That's the biggest struggle—convincing men that it's not the same for a lot of women because they come from a different place in life.

It's interesting that you said there's so many podcasts that are run by men. One of the things I want to do with this book is—of course it's about Laura Palmer and *Twin Peaks*—but my impetus for writing

the book was there's so many women out there who are inspired by the show and doing things creatively, but the men seem to have the most vocal voices and platforms in the community and have that exposure. For me, it was critical to highlight these women's voices too.

Marya E. Gates: So far on my podcast all of my guests have been women. I've had men ask if they can be on, and I've said no. I don't mean to be insulting, but the podcast sphere is so chock-full of men that I want my podcast to not only be about female filmmakers but about female critics talking about female filmmakers. Female voices are underrepresented, and I just wanted to be a conduit for female voices.

Let's talk about *Twin Peaks*. What was your initial reaction to the show?

Marya E. Gates: I started by watching all of David Lynch's filmography in chronological order, so I started with *Eraserhead*, which I watched while I was packing up a house in a blizzard and I had no heat, so it was kind of like I was in *Eraserhead*. When I was younger, I didn't know who David Lynch was, and I had seen *Blue Velvet* in college because it is a cult classic. The person who introduced me to *Twin Peaks* was my first boyfriend. He had just finished watching the whole series with his friends, and he didn't want to rewatch it with me. So after I finished the filmography I watched it. In one of my past lives, I wanted to design suits. When I first went to grad school, I was there for fashion design because I wanted to make suits. When I saw the nice, slim-cut suit on Dale Cooper, I was like, "Yes!" All of the girls reminded me of dark characters in earlier films, like Anna Karina in *Band of Outsiders*—those sixties girls—especially Audrey Horne. She seems like she fell out of a Jean-Luc Godard film. I am a big connoisseur of pie, so the fact that pie is the most amazing thing you see on this show is incredible. And the coffee: I've been a coffee drinker since I was twelve. The show has suits, coffee, Godard, pie, small town, and all of that all mixed together is just too much of everything that I love all in one. And then there's this great mystery on top of everything, and I've always been a fan of mystery. I used to watch this show from the early nineties called *Silk Stalkings* that was a Canadian version of *SVU* [*Law & Order: Special Victims Unit*] a decade before *SVU* started. I used to watch that with my mom. *Twin Peaks* reminded me of that, with the ongoing murder mystery. I tried to get my mom into *Twin Peaks*. She didn't watch it when it was first on because my brother and I were young and she wanted to watch shows she didn't have to think about. She was getting a master's degree and raising toddlers at the same time, so it was too much for her frazzled brain. But when I reintroduced it to her and explained what I thought some of the references were, she said, "This is so much better than I ever thought.'"

I met you when we were in line to see David Lynch at Whole Foods in 2013. We discussed our love of Lynch while waiting to meet him for the first time. Can you talk about your love for David Lynch?

Marya E. Gates: Basically I watched his entire filmography in a short period, including all of *Twin Peaks*. It happened in November and December of 2009. I loved all of it so much. I think his point of view is so unique and so fascinating. When I went back to grad school I used to go to this bookstore all of the time that had great film books. And I found a copy of *Lynch on Lynch*. And I read *Lynch on Lynch*. Reading his point of view of pretty much everything was just, "Yes!" Part of it for me was he sets a lot of his work in a small town, and having grown up in a small town you see facets of humanity that maybe you don't have time for in a city. There's also an idea of safety in a small town that you don't have in the city. And in this book, he has this great quote about why he won't explain his films, because he puts his art out there and art is subjective and he is not going to explain it because whatever the film is to him, it's not that to you. What I see in a film is not what anyone else will see in a film. Each person brings their own experience to a piece of art, and that includes film. Lynch really understands that, and I respect him for that. He is also exploring different facets of his creativity—he makes music and he writes and paints and mixed media. As much as I would want him to just make films over and over again, I like that he is not afraid to express himself in a plethora of ways.

There is a perception by some that Lynch is misogynistic, but I don't think that's accurate. A lot of that comes from people's ideas of *Blue Velvet*, and Roger Ebert was against that film. Roger Ebert and Gene Siskel both hated *Lost Highway*. The thing about Lynch is not that he hates women. I think he's acutely aware of the violence that women face, both emotional and physical. I think he's not afraid to show that. I think he does it out of reverence for women and not out of hatred of women—especially the emotional violence. He's so great at showing emotional violence and not afraid to show you that when these people are out in public, they may be perfectly fine, but behind everything the emotional violence is so deafening. He is not afraid to shy away from that. That's part of the reason why I love him as a filmmaker.

Mary Hütter
Filmmaker

"It's like anything with any woman working in any industry, you know? You have to prove yourself a little bit more, go out of your way, getting passed over for things by men who know way less than you."

Before I met Mary Hütter in person, I watched her on the 2007 *Twin Peaks Definitive Gold Box Edition*. Hütter was a featured fan on the DVD extras, which covered the fan-run Twin Peaks Festival in Snoqualmie, Washington. Originally from Bay City, Michigan, Hütter loved *Twin Peaks* so much she moved to the "real" Twin Peaks, Snoqualmie, in 2014.

Hütter is a video editor and filmmaker and has made her own series of *Twin Peaks*-inspired films over the years. More than anything, Mary Hütter is an ambassador for the *Twin Peaks* community. She represents the best of the *Twin Peaks* fandom to the people of Snoqualmie, and she hosts visitors from all over the world by taking them to filming locations and talking for hours and hours about the show and its impact.

The Twin Peaks Festival used to screen your films, and you've won some awards for them. Can you talk about some of your short films and your filmmaking process?

Mary Hütter: I wasn't going to do the first one, because I hadn't been behind the camera for many years, since college. I'd mostly been in the edit suite. But another friend from the festival basically forced me to do it, and I'm really glad she did. So I wrote this little short story. For me, there are many parts of *Twin Peaks* I love, but I just love the town and I love the little things that make up the town. I love always knowing little tiny details like the name of the dry cleaner in *Twin Peaks*, because, for me, it makes it more of a real thing. When I first moved here and moved to Snoqualmie, it became strange for me to actually be living in the town and seeing the difference between Snoqualmie and Twin Peaks. I decided to tell a story about Twin Peaks now. When we first started thinking about it, the show wasn't coming back. And then we found out in the process of writing it and making it that it was going to come back. So I decided to tell the story of the town of Twin Peaks and the people who are still here and what Laura Palmer would mean to them now. The film was about this teenage girl who had always heard stories about Laura Palmer, because nobody talks about it anymore out loud, but it's a thing in the town and almost like a ghost-story legend. And so she's trying to find out the real story of Laura Palmer. And she gets obsessed and she starts interviewing people YouTube-video style in the town—like Joey Paulson's brother and I also included Danielle, who's a character from *The Secret Diary of Laura Palmer*, because I love *The Secret Diary* and was really attached to it when I was in high school.

I thought your film was so interesting because you had people

speaking against the backdrops of Snoqualmie. It felt authentic, like a real documentary. Can you talk about how long you attended the Twin Peaks Festival and your relationship to the fest?

Mary Hütter: I wanted to go to the fest ever since I first heard of it in *Wrapped in Plastic* [the defunct *Twin Peaks* fanzine] when I was in high school. And I didn't ever have a regular subscription to *Wrapped in Plastic*, but I would pick it up whenever I would be at different places. But I lived in the middle of Michigan and didn't have any money, and there was no way I could go across the country by myself. I was getting married in 2000 and I looked up when the fest was going to be, and it was a few weeks away from when I was getting married, so I couldn't tack it onto my honeymoon. Then in 2006 I said, "I am going to the festival this year," went, and I fell in love immediately. That weekend changed my life. I met all these people who I had things in common with that I didn't have in common with anyone else. I felt like some of those people were my soulmates, and I loved them. And I knew a couple people from davidlynch.com, like Josh Eisenstadt [Eisenstadt's parents ran the festival for a while, and Eisenstadt ran the trivia contest and was a pivotal part of the fest for many years]. The weekend I was there, Paramount was there filming a documentary about the festival that was going to be for the boxed set that was coming out the next year. I ended up getting in that documentary because I won the trivia contest and I came in third place in the costume contest. So I actually got into the documentary, which was pretty cool. Winning the trivia contest—I want that in my obituary someday. I'm very proud of that. My relationship changed with the recent US Twin Peaks Festival. The organizers who took over the festival in 2013 have taken the festival in a direction that I could no longer stand by and watch. There was a disrespect for the fans and the Snoqualmie Valley that I found appalling. It was a sad situation, so I went to the UK Twin Peaks Festival in London, which is kind of hilarious, since I live in Snoqualmie.

What is it like living in Snoqualmie? We have a romantic idea of a place, but when you live there it may be different. Is it wonderful as a *Twin Peaks* fan? Has it let you down in any way?

Mary Hütter: It's a little of both, I think, because it isn't Twin Peaks and then it is at the same time. And so whenever it's not Twin Peaks, it's a letdown. But then every morning when I wake up and I walk outside and I see the mountains and the mist, I'm like, "Holy shit, it's Twin Peaks!" And that has not worn off yet, and I was afraid that it might. But I feel nerdy and I listen to the *Twin Peaks* soundtrack in my car. Actually, my kids asked me to stop at one point. The thing that was the most disappointing is a lot of the town not having a very positive view of *Twin Peaks*. Some people, because they felt the show was making fun of them, think people are making fun of them as hicks. The tourism was bananas in '90 and '91, when it was a much smaller town than it is now. They still complain about the Japanese tour buses that would come into town and stop traffic. And then people say, "That's a weird show. I didn't like it." So there's a lot of negativity about it from business owners in town. A lot of us had thought when we came into town that the town just doesn't want us there, and a little bit of that's true. So what I've been trying to do since I've moved here is try to change that. I'm trying to get to know people and create more of a positive view of *Twin Peaks*. And I've been able to do that a little bit.

What was it like living in the real Twin Peaks during the filming of Season 3?

Mary Hütter: Living here during the rush of new *Twin Peaks* was overwhelming. Watching the filming of Season 3 was the highlight of my *Twin Peaks* fandom. I got to sit outside the Double R Diner, under the newly re-erected "Mar-T" sign, and watch Double R waitresses pour coffee for patrons in plaid shirts. I saw Ed and Norma talking to Bobby Briggs through the window on a warm September night. I cried. *Twin Peaks* fan tourism to the valley definitely increased, as did the awareness by locals. This time around the Snoqualmie Valley opened its arms to *Twin Peaks*! Both North Bend and Snoqualmie held Season 3 premiere events. Snoqualmie had a valleywide *Twin Peaks* Scavenger Hunt. They showed *Fire Walk With Me* in a former drying shed of the former mill, which doubled as the Packard Mill [currently a DirtFish rally school]. North Bend held a premiere party the night of the Season 3 premiere, complete with a Red Room, signature *Peaks*-y cocktails, and tours of filming locations. After explaining to local businesses that they are seen by fans as not really wanting them around, businesses put up signs that said, "Welcome, Twin Peaks Fans!" to let them know that times have changed. The city of North Bend even erected a replica "Welcome to Twin Peaks" sign in the original location from the opening titles (which was quickly stolen . . .).

You really are an ambassador for fans.

Mary Hütter: I'm trying. There is now a loosely based group of local fans who continue to make a positive impact on the local community in the name of *Twin Peaks*. We raised money in the summer of 2018 and donated it to a local charity for domestic abuse, because of the obvious correlations and issues brought up by the series. Karl Reinsch, a local fan whom I met during filming, successfully petitioned the North Bend and Snoqualmie city councils to proclaim Twin Peaks Day every February 24.

You've been working as an editor for years now. What is it like being a woman in the entertainment/creative industry?

Mary Hütter: It's like anything with any woman working in any industry, you know? You have to prove yourself a little bit more, go out of your way, getting passed over for things by men who know way less than you. That's definitely happened to me. In my job, at least, in a tech field, where I would see so many men talking out of their asses, literally making up words that sounded fancy, and everyone would believe them, I would be like, "Are you fucking kidding me?" And then other people, mostly other men, not wanting to seem dumb would just go with it. But also there are a lot of women editors in the entertainment industry. That was one of the first fields women were allowed to be in, that women kind of took over at the beginning. I don't know if my experiences were any different or better or worse than any other job.

When did you first watch *Twin Peaks*?

Mary Hütter: I first watched the show the day the pilot premiered. I was fourteen. I should preface it with the fact that my father had died the year before, and to deal with it I was throwing myself into television as an escape. I was looking back at my diary the other day from back then, and half the diary entries were what I did that day and the other half were what was happening on my soap operas. So that was how I was dealing with the world. And I was excited that there was a new nighttime soap opera starting. I was a huge fan of *Dallas* from the time I was young. I didn't know anything about David Lynch or Mark Frost or any of that. I had no idea. So I watched the pilot by myself in my living room, and I fell in love with it. I still remember watching it and not even understanding exactly what I was watching except I loved the entire thing. So I told all my friends at school and nobody cared. I started keeping a little thing of who I thought was the killer. I was completely obsessed. I made my mother buy *The Secret Diary* for me when that came out, and I'm glad she didn't read it before she gave it to me, because I never would have gotten to read it.

You have posted a photo of yourself as a teenager dressed up as Laura Palmer covered in plastic wrap—

Mary Hütter: I used Saran Wrap. It was Halloween 1990, and I wanted to be Laura. I didn't have any slinky-slip thing to wear, so I got a white T-shirt and got it dirty and then wrapped myself in Saran Wrap and tied my wrists and glued an "R" on my fingernail.

You've met David Lynch a couple of times. Can you talk about your thoughts on Lynch and his films?

Mary Hütter: Well, *Twin Peaks* got me into David Lynch, and then in high school I started to watch all the movies of his I could find. I actually have a scrapbook where I would cut little pictures out of *Twin Peaks* people and David Lynch people. So I had a lot of pictures of David Lynch because I had, of course, a crush on David Lynch after that. In 2005 he was doing his Transcendental Meditation talks. And I found out he was going to the University of Michigan. I went to the talk, and

I wore my davidlynch.com T-shirt. I waited until it was done, and then I went to the stage. He was standing on the stage and I was on the ground and I said, "Oh, I don't have anything for you to sign, but I'm in X room [the chat room on davidlynch.com; Hütter was an original member] and I just wanted to say hi." And he said, "Who are you?" I said, "Oh, I'm Grrlskout," and he said "Grrlskout?! Hot dog!" Like, he knew who I was! And I was like, "Um, yeah, well, I wondered if I could get a picture of the two of us together?" And he said,

Photo courtesy of Mary Hütter

"Of course you can! Come on up here!" And then he pulled me onto the stage. And these other guys who were standing next to me were looking at me like, "What's happening?"

I realized that he seemed like he was more excited to meet me than I was to meet him. And then I no longer had a crush on him, because it just seemed wrong. He just seemed like . . . Dad. I didn't get a crush vibe at all. He seemed like a father figure. He just seemed nice, and he seemed like a safe person. It meant a lot to me. And he asked me to send him a copy of the picture, which I did. It was awesome. And then I met him again a couple times in 2015 when he was filming in town, because he was around town a lot. I didn't remind him who I was because he seemed really busy. He was working. So I just said hi and thank you and I shook his hand and stuff. But he still seemed like a nice person.

So what was it like watching David Lynch and his crew film Season 3?

Mary Hütter: I saw a lot filmed, and I couldn't even give people spoilers because the more I saw filmed the more I realized I had no idea what was happening at all. Any preconceived notion I might have had about Season 3 went out the window. I did see some things filmed in some locations, like the diner, and that was one the best nights of my entire life, because I not only got to watch David direct, but it was totally breaking the fourth wall for me. It was messing with my head because I was standing and sitting at some points until five in the morning in the parking lot of the diner, looking in and seeing characters in the diner right in front of me. And I was just like, "What is happening?" We were in Twin Peaks, and it was twenty-five years later and there were the people: gray and older, and holy shit, it was crazy. Also, there were random Twin Peaks Sheriff's Department cars parked around town. It was so confusing and amazing at the same time. And just to see David direct. He seemed so nice and caring and was taking actors aside and talking to them and then going back to directing.

Anita Rehn
Artist

"I was in the backyard yesterday. I walked past a tree on the side of the house that's not really supposed to be growing. I was thinking about the Evolution of the Arm. I walked past that tree and thought, 'Oh, I'm just going to snip this right off.' I put a papier-mâché head on it. It was fun when Dougie showed up because then we could take a picture of Dougie with the arm."

When Anita Rehn met Julee Cruise, American singer and songwriter, I was there. Well, not physically in front of them, but I was nearby. I heard the screaming and cursing from outside the restroom at the Salish Lodge and Spa (the location for The Great Northern in Snoqualmie, Washington) back in 2016. There was a smell of eucalyptus and pine in the air while these ladies squealed in delight because they were finally meeting each other in person. The *Twin Peaks* fan community has many prominent leaders, but Anita Rehn is its reigning queen. Rehn helped create the Facebook group Ronette's Bridge, originally as a way for folks to communicate while they attended the US Twin Peaks Festival and later as a kind of reunion site for festivalgoers. The group has since evolved into a place of joy and community beyond the fan-run festival. Rehn has traveled across state and national lines to attend official festivals and events as well as fan meetups. She dragged a Dougie stand-up throughout the Pacific Northwest and documented his journey on social media, increasing his fame and hers. Rehn is incredibly kind and strong. Rehn said she survived a dysfunctional family and an unhappy marriage. She became a mom at a young age, something she said she really wanted. She's a nurturer and a survivor. More than anything, Anita Rehn is a giver. She's a caretaker for the elderly and has been a surrogate mother. And for a fan community that mostly touts kindness and giving, Anita Rehn espouses both.

So it seems like you've been drawn to being a mother but also a caretaker. Have you ever thought about why that is? Is it innately in you, or is there another reason you've taken on this role?

Anita Rehn: I'm not exactly sure, but it does seem like something I need to do. When I was working in hospitals and nursing homes when I was a teenager—which is hard work and emotional—I'd think, "I just want a job where I put sauce on pizza." Not that that's brainless, but I just wanted a job where people aren't crying or people's lives don't depend on you helping them or feeding them. I tried other jobs and I thought, "I hate this." So even now I take care of seniors.

You're a high-profile woman in the *Twin Peaks* fan community and

a mother to women. You've talked about your feminism online and in person. What is your perception about how women and girls are treated in the world?

Anita Rehn: The last five years or so I've felt my eyes are much more open than they ever were regarding gender, women's issues, abuse. And once I started seeing things, I can't unsee things, I can't unhear things. I have young daughters—they're in their twenties, and thankfully they help keep me on track. They are supereducated, informed, strong women. They're everything that I wished I was when I was younger. But there's a lot of stuff that's very disturbing to me out there now, and some things I don't understand, and I don't know if I'm doing the right thing or thinking the right thing. For example, I've always thought of myself as very progressive and trusting. I was a very supportive parent, but I wasn't afraid of discipline because I felt growing up I would have liked more boundaries. So I always made sure my kids knew how much I cared about them. The girls' high school has a dress code. My older daughter wasn't an average teen, but my younger is a bit more average. She is more fashionable, and we had a battle all the time about what she could wear to school. The school had a dress code that you weren't supposed to wear short shorts, but everybody did it. And so we would go head-to-head all the time about it. Now I feel terrible about that. I feel terrible about forcing her to change how she wanted to appear, to conform to other people's attitudes about what makes them comfortable. So those are the kinds of things I think about now. Why should anybody have to change what they want to look like? It's the whole rape-culture thing—don't walk by yourself at night. People should be saying, "Don't rape me," how about that? I did have good intentions, but I have since apologized because now I realize you do whatever you want to do and I'll back you up. I'm such a people pleaser and polite, and it's scary to me that I may have raised my children to be too polite, especially my girls. You don't have to be polite to strangers—especially if you feel uncomfortable.

How and when did you first watch *Twin Peaks*?

Anita Rehn: I was twenty-four when it started, and I looked forward to it for a long time because I absolutely loved *The Elephant Man*. So when I heard David Lynch was doing a television series I was like, "No way." I was immediately hooked. I watched every week, and was pretty obsessed. I read Laura Palmer's diary right away and listened to the soundtrack constantly. Full out. And then did the whole campaign, you know, "Give Peaks a Chance," and wrote letters, and all of that.

***Twin Peaks* is a show that's unlike any other show. What was your reaction to seeing something like the Red Room on TV?**

Anita Rehn: I didn't appreciate the Red Room as much when I was younger as I do now. I was more hooked on the characters, the character development, the complexities of all of that. While the Red Room fascinated me, I didn't really understand it. I always crave happy endings, and to not have that given at all was very frustrating. That's why I fought so hard for the show to return, because I thought it would be nice to have endings and not have this unknown. Even though certain things were never going to be happy. There's so much violence and tragedy in the show. It would have been nice to have some more warm, fuzzy at the end. But the whole concept of dark and light, and black and white, and good and evil, and doppelgängers, it's amazing to me now. It just gets more fascinating and complicated. The more you think you've figured out, the more you know you don't know. That whole otherworldly thing is great to me now.

It's interesting how your perspective has evolved with regard to the stranger things on the show. What was your reaction to *FWWM*? Because it's a prequel/sequel, but in a way it has a happy ending.

Anita Rehn: Very hard to watch. *FWWM* is a difficult movie. Sometimes I see teenage kids watching it. At my first Twin Peaks Festival, I sat behind a couple from Texas who brought their young teenage boys. Some scenes make me so uncomfortable and are so hard for me to watch. I think, "I don't know how you're doing this!" But then I realize not everybody sees the same movie. Not everybody attached the same emotion to it. Since *The Missing Pieces* came out, I've seen it a lot more. I don't know if I'm a different person now or I've become a little bit more desensitized to the harder parts.

You were involved with the *Twin Peaks* festival in the US for a long time and met Julee Cruise at the Fest. Tell me about your friendship with her.

Anita Rehn: Julee Cruise and I knew each other from Facebook, but we had never actually met until the 2016 fest. When the fest organizers asked her to attend, she just flat out told them she wouldn't go unless I could be the one who was helping her. So they asked me. It was quite an experience. I would not trade it for anything, but it was a challenge. She was a challenge. But I enjoy challenging people. I feel like I have a gift, like a challenging-person whisperer.

I was there when you first met Julee Cruise in person. We were at The Great Northern, and you were looking for Julee Cruise, and then she was looking for you. She went into the bathroom and then you ran into the bathroom. Then I heard screaming when you finally met each other. What was it like when you met for the first time?

Anita Rehn: It was hysterical. It's like, "Buckle up!" It was perfect. I'm in the bathroom stall, and Julee kicks the door open. I heard this bang. And then I heard, "Are you fucking in here!?" And I think, "Holy shit, what is that? Oh my God, I know what that is." So, I poked my head out of the stall and there she was: a tiny little tornado of energy. That is Julee Cruise. And then it was like, "Whoo!" from then on. It was a crazy ride.

You were Julee Cruise's handler at that fest. And you witnessed her performance at the theater during the fest. It's been many years since she recorded those songs, but she did it even though those songs are in a different pitch than her normal singing voice. What was it like watching Julee Cruise perform her iconic songs from the show all these years later?

Anita Rehn: She was a mess leading up to it. She's an artist. She's a perfectionist. And she was afraid. We worked on a set list before, and there were a lot of things she thought weren't right or weren't going the way she wanted them to go. As it got closer she got more anxious, and she was late getting to the sound check. It was so close to the performance that I was starting to get nervous. But I'll tell you, when she opened her mouth and sang at that sound check, I almost lost it. The original soundtrack to *Twin Peaks* was like the music from my heart. It was so emotional. At the sound check, she sounded flawless. Finally, we left the sound check when we were supposed to be arriving back at the theater, and then she had to go back to the hotel and get ready. She was not moving very fast. I was trying to gently nudge her along, and I'm not a very assertive person. Anyway, I could tell she was nervous, so on the way over, when I finally got her out of the hotel, I still was not sure she was going to go through with this. I was as scared as she was, and I didn't have to stand up there on that stage. So we got to the theater and of course they had started the film *Mulholland Dr.*, even though I told them, "She's coming, she's coming!" I kept telling everyone she's coming. It turned out to be very Lynchian: start the movie, stop the movie, and here's Julee Cruise. She walked onto the stage and I could tell how scared and how nervous she was. Then she started singing and I thought, "She doesn't sound anything like she sounded at sound check, oh my gosh." Her voice was cracking because she was scared. But it was like magic, because she's a performer, so she knows how to connect with an audience. She felt that love and just opened up. She completely changed after that. For weeks afterward, she wasn't even the same person. She was so happy and so confident. That audience gave her so much love. I still get emotional when I think about it. She did fashion week [New York Fashion Week in 2016] after that. She would have never done that fashion week had she not received such an amazing reception. I'm so grateful to the fest people who stayed and gave her a standing ovation.

You are known in the fan community for many things—among them are your travels with Dougie. Tell me about your adventures with the Dougie stand-up.

Anita Rehn: Showtime had a special, and I had always wanted a Cooper stand-up. So I ordered the Agent Cooper stand-up from Showtime during that sale and was delighted when he arrived at the door in the cardboard box. I opened the box, and I'm like, "Oh my God, it's Dougie!" I took him out immediately and stood him all up. I thought, "Wow, looks like I made a mistake, I guess." Then I realized I didn't make a mistake, because I remembered they sent a picture of the stand-up when I ordered it. I looked in my email, and sure enough it's a picture of Agent Cooper and says "Agent Cooper." I sent an e-mail to Showtime—that I was really proud of, by the way. It began, "HelllooOOOO." I said I hit the Mr. Jackpots and all this stuff. I never heard back from Showtime. The next day I was talking to my husband about it. He lives for making phone calls to people about things. He thinks he's Mr. Fixit. I said, "If you want to call Showtime and ask them about it, go ahead." So he called them and put it on speakerphone, and they said, "Oh, yeah, we sent you the wrong thing. We'll send you the right one." So I brought him with me to the fest. He was just so much fun. Because Dougie, uniquely, has a blank expression, he lends himself perfectly to a cardboard stand-up. I was putting him places and taking his picture.

I had also made the Evolution of the Arm and Johnny Horne's teddy bear. So we piled all of our things in the car and took Dougie too. When we stopped on the road, I took pictures of him across three states. I took a hilarious picture of him in the town of Weed, California. I wanted to check him in to Weed, and I put my big straw hat on him and sunglasses and gave him a package of Cheetos.

In the meantime, I had searched Showtime's site and noticed they didn't offer a Dougie stand-up. When everyone started seeing the pictures they'd ask me where I got him. And I said, "Showtime just sent him to me," and they're like, "Well, he's not on there!" After a day at the festival, my husband sends me a picture and all it is is a box that's shaped just like the box that Dougie came in. I thought, "Yay! That's Agent Cooper. Open him up!" And he sends me a picture text and it's another Dougie. I thought, "How can that be?" I look on the site again and still no Dougie. A day or two into the fest, Sabrina Sutherland had gotten wind of it, because Dougie was all over the festival. Sabrina said,

"I've solved the mystery of Dougie." She said Showtime had sent out fifteen by mistake, and they weren't approved yet by Kyle and David, so they were prototypes but not official. So hold on to those Dougies because they could be a collector's item. I guess they weren't supposed to be sent out. I told my husband, "Don't take that other Dougie out of the box." So I left him the box. In the meantime, I did get Agent Cooper. I left original Dougie in Washington, because it seemed like he belonged there with the original diner counter. So he's in Washington at Mary Hütter's home.

I thought it was perfect seeing Dougie everywhere. What prompted you to make the Evolution of the Arm and Johnny's weird teddy bear and take them to Washington for the fest?

Anita Rehn: I just thought it would be fun. I have too much time on my hands lately. You know, the kids moved out. I thought, "I wonder if you can make that?" The bear was fun. I looked at him and he just struck a chord with me. He's so fantastically bizarre. I was getting something in my cabinet and I had a plastic cookie container, and I thought, "Oh my God, this looks like his head if I just turned it upside down and put it on top of the headless bear. I could probably even draw those eyes." And then the arm, you know, is just a tree branch. I was in the backyard yesterday. I walked past a tree on the side of the house that's not really supposed to be growing. I was thinking about the Evolution of the Arm. I walked past that tree and thought, "Oh, I'm just going to snip this right off." I put a papier-mâché head on it. It was fun when Dougie showed up, because then we could take a picture of Dougie with the arm. And then to see Dougie in the Red Room at the fest with Al Strobel [Philip Gerard] was very fun. That was Al's idea. I said, "Do you mind pointing at him and saying, 'Don't die'?" He said it three times and said it backwards, because Al Strobel is so good at talking backwards. It was awesome.

Is there anything else you want to share about yourself or thoughts on *Twin Peaks*?

Anita Rehn: I know I told you before, I'm happy that someone like you is able to articulate how women can identify with this character Laura Palmer so much, and Laura coming away like a champion for complexity and strength in light of difficulty and challenges. I think it's an important story to tell. It's an important piece of the show and the fandom that I don't think everybody understands, but there's a large group—I feel like it's a quiet group—and I appreciate someone giving a voice to this group. Because there are a lot of people who identify with Laura Palmer, but they're not the people talking the loudest, you know?

Francine "The Lucid Dream" Performer

"People have difficulty connecting burlesque to being a feminist statement, but I strongly believe it is."

Francine "The Lucid Dream" is a vision in whatever Lynchian character she chooses to be during her burlesque performances dedicated to David Lynch. Whether on stage or behind a camera, Francine is aware of what the viewer is witnessing. She studied cinema and photography in college and started *The Pink Room: David Lynch Burlesque* show a few years back. Francine owns her sexuality as a woman. Burlesque is a space for women and all genders to explore feminism and equality through art.

You made a film called *A David Lynch Movie*. Tell me about it.

Francine "The Lucid Dream": For most of my life I concentrated in still photography, but I was always interested in film, which was part of my degree at college. But I didn't attempt filmmaking, because I felt like I didn't have the resources for a big production. Basically, Schaffer the Darklord, who is one of the most passionate *Twin Peaks* fans or David Lynch fans I've met, wrote a rap, because he's a nerdcore rapper. He wrote *A David Lynch Movie*, and he performs it at all of our shows. So for a long time we thought we should make a music video for the song. For a while I wanted to find the money to hire someone to make it. And then I realized I should just shoot it myself because now I have a camera with the capabilities and I have people who can help me out with it, so we just did it.

There are a lot of misconceptions about what burlesque is as an art form. From your perspective, what is burlesque?

Francine "The Lucid Dream": The humor, the "making fun of" part, is the burlesque part. Some people think burlesque is just stripping and, of course, there is a component of that. But burlesque is usually a lot more than that, especially with neo-burlesque. Some classic burlesque performers have definitely gotten edgy and political, but neo-burlesque is a very political art form here in New York City. It really is stemmed in the performance-art scene, which is often very political. So a lot of people have difficulty connecting burlesque to being a feminist statement, but I strongly believe it is. I suppose it's like any art form; a movie could be feminist or not feminist, depending on what you do with it. But to a large extent most of the burlesque I've seen here in New York City has a strong feminist base. The word "burlesque" stems from "to mock," and we do mock things. Even though all of us love *Twin Peaks* and we love the work of David Lynch, it doesn't seem to make sense to just try to cosplay or just straight up copy the art. We can all go home and watch the show over and over again, so we try to add a little twist to it, something funny—either our personal opinions about some of the characters or we just add a little different twist to it to make it interesting.

As a woman working in this field, it can be difficult to put yourself out there as an artist, as a performer, as a filmmaker. Can you talk about what your experience is as a woman working in this creative environment?

Francine "The Lucid Dream": When I began my work in photography, it was very male dominated. Most of the photographers I worked for were men. There were a couple of women, but there were hardly any female photo assistants even when I first began. I always tried to power through it. I always tried to fit in with the guys, and I liked that challenge for a little while, but when I became involved at the burlesque scene it was an opportunity to embrace my more feminine side, which is something I had to ignore to be taken seriously in the photography world. So that was nice, and I still feel like I go back and forth between, you know? I'm kind of like a tomboy, but I also like to dress up in feminine ways sometimes, so I like the option of having both. But more importantly I found that it was a great way to network with women in this city, as I know a lot of women post-school days have a hard time making good girlfriends—especially in New York City; it's tough. I found a huge space of wonderful and diverse and funny and awesome women. So that's been great.

When did you first watch *Twin Peaks*? What was your reaction to it?

Francine "The Lucid Dream": I was very young when I first watched it. I was a young teenager, and I got sucked into it right away because there were so many teenagers in the show, and I was a little bit younger than those characters when I first saw

Photo courtesy of Francine Daveta Photography

it. Laura Palmer—although I did not go through anything like what she went through, I think a lot of girls my age could relate to the confusion and dealing with a newfound sexuality and with general problems in the world but also trying to figure out life.

Laura Palmer. Sexuality. Dealing with problems as a teenage girl in modern-day society. I think that was the first time on TV, even though there's some dark paranormal elements happening, there was a really honest discussion about a young teenage girl's sexuality. And her story got into more detail with Jennifer Lynch's *Secret Diary* book. These things weren't talked about in the media, because I don't think parents would have been able to handle that, you know?

What kind of feedback do you get from your shows—especially when you're tackling more of these controversial topics? Do you get a different kind of feedback from women?

Francine "The Lucid Dream": The fan base is always so amazing. I always get wonderful feedback from everyone who comes to the shows. There are a lot of people who come year after year—fans who have now become friends of mine. Then there are also new people who have never seen the show and just heard about it and came to check it out. I've never heard of anyone who did not have a total blast. I've only gotten one negative message, sent via Facebook, and it was a person who had not seen the show, so that's why I discount it, because how can you judge it if you haven't seen it? They were saying, "You say you're something else but you're really just all strippers; you're just basic strippers." I think they had maybe seen part of my video, an online video of a performance. You can never judge an online performance, or even a piece of it. You have to be there and see it and understand the context. So that was a little disheartening. And there's nothing wrong with being a regular stripper. I love strippers and strip clubs. I have nothing against that. But I think a lot of people outside the scene are quick to judge. But like I said, anyone who has actually come to a show has had a great time—even with the darker performances. A lot of the acts are tongue-in-cheek, and I think we create a safe space to say things with our performance. And people understand the context of it. I think people generally tend to get our sense of humor.

In the story of Laura Palmer, there's incest, there's rape. One of our performers has done a Ronette Pulaski act, and it's very dark. It's almost too hard to watch. If you come to watch a burlesque show and you just want to see showgirls and pretty sparkles and that kind of a thing, this is going to be kind of a downer. Bunny Buxom does the Ronette act, and she finds a way of doing this act that's largely about rape but gives this woman, the character she's playing, this empowerment. And parts of it are sexy, because even if you've been through an experience like that, that doesn't mean that you can no longer be sexy or sexual. It's just another thing that adds to your experience as a woman. And it makes people uncomfortable. It should make people feel uncomfortable. That's the point of the act. I think someone once laughed at it at one of our shows when we went on tour. A man was laughing at it, but he felt bad later. He told her afterwards, "I was laughing. I wasn't laughing at you or laughing because the act was funny. I was laughing because I was nervous." It should make you nervous. What happened to Ronette Pulaski was . . . I'm getting chills just thinking about it now. It's a very haunting act. Very beautifully done too. I like doing this. I like having the freedom of expression to tackle some difficult subject matters and put it on stage. For the most part everyone comes up with their own concept, music, costumes, all of that, which I find very empowering for the individual. But ultimately, at the end of the day, I make sure it's a fun show. I want people to walk away and feel good and laugh. Especially given the circumstances, I think we all need more laughter.

In years past, David Lynch has been criticized for being sexist or creating sexist characters. That always troubled me, because his characters are complex. He's had some female characters who are twisted—they're a lot of things. But I think women can be a lot of things. I think most of these criticisms probably came out of the eighties, where people had really narrow views of what women are or should be. But if all his male characters were simple, good dudes and it was just all these horrible women, then I may be able to question it, but I think everyone is supercomplicated. But that's what makes drama interesting.

Joyce Picker
Writer

"I wrote a lot of comedy when I was in my twenties. It's just tough. You have to prove yourself more when you're a woman."

"They're all going to laugh at you!" Piper Laurie squealed at the 2013 Twin Peaks Series Retrospective at the University of Southern California. I almost squealed, too. An audience member had asked Laurie to re-create her iconic character Margaret White from the 1976 horror film *Carrie*, based on Stephen King's novel. I found out it was Joyce Picker who had made the bold request, and Piper had surprisingly obliged. Maybe, like many of us, she couldn't deny Joyce's sincerity, kindness, and absolute joy. Picker is originally from Detroit and moved to Los Angeles more than twenty years ago. She's been an actor and a comedian. And she's a longtime writer, film critic, and columnist who writes about late-night television. Recently, she's written for *The Blue Rose* magazine and is a regular writer for *25YL—25 Years Later*—a site that covers film, television, music, and sports.

Tell me about when you first watched *Twin Peaks*.

Joyce Picker: I watched it when it originally aired. I was always reading *TV Guide* and interested in TV. I've been a couch potato my whole life. I wasn't too familiar with Lynch's work beforehand. I had a bad experience with *Eraserhead* when I was way too young. So I watched *Twin Peaks* live on ABC. Then, during the summer hiatus, I watched it again, with my dad. And I watched Season 2 with my dad. It's the only television bonding experience I ever experienced with my dad. He was the one who took me to horror movies, but we never had an interest in the same television show before. It was actually a time when I first got to know him, even though it was late in his life. And I shared this time with him not expecting in a million years who killed Laura Palmer. And that was fine during the run of the show, but during *FWWM*, when I saw it with my dad . . . that was pretty uncomfortable. I couldn't watch it with him again.

You've been a comedian as well as writer. What is your experience being a woman in the world and in your career?

Joyce Picker: It's been a challenge to be taken seriously unless you look a certain way. When you don't look a certain way, Hollywood's a very rough town. I moved here twenty years ago, and I knew I didn't have the ingénue look. I knew I was going to be going for character roles, if any. But the competition is too much. I couldn't get an agent or a manager. I wrote a lot of comedy when I was in my twenties. It's just tough. You have to prove yourself more when you're a woman. When I started in comedy, there were not a lot of female comedians. I got nervous about the prospect of actually moving further as a comedian. Like, "If I really want to do this, I'm going to have to travel and stay in these comedy condos, and they're filthy, and you're staying with single men." I wasn't prepared. I was barely prepared to drive myself to downtown Detroit, rather than drive myself all over the country to do gigs as a comedian. Every comedian bombs—I could not emotionally handle the bombing. So I got out of it. The alternative scene was created after that. I probably could have done something there. I have a lot of "would've, could've, should've" in my career as an actress and comedian.

As far as writing about *Twin Peaks*, this show has such an impact on me. This is one of my two favorite TV shows of all time, the other one being *SCTV*, which influenced me to want to be a sketch comedian. *Twin Peaks* was the most interesting thing I've seen on network TV. I couldn't believe what I was watching. The TV show itself never got out of my mind, and when the opportunity came up to write for *The Blue*

Rose, which I knew was a descendant of *Wrapped in Plastic*, I needed to write for this magazine. I needed to express myself. This TV show is such an inspiration for any kind of artist, whether they're a writer or an actor or a painter. This type of show is so inspirational and opens your mind, gets to that part of your head that's the creative side, opens that up, opens up the right side of the brain. It's just something I always find so beautiful, that all these years later people are still finding new ways to talk about it, new art to make influenced by it.

Gabrielle Norte
Filmmaker

"I am Native American and a female. . . . It pushes me as a female filmmaker to do my very best work, because sometimes people are expecting me to not do the same work my male counterparts are doing. Maybe I can't handle something that they can handle. The reality is it drives me to want to do even better than them."

A group of young girls dressed in all black, their faces covered with a blood-red kerchief, emerge from the darkness and confront two stunned people in the middle of the street. Scarlet smoke billows. These are the missing and murdered Indigenous women. The two characters bear witness to their humanity, their pain, their tragic death. This is the culmination of Gabrielle Norte's short film *People Watching*. Norte is an award-winning filmmaker and a member of the Los Coyotes Band of Cahuilla and Cupeño Indians located in Southern California. At the time of this interview, she was a student filmmaker making the rounds on the festival circuit, and winning every time. Her work is powerful and visual, and she often uses her platform to highlight her community. She's also quirky and hilarious and loves *Twin Peaks*.

What made you want to be a filmmaker?

Gabrielle Norte: I developed an interest in film specifically in high school because I had grown up on the reservation. I grew up going to powwows. Storytelling is such a huge part of my culture, both song and dance. In high school, I started looking for ways to use my creative aspects, because I always had an interest in the arts in general but I was looking for a specific thing I could do while also bringing my culture into the mix. I loved making videos, and I felt like it was time for Native American people to be represented in film and TV. I grew up watching all these shows and movies, and I never saw myself represented on the screen. I said, "Well, maybe it's time that I be the person to change that." But deciding to be a filmmaker and being a filmmaker are two different things. After producing my first short film, I learned all of the time and effort and work that went into it. Being able to get into film festivals—specifically Native American film festivals—helped a lot, because it's discouraging sometimes going to a school where there are no Native American people. It's been an interesting experience to see how non-Native filmmakers have reacted to what I have to say.

When did you first watch *Twin Peaks*?

Gabrielle Norte: I first watched *Twin Peaks* about two years ago, for the first time. I did a presentation for a class, and my topic was on diversity and small-town life. I had mentioned *Twin Peaks* in it, but I had never seen *Twin Peaks*. I finally made the decision to watch it. I enjoy this style of storytelling. It was different from any other show I've ever watched in my life. It was great to see Michael Horse, of course, because I wasn't expecting to see a character like that in that show— especially not one that wasn't extremely stereotypical.

What do you think stands out about Hawk's character or Michael Horse's performance, because, like you said, if there is representation

it's usually very stereotypical. Was there anything in there that was stereotypical or wasn't?

Gabrielle Norte: His character was written extremely well, because Native characters are always just the historical shaman or medicine man. His character was just an everyday guy, but he had this position of leadership and power. He talked like a normal person, and he had this normal life, but they didn't saturate his character with the normal Native stereotype. He wasn't this mystic being at times. He talked about Native American folklore, but it wasn't done in a way that was just out there. He was presented as an everyday contemporary image of a Native person. That was important.

Michael Horse has said, "I'm not The Hawk"—he calls him The Hawk, which I love. Even though Hawk is not represented as a stereotypical spiritual person, he said, "I am not as in tune spiritually as he is." He said, "I respect my elders and where I came from," but he said he's a goofy guy. You see a little bit of that goofiness that comes out in Hawk. Mark Frost and David Lynch tend to cast people who are somewhat like their characters. There's a little bit of truth in the characters that comes from the person who is cast. It's interesting, this distinction, that Hawk is not a stereotype, and neither is Michael Horse the same as Hawk. What about your identity—as a woman and as a Native American? Can you talk about how your tribe affected your identity and how you bring the culture that you come from into your work?

Gabrielle Norte: I come from a tribe called the Los Coyotes Band of Cahuilla and Cupeño Indians. It's very rural and isolated. That whole experience was unique. I grew up wanting to get out of that because there wasn't a whole lot to do. But once I left the reservation I realized just how big of an impact it had on me—going into something I didn't have a strong background in. My family aren't filmmakers. I don't know anyone who is a filmmaker. I barely got a camera as soon as I got to college. So I realized how important my culture was going to be in my college journey as well as a symbol of pushing me to actually finish.

Do you find that people treat you differently when they find out that you are a Native person? Do they look at you differently?

Gabrielle Norte: Yes, all of the time. I think a lot of people think I'm joking, because I'm not extremely dark-skinned, so that throws them off when I say that. I had an experience last week when I told someone. They didn't believe me at all. I pulled out my tribal ID and showed him, and he's like, "Is this real?" A lot of people in general just don't understand that Native American people even exist and that they are just normal people, but also all of the things that have happened throughout history are still on our mind. We're still trying to change a lot of things.

What about representation on TV and film? You touched on this a little bit, because there are so few Native people who are telling those stories behind the camera and in front of the camera. What have you seen in terms of representation, and what do you hope to change in your own storytelling in terms of how Native people are represented?

Gabrielle Norte: I think we are seeing a lot more Native actors get Native roles, but these movies are typically historical movies, so it's still in the realm of "This is a stereotypical historical telling of our culture." You never just see a Native American going about their normal day, driving a car or going to a job. Of course with *Twin Peaks*, that's a great example. I just finished watching *The X-Files*, and Michael Horse played a role in one of the episodes in the first season. That was really important too, because that showed a lot of great things by actually including Native actors and having it set on a reservation. It wasn't overly "Native American." That was one recent example I saw, and that show was in the nineties. A lot of the movies that are coming out nowadays have Native actors, but they are always in a supporting role. They are never the protagonist. You never see a Native face as the face of a movie poster or Native stars carrying a movie. It's like they are there, but they are not as important. You typically have a white protagonist who is there to play the white savior role and save the Native supporting actor. That needs to be changed to depict Native Americans in a contemporary sense, because we are still stuck in a historical sense.

Your film *The Wounded Healer* won for best cinematography at the ReelStories Film Festival. It had a striking recurring image of a ceiling fan in it. Was that inspired by *Twin Peaks* at all?

Gabrielle Norte: I think subconsciously it was. I did catch that the second time I watched it, and my roommate pointed it out. She said, "What's up with the ceiling fan?" I really don't know. There is something about ceiling fans as a motif that I had to use as a way to tell this story and incorporate the theme of it. I don't know if I drew directly from *Twin Peaks*, but maybe subconsciously I did.

I loved your use of the fan. It had this idea of wind and movement and technology. What was the process of making your film *The Wounded Healer*?

Gabrielle Norte: It was a challenge, and I learned a lot because I had never done something like that to that extent and especially not by myself. I just sat down and wrote it. I typically get an idea of one shot and then I build upon that. I didn't know where to start when making it. None of it went according to plan, of course, because that's how filmmaking works.

Do you see any challenges or opportunities being a filmmaker who is a woman?

Gabrielle Norte: A female filmmaker is still rare in the industry. We are getting there. For me it's kind of like a double whammy because I am Native American and a female, so with that combination I am in the extreme minority. I think it's hard to balance both of those things, because there are issues in both of them. It pushes me as a female filmmaker to do my very best work, because sometimes people are expecting me to not do the same work my male counterparts are doing. Maybe I can't handle something that they can handle. The reality is it drives me to want to do even better than them. It pushes me to be better than myself.

Often women and people of color are underestimated, so they have to work twice, three times as hard unfortunately to get recognized. That shouldn't be the case, and it is changing, but I hope it changes more. We all have days where we have self-doubt or discouragement or maybe someone says something to you that makes you realize that they are seeing you as something other than what you see yourself as. How do you come back from that? How do you keep going and keep producing art?

Gabrielle Norte: I experience that a lot actually, because of my background. People from my reservation or people from Native communities sometimes look down upon Native students who go off the reservation to better themselves. They call us selfish and say we are whitewashing ourselves. We are looked down upon, yet we are going to be the people to bring positive change to the issues that are occurring. That has always pushed me. It's hard to hear people who are supposed to be supporting you talk down to you about what you are doing, but it actually fuels the need to go out and do it. For me a big focus is supporting Native youth. I always have the statistics of the things that are happening to Native youth, the alcohol and drug addictions and the suicide rates on the reservations. I want to use what I am doing as a way to bring positive change to all of those statistics. Maybe they will see me and think, "I can do that too." Then they can be the ones to bring the change.

Lindsey Bowden
Producer

"I always had a burning ambition, from a young age, and I think Twin Peaks spurred me on even more."

Lindsey Bowden is a powerhouse. Bowden single-handedly founded the Twin Peaks UK Festival in 2009. She is a producer, a performer, and an author who has worked with an impressive array of talent, including Paul McCartney, George Michael, and the Red Hot Chili Peppers. She's published a *Twin Peaks*-inspired cookbook titled *Damn Fine Cherry Pie,* and contributed a chapter to *The Women of David Lynch* collection of essays. But the Twin Peaks UK Festival has a special place in her heart. Unfortunately, the festival disbanded in 2020 when CBS did not renew the license. This interview took place before she was notified by CBS. When the festival ran, she worked hard to create an experience for fans, which included re-creating the iconic Red Room, hosting an array of celebrities from the show, showcasing live owls jaunting across the halls of London, and featuring The Double R Club, one of the darkest and most Lynchian cabaret acts around. When I first met Bowden, I was struck by her warmth, her strength, and her vulnerability. Lindsey Bowden loves *Twin Peaks*. I had the honor of accompanying her on her first visit to Snoqualmie, Washington—the home of the real Twin Peaks. When she stood on the cliff overlooking The Great Northern hotel and the falls, the iconic image of the opening of every episode of *Twin Peaks*, she was breathless and quiet. Her eyes became large and watery. Her lips curled into a gentle smile. She was home.

Did you watch *Twin Peaks* when it originally aired?

Lindsey Bowden: I watched it from the beginning. I watched it right from the get-go—nine o'clock on BBC Two. It was amazing and had a real effect on me.

When you think about your younger self watching the show, what would she think about you now that you are putting on this festival where fans from all over the world attend and celebrities from the show attend?

Lindsey Bowden: We had a club in school, and you couldn't be in that club unless you watched *Twin Peaks*, *Northern Exposure*, and *Quantum Leap*. So fourteen-year-old Lindsey was very ambitious. I would spend all my time in my bedroom just dreaming about being on a West End stage, working hard to make sure it happened. I always had a burning ambition, from a young age, and I think *Twin Peaks* spurred me on even more. I was inspired by the writing, the acting. I had the biggest crush on Sheriff Truman [Michael Ontkean]. I could never have predicted that *Twin Peaks* would become such a big part of my life. Obviously it's not the only thing I work on, but it's a big part of my life.

There is something about this particular fan community where people tend to be creative, sensitive, and misfits or outcasts. Why do you think that is?

Lindsey Bowden: I see it in the fans who come to the festival every year. A lot of them come on their own and they make friends, and they've become very good friends and come back year after year. I've become very good friends with a lot of the fans, and some of them talk about what they're going through to me, which is lovely. I believe in being kind to one another and supporting one another. Rebekah Del Rio [*Mulholland Dr.*] told me a really good story about a crab needing to get out of a pot. If you don't support one another to create a ladder, the crab's not going to escape the pot. The one thing I do try to encourage at this festival is friendship. We are completely inclusive, and anyone is welcome. And automatically you have friends and you have a family. The one thing I'm grateful for above anything else is how me and Rose Thorne and Benjamin Louche and everyone who has made this festival what it is have helped people. I believe firmly that you treat everyone how you want to be treated. And you speak to everybody with the same respect you want to be spoken to. You never know what someone is going through. If the festival has helped people in some way, then I think that is the richest thing I could ask for.

Sheryl Lee really embodies the character of Laura Palmer. Of course you know Lee's performance in *Twin Peaks*, but you also know her personally, and she's been a guest at the festival. What are your thoughts on Sheryl Lee?

Lindsey Bowden: Sheryl Lee is one of the most genuine people I've ever met in my life. We had been talking for a couple of years before we actually physically met when I picked her up for the 2014 festival. The first thing she did was grab me by my cheeks and shake my cheekbones. We spent the afternoon together, and it was lovely. Catherine Coulson actually introduced us by e-mail. I think Sheryl is a phenomenal actress. I think she embraces a character, and not just Laura Palmer, but other characters I've seen her play. She lives that character. I think she deserves to go a lot further in her career. She deserves to have proper recognition. She should have gotten it from *FWWM*. That was a hell of a performance. I often wonder if that performance in *FWWM* actually stayed with her for a while. She embodies that character so much and the way she plays that dual role of a normal teenager with this angst and this self-destruction going on underneath it. I like the fact that she is a private person as well. It makes her even more attractive as an actress.

I often wonder if there is a protective element of that, particularly because she came to the spotlight so quickly and so young and had that incredible performance in *FWWM*. It had to be an exhausting performance.

Lindsey Bowden: Especially being that young—it had to conjure up those emotions. I think it was Helen Mirren who said acting is about what you are feeling inside and not about what is happening on your face or the lines you are speaking. You have to actually feel it to give a true performance. For someone so young to feel she was being tormented by this demon soul, and this demon soul actually turns out to exist in the body of her father—the person who is supposed to love her and protect her is the person who is going to ultimately destroy her. She came from a stage background. She did a lot of theater in Seattle, which probably helped, because you can't get away with everything on the stage. You have to be in it 100 percent.

After running the festival for so many years with *Twin Peaks* being a part of your job, has it changed how you view the series?

Lindsey Bowden: My emotions about *Twin Peaks* are very different now. When I first watched it, it had a big effect on me, but now it has become a business to me. I see things with my producer head rather than my fan head. But there are two things that always get me emotional and back to being a fan: at the festival when we are testing things on the big screen, like *FWWM*. When I hear the music being played really loudly, that always makes me emotional. The other is when the fans enter the festival and they see everything we have created for them.

Rose Thorne
Performer

"Every now and then we turn up, sing a few songs, everybody takes off their clothes, and everyone gets excited!"

At The Double R Club performance at the Twin Peaks UK Festival, the final act is "The Elephant Woman." A beautiful woman with shocking scarlet hair emerges from behind the curtains. She's dressed in the finest boudoir style and is wearing an elephant's trunk on her face. This is Rose Thorne performing a play on David Lynch's film *The Elephant Man* not long before her fiftieth birthday. Thorne said when people ask her if she used to be a burlesque performer, she tells them, "I *am* a burlesque performer." Thorne doesn't just run a club of burlesque performers. She is one. Rose Thorne and Benjamin Louche created The Double R Club in 2009. Thorne and Louche, who are married, met at a Halloween party in the nineties. Their personal relationship led to a professional one with The Double R Club. The club is based in East London and hosts shows the third Thursday of the month year-round except for Christmas and late summer. Thorne also created and runs Cabaret vs. Cancer, a charity organization that supports cancer research and the families of those diagnosed with the illness. The charity hosts a variety of events year-round. The cabaret shows are directly or indirectly inspired by David Lynch. The Double R Club describes its show as "mystery and nightmares inspired, directly or indirectly, by the dark and beautiful worlds of David Lynch, an absurdist and darkly surreal cocktail of 'Damn fine' Lynchian cabaret & burlesque, comedy & live music, bolstered by twisted rock 'n' roll, slow sinister jazz and wailing junk-blues; and all brought to you from the deepest river of your dreams ……" on its website.

How did The Double R Club come about?

Rose Thorne: It was back in 2009. At the time I was a burlesque performer and had been for three or four years. We've always been drawn to the darker side of things. I started to think that maybe David Lynch would be a good frame to hang such a show on, because it occurred to me that in a lot of his films and in *Twin Peaks* there's what you could call artificial performance spaces. Even all the way back to *Eraserhead*, there's the stage and the radiator, and in *Twin Peaks* you've got The Bang Bang Bar. You've got Silencio in *Mulholland Dr.* You've got The Slow Club in Blue Velvet.

The Double R Club was part of the Twin Peaks UK Festival for ten years. What was that experience like?

Rose Thorne: We got in touch with Lindsey Bowden, and then we became good friends with her. We have a good working relationship. She leaves us to do our bit, and she does all the other stuff. Every now and then we turn up, sing a few songs, everybody takes off their clothes, and everyone gets excited! So yeah, we've been part of the festival right from the start and met so many lovely people. Everyone has been so generous with their hearts and minds. They have also supported the charity that Ben and I have. Considering we see these guys one or two days a year, it feels like it's a family that's been around us for a long time.

Have you always incorporated *Twin Peaks* and David Lynch in your show in some capacity?

Rose Thorne: We use the phrase "Lynchian." Sometimes things are quite clearly Lynch and quite clearly *Twin Peaks*. But other times they just leave you with that sense of Lynchian. Sometimes an act will come on stage and we think it's a hilarious act, but the audience is thinking, "Are we supposed to laugh?" because they're really nervous. Benjamin Louche sets the tone of each show by starting it off in the style of Ben from *Blue Velvet* with a work lamp and a lip sync to different songs every month. That always sets the tone. We welcome people into the venue with shots of our Agent Cooper coffee cocktail and a little miniature doughnut. The room is filled with haze, and the walls are wood paneled, the lights are red, and it feels like you are stepping into another place outside of East London.

The Double R Club does a great job of interpreting the show, particularly Season 3, and going to those dark places. You're not just mimicking the show, you're creating something new. You take it to a different place. How do you do that?

Rose Thorne: We are fortunate to have a lot of performers who are also Lynch or *Twin Peaks* fans. So we were all watching it in different houses, and every now and then on a Facebook message somebody would come up with something and say, "I've got an idea." And it's like, "OK then," and then a lot of dialogue goes between us sometimes and Ben mixes some of the music. It all comes together.

Tell me about your charity, Cabaret vs. Cancer.

Rose Thorne: I founded a charity called Cabaret vs Cancer. We support families who are affected by cancer and, in particular, families with young children, so that the stigma of death and the fear of death is something they can start to talk about before somebody dies from cancer. We work a lot with child bereavement teams and getting them the right tools and supplies that they need in order to help those conversations start earlier in the process. So if somebody has cancer and is getting cancer treatment and they just need a little financial support, we can provide that. And we give some money to cancer research so that one day some cancers will be wiped out. We have been a registered charity now since 2016. We did a big event at the start of 2016 to celebrate the life of David Bowie and raised so much money my accountant said, "You need to be a charity now." So we've become a registered charity, and the festival is a huge supporter of the charity. The people who come here are very generous with it. We raise a lot of money and hopefully help people and families who are affected by cancer and death. Lindsey and I both lost our mums to cancer just days apart and just about two weeks before the 2010 festival, the very first festival. Lindsey's mom was in a hospice and my mom was in hospice. They both had cancer. Both our moms died within a few days of each other. It's given another dimension to the relationship Lindsey and I have that we don't have with anybody else.

I am so sorry for your loss. I think it's fantastic what you are doing.

Rose Thorne: She would be proud of everything that we've done. She would be amazed that we've managed to do so much just because she died of a disease. Good things came from a very bad thing happening.

Cheryl Lee Latter
Writer

"Some people seem to be alone in their lives, so they like to check in with the [Between Two Worlds] group every day to chat, and they feel like they have real friends. And we notice when people aren't around-37,000 people, yet we'll still notice if someone hasn't been around in a while! And we check in with them."

Cheryl Lee Latter was destined to be a *Twin Peaks* fan. She shares the same name as Sheryl Lee, after all. Although Cheryl's name is spelled differently, she shares the same magical quality that Sheryl Lee has of being able to connect with everyone she encounters beyond the superficial hello. Latter's waters run deep. She's a leader, along with creator Carl Hershberger, of a place for *Twin Peaks* fans around the world to connect: the Facebook group Between Two Worlds. Latter has written extensively about *Twin Peaks* through her blog, *Between Two Worlds*, and also through *25YL* and *The Blue Rose* magazine. She's published a few novels, too, including *Naughty Alice* and *Pirates and Princes*. Latter creates worlds and invites you in. And you are lured—by her intellect, her scarlet hair, and her bright blue eyes. How could you not be drawn in? She is Cheryl Lee, after all.

When did you first watch *Twin Peaks*?

Cheryl Lee Latter: I discovered *Twin Peaks* when it was brand-new. I had a friend who said to me one day, "Oh, there's a new TV show coming on about a murdered prom queen, and it's directed by David Lynch, and you would absolutely love it; it's made for you." And I was like, "Meh, I don't really watch TV." And she said, "No, he's a really weird director, and it would be perfect for you." So I thought I'd give it a whirl. And I remember sitting in my bedroom in the dark in front of my little portable TV, because I wasn't allowed to watch TV at nine o'clock, and I remember the credits came on and I just knew it was for me. It was so weird—like a homecoming. And I saw "Sheryl Lee" in the credits, and my name in England at the time was never anywhere—never in books, never on key rings—like, my name was never anywhere. To see the name Sheryl Lee made me think this was meant for me. I lived in a small town that was very much like *Twin Peaks* and had the same kind of feel. I would walk around feeling like I was in the show and was a part of it; I felt as if I belonged more in the fictional town than the real one.

I went through my whole life like this was always my private thing—I never had people to share it with. Then, a few years ago, I remember following pages like Welcome to Twin Peaks, so I thought I'd give some groups a try, though I'm not that sociable. I joined a couple of massive ones and a couple of teensy ones just to see what was going on and find out what kind of people are out there. When you think about fandoms, you think about *Star Trek*—which seems so alien in concept to me—where everyone gets so into it. I thought it might be like that—that maybe people wouldn't be as welcoming to other people, to new people. I tried a few *Twin Peaks* groups, and then for Mother's Day my daughter created a picture of Cooper for me. I wanted to share it with somebody, but obviously I didn't have any friends to show it to, so I thought, "I'll stick it in one of those groups and see the response, and if people are horrible I'll just leave and never be involved again—and if people are nice I might meet some people that way."

I put the picture in a Facebook group, and it was amazing. People were just so lovely and so friendly. I remember meeting Christian Hartleben on that thread, I remember meeting Jill Watson—all people who I'm such good friends with now and who I talk with every day. All came into my life on that first post. And from that day, it changed everything.

Two weeks later, Carl Hershberger asked me to be a moderator in the group, and it just opened up a whole new door of people, and it was amazing.

The *Twin Peaks* community is generally kind, but every now and again a troll gets in and arguments happen. Can you talk about moderating that group?

It all started with Carl Hershberger. It was his group and his vision. We all share that vision, so we all work really hard at it. We want it to be an inclusive place. We have so many people who visit it every day; it's like their place to go to hang out with friends. Some people seem to be alone in their lives, so they like to check in with the group every day to chat, and they feel like they have real friends. And we notice when people aren't around—37,000 people, yet we'll still notice if someone hasn't been around in a while! And we check in with them. It's really nice. And people respond to that so beautifully, and they understand what we're trying to do.

We do everything assuming that Sabrina Sutherland's watching it. We know that David Lynch isn't going to read us, but we act as if he does and as if a little Mark Frost is sitting on our shoulder. We don't want to do anything disrespectful, and we want to honor their work and ideas, so that's what we focus on—to keep the conversation alive and going. They gave us this, and this is what we can give back. Whenever we do get a troll we have zero tolerance; we just squish them. We can recognize them miles away, and then we block them—no chance.

You have written about *Twin Peaks* on *25YL* and on your blog. You also contributed to "The Women of Lynch" issue of *The Blue Rose* magazine. Who was your favorite character to write about?

Cheryl Lee Latter: Ronette Pulaski. As a character, she's always forgotten about, always sidelined. Everything Laura went through is magnified in *Twin Peaks*, and what Ronette went through is parallel to that, a lot of it, in the real-life world, if you take BOB out of it—though I'm sure she had her own demons. It's always nice to give her a voice as a character.

She's the one I was most proud of writing about. I never knew how much people loved Audrey Horne until the last couple of years. I never knew she was so popular. As a teenager, she was the one I always related to the most, so writing that piece was personal, because a lot of me went into that. I could really empathize with her. Lynch and Frost, they've given us this escapism and these stories and these dreams, and it feels like you're giving a little something back, to do that.

Laura Stewart
Writer

"Twin Peaks has been a strange journey for me. It started off as a very sweet, quirky, young-girl thing, and then it became a hugely important emotional constant. That's why I love writing about it so much, because it is, in a sense, therapy too: because I have experienced something so similar, I can imagine how Laura felt."

"Lynch loved Lula as tenderly as Sailor did and rewarded her faithfulness and courage by giving her the happy ending she really deserved, making her the poster girl for wild-hearted, feminine rebels."[1] This is an excerpt from Laura Stewart's essay about Lula Fortune from *Wild at Heart* for *The Blue Rose* magazine's "The Women of Lynch" issue. Lula is Stewart's favorite Lynch character. Like Lula, Stewart is wild at heart, intelligent,

---

1   Laura Stewart, "Lula Fortune," *The Blue Rose* "The Women of Lynch," August 2018, 14.

and vulnerable. She's also a prolific writer. She's the assistant editor in chief of *25YL*. Laura shares the same name as Laura Palmer, and there's a kinship there. In the following interview, Laura Stewart shares her very personal connection to *Twin Peaks*.

Andrew Grevas, who runs the site *25YL*, covering *Twin Peaks* and more, always says he had no idea how big the site would become. You and Grevas were covering Season 3 as it was happening. You're still covering *Twin Peaks*, in addition to other television shows and films. What was your favorite *Twin Peaks* piece that you wrote?

Laura Stewart: It's about Sarah Palmer, actually. "See No Evil, Hear No Evil, Speak No Evil," which was a big theory about Sarah after Season 3: She probably did know what was happening to her daughter and maybe, whether intentionally or not, turned a blind eye to what was happening in that house. Then that became a demon inside her—her guilt and regret at what happened to her daughter, and how she lost her family and ended up an alcoholic, alone, because she didn't speak up. It's kind of a "woman's fate." I'm not blaming her at all. It's kind of a "This is the burden that women often have to bear" in keeping quiet and trying to keep peace. It was just sort of manifested in her face and her actions in Season 3. She'd become the demon, and Laura's ghost, in a sense, haunted her so much that it actually became a living, dark entity within her that had Laura's smile, and she could never forget it. No matter how she tried to get rid of that photograph, she couldn't smash through the glass. It couldn't go away. It will be with her the rest of her life—that burden, what happened to her daughter in her hands. So that was probably the article I enjoyed writing the most, because I could really dig into that side of things a bit.

People had so many different interpretations of Season 3, including Sarah Palmer's role in it. What feedback did you get on that piece?

Laura Stewart: I did have mostly positive feedback. With *Twin Peaks*, you can see it in so many different ways. I have always taken it as that sort of "BOB is the evil that men do." He isn't really an actual demon. It's just what could happen to any single one of us depending on what happens to the people you have in your life and the choices you make off the back of your experiences. So I have always taken it as a metaphorical/psychological thing, and I've always thought of the Black Lodge as the psyche, not an actual physical place or anything like that. And I suppose Cooper's journey felt the same for me. It's always been his journey through his own experiences and whether the good or evil in him wins through. And I think that's why BOB was such an easy kill in the end, in comparison to what some people thought he should have been. Because everybody's got a BOB in them, if they let it happen. Not even if they let it happen; sometimes it happens whether you want it or not. It's a powerful force. So yeah, I mostly had positive feedback about it, because I think it made a lot of sense to a lot of people, my interpretation. But I know it's different. One guy did comment that I clearly didn't understand *Twin Peaks* at all.

You've also written a few pieces for *The Blue Rose* magazine, including "The Women of Lynch" issue. Can you talk about the characters you covered?

Laura Stewart: Lula from *Wild at Heart* is always my favorite. I've always loved her. I've loved that film for so long. She was always misunderstood. On the surface she's ditzy, and she's overly sexual, and people didn't really take her seriously. But I've always seen that deeper side of her. She was very thoughtful. She thought too much and put everyone's needs before her own. And she had to battle against some terrible things that happened in her life. David Lynch often writes women who have had bad experiences, especially with men . . . and also mothers. She had a terrible, controlling mother as well, not that Laura Palmer had a terrible mother, but similar there were issues in that their mothers allowed bad things to happen to their daughters. Lula is definitely a favorite. I loved writing about everyone, to be honest. But Lula is always my pinup girl. And I had the honor of writing about Norma. It meant even more after Peggy Lipton's death, which was so, so sad. It's probably the most I've ever cried over a celebrity dying. And I think because I'd written about her for *The Blue Rose* magazine, I thought, "Oh my God, she's mine,

Laura Stewart wrote for Issue #7 of The Blue Rose *magazine. Cover by Blake Morrow.*

and she's gone."

She was brilliant. And it was like I had the two best love stories. Lula's and Norma's were two of the best on-screen romances to me. So it was a pleasure to write about. I also loved writing about the girl in the accident in *Wild at Heart*, who was played by Sherilyn Fenn. Even though we didn't get to know her name, and we saw her for probably two minutes on-screen, it actually gave me liberty to just say what I thought rather than what I knew. That was a nice creative experience for me, because usually you've got all the information there and you have to interpret it. But there wasn't that much information, so you could be a bit more imaginative with it. I wrote about Sarah Palmer as well, and Josie. I love Josie because, again, I think she was another misunderstood person. She was disliked by a lot of *Twin Peaks* fans, but I liked Josie. I felt she was just another Laura at the end of the day, but she's come to face her demons in a different way.

Josie was used and abused in her life early on too, and had to survive. The background explained her character and why she was making

the choices she did. You didn't always know where she stood, and I thought that made her interesting. You didn't always know if she was doing this to stay alive or for altruistic purposes or if she was an opportunist. She was a really interesting character.

Laura Stewart: Right? We got to learn about Laura's story, and we have a lot of empathy for her even though we know that she was pretty manipulative and she did some pretty unpleasant things to people. But we love Laura. We absolutely love Laura. But Josie doesn't get the same sort of forgiveness, because we didn't see it play out, I guess. We didn't see what happened to her. But she did experience very similar things. I mean, she did manipulate men, and women, but again so did Laura, and they were both fighting their demons.

When did you first watch *Twin Peaks*?

Laura Stewart: I was ten. I was with my dad because I think my mum must have gone to night classes. I'm pretty sure it was a Tuesday night in the UK on BBC Two. My dad let me stay up and watch it with him as a father-daughter bonding session. Obviously he didn't know how the story was going to turn out! I caught the first one and thought, "Wow, this is brilliant," and then, from that point on, he couldn't stop me from watching it every week. I know he loved the music. He loved Julee Cruise. I remember him getting the *Twin Peaks* soundtrack on cassette tape, which had the long inlay sleeve with the caricature pictures of the cast. Of course I stole that from my dad. I just played it constantly and looked at that tiny picture of Bobby. When I was ten, I thought he was amazing. Now it's Harry who I crush on, because I'm older. Bobby's too young for me now. It was more the soap opera element that I loved back then. I didn't see *FWWM* for a long time afterwards because I couldn't go to the cinema, as I was too young.

I remember being in my bedroom and having a little black-and-white TV that you had to tune in. My TV was covered in stickers from *Smash Hits* magazine, and a lot of them were *Twin Peaks* stickers that said things like "Who Killed Laura Palmer?" and "I Love Bobby." My name being Laura and it being about Laura made it extra special for me. I had just started secondary school—high school—when the second season aired.

What are your thoughts on *Fire Walk With Me*?

Laura Stewart: Things happened to me in my life which made *FWWM* mean so much more to me emotionally than what the TV series had. My best friend and I were both sexually assaulted by the same man when we were fourteen. Watching Laura's story play out and reading her thoughts in *The Secret Diary*, *Twin Peaks* had a totally new impact on me then. Jennifer Lynch, in the diary, has got all those feelings so spot on—how you feel self-hatred and blame yourself and then you become promiscuous, almost as a self-punishment, because even though you haven't done anything wrong, you feel dirty or think, "I may as well just let everyone do this to me now." Both my friend and I lived that life for a while. We went a bit off the rails and did a lot of drugs and had too many boyfriends. We did things we wouldn't normally have done, things we probably wouldn't have done if the assault hadn't happened.

Many years later I found out my friend had been in a very similar situation as Laura Palmer, with a terrible father who had been abusing her for years. He seemed like such a great dad from the outside. She eventually committed suicide by intentionally overdosing on heroin. That was only a few years ago. She had been struggling with addiction for years but had been clean for a while, but those demons didn't go away. I think Laura's story has helped me deal with my friend's suicide, because I think, "Well, Laura chose to die too, in a sense." She wanted to end it there—that she was going to win this battle, and if she went down, her demons went down with her. My friend had her own daughter who was eighteen when she took her own life. It seemed like, "Well, now that my daughter is not around, and I know she's safe and she's away from him, so it's OK for me to do this now." She didn't do it while her daughter was growing up. She waited for her to be an adult. It sounds terrible. But it certainly helped me get over her death, in the fact that she's free of her demons now and she broke the circle of abuse.

Twin Peaks has been a strange journey for me. It started off as a very sweet, quirky, young-girl thing and then it became a hugely important emotional constant. That's why I love writing about it so much, because it is, in a sense, therapy too: because I have experienced something so similar, I can imagine how Laura felt, and I can imagine how Donna felt in the same situation, losing her best friend. Donna gets a lot of grief. She was only seventeen when her best friend was murdered. But she's given such a hard time by some fans. They treat her like an adult—yes, she made some bad choices, but she was a kid. I can't imagine any seventeen-year-old would deal with it totally levelheadedly. When she visits Laura's grave and says, "It's like they didn't bury you deep enough," I totally get that. It sounds like such a harsh thing to say, but no, I totally get it. I remember my friend, a long time before she died, ran away from home for a while with this guy who was much, much older than her. She was fifteen, and he was thirty. She was missing from school for ages, and the police were around my house all the time questioning me. It was in the national newspapers. It isn't nice for the people who are left behind. Obviously it wasn't nice for her either, but for the people who didn't have anything to do with it, it's a big impact on them as well, because you're thrown in the spotlight.

I had no idea where she was, but I was presumed guilty by association. The police definitely thought I was in on it and that I knew where she was because I was her best friend. Eventually, they did find her and brought her back home. But it was too late by that point. She had begun using heroin and was already on the road that would lead to the rest of her life. The great thing about *Twin Peaks* is how spot-on Lynch and Frost got it. They got how teenage girls behave—which they shouldn't get so spot-on being middle-aged men, right? But they really did. I imagine Jennifer Lynch had a lot to do with that. I'm sure she must have talked to her dad about how these characters should act. *The Secret Diary* is so accurate. That's what makes it so hard-hitting. It's a tough read. But it's probably the most honest book I've ever read. I think every girl, in fact every person, should read it at some point in their life to understand people better. We are so judgmental about people, but we don't know what has happened to them in their lives, and we need to be a bit more forgiving.

Melissa Reynolds
Filmmaker

"Here comes David Lynch, who breaks all the rules and says you don't have to follow them. You can have a scene that's seven minutes long of someone sweeping the floor. Who's to say you can't do that? That's what I love about Lynch. For me that was a massive revelation, because I'm a real rule follower in life, but I think in art you don't always have to follow the rules."

"Donna Hayward is Laura's counterpart. In Laura's mind she's almost saintlike, a paragon of goodness representing the innocence that Laura has lost,"[1] writes Melissa Reynolds in "The Women of Lynch" issue of *The Blue Rose* magazine. Reynolds, a filmmaker, editor, music composer, and writer based in London, turns a filmmaker's eye onto *Twin Peaks*, not only analyzing how the characters interact but also learning and absorbing David Lynch's filmmaking techniques. Reynolds has immersed herself in the *Twin Peaks* community, writing for *The Blue Rose* magazine and *25YL* as well as working for the Twin Peaks UK Festival. She has personally served as the handler for Michael Horse (Deputy Hawk). Like Donna Hayward, Melissa Reynolds represents a paragon of goodness, with the fierceness of an artist's all-seeing eye.

Tell me about yourself.

Melissa Reynolds: I am from the southwest in the UK. I'm a filmmaker, writer/director mainly, but I do a bit of editing and music composing

---

1   Melissa Reynolds, "Donna Hayward," *The Blue Rose* "The Women of Lynch," August 2018, 21.

as well. I try to do it all myself at the moment, mainly to save money. That's what I'm doing now, and I've also been working on a feature script for about ten years that is slowly starting to draw some interest. I'm also working on short films and things like that. The script I've been working on is a drama about family, mental health, and human connection and three people who are all trapped who learn through their connections with each other that the only way to get out of the self-imposed prisons they've created is to start from within.

You're a filmmaker. You're a woman. You're a writer. This book is about elevating women's voices and empowering women. In the industries that you've been in, what's been your experience as a woman?

Melissa Reynolds: I was a runner at a TV postproduction house where there were a lot more women on the running team than there were men, which was nice and doesn't always happen. We were treated very well, but there was a certain man of a higher position within the company who got fired for reasons to do with inappropriateness toward women. I haven't experienced it firsthand, but I've seen it happen to women in my work environment. In that case it was thankfully handled and dealt with, but sadly isn't in a lot of instances. The company I worked for was actually owned and run by a woman, and that definitely made a difference to the work environment. She was a very kind and supportive boss, and that trickled down throughout the whole company. As far as production, I've been the one in control other than the film courses as a student (which were obviously in a school/college environment, so were very protected). On my other projects I've been the one in control, so I was able to make sure that everything was good and safe for everyone in every way.

In terms of how hard it is to break into the industry as a woman, and how we are treated, I've only realized just how difficult it is in the past three or four years. I've known it's going to be a lot harder for me to break in just because I'm female and historically there hasn't been the same support as there has been for men. I mean there are so many female filmmakers, but not enough of us are given the opportunity.

But I'm optimistic because of the sea change that has happened in the last few years. The Me Too and Time's Up movements have brought all the injustices out into the open, and that needed to happen. Now so many doors are opening. I'm very lucky because I've found a mentor—a writer/director—who actually happens to be a man, who is incredibly supportive and believes in me and my ideas and is helping get me and my work out there. We need that as women in this industry. We not only need to support each other, but we need male allies.

Tell me about your experience watching *Twin Peaks* for the first time. What was the context and what was your reaction?

Melissa Reynolds: There's quite a big history to this because, being a filmmaker, I knew about David Lynch. I'd watched *The Elephant Man* when I was nine, and it absolutely devastated me. I couldn't watch it again for ten years. I think I've only watched it about twice since. I just can't do it. It's an incredible film, but I find it so upsetting. I didn't see any more of his films for years but kept hearing about *Mulholland Dr.* and how amazing it was. So I watched *Mulholland Dr.*, and I was completely blown away. Then I knew I had to watch *Twin Peaks*. Even people who didn't know too much about TV seemed to have heard of it because it was so groundbreaking. So I told my mom (who I watch a lot of things with) that we needed to see *Twin Peaks*. We literally would watch about five of them a night. We would be up until two in the morning. I had never seen anything like it. I thought it was completely bizarre but also incredibly moving and funny in equal measure. It was unlike anything I'd ever seen. It completely blew everything out of the water for me from a filmmaking perspective.

Watching it with my mom was great because we love analyzing and talking about what we watch. We really go deep, like scary deep, into some things analytically. People must think we're crazy. We have a show over here in the UK called *Gogglebox*, which is basically just a bunch of ordinary people reacting to TV, so when *The Return* happened I suggested my mom and I film ourselves watching the finale to show our reactions, just for a laugh. Watching it back was just hilarious. We have a great bond when it comes to watching things,

Did David Lynch influence your filmmaking?

Melissa Reynolds: I would say it's a case of pushing boundaries. When I first watched *Twin Peaks* I was deep into learning how to be a screenwriter, how to be a director, and of course my teachers were just teaching the rules, because you have to learn the rules. Then here comes David Lynch, who breaks all the rules and says you don't have to follow them. You can have a scene that's seven minutes long of someone sweeping the floor. Who's to say you can't do that? That's what I love about Lynch. For me that was a massive revelation, because I'm a real rule follower in life, but I think in art you don't always have to follow the rules. Lynch, when he was younger, was not given coloring books because that's just adding boundaries. I learned from Lynch that you can push those boundaries. You can break the rules; you can do anything. There are all these supposed rules in storytelling: this has to happen on page twenty and that needs to happen here. Obviously you have to learn about structure because it's so important, but structure can be so many different things. If you look at the structure of so much of Lynch's work, it completely subverts everything.

Lisa J. Hession
Writer

"*Twin Peaks* had the darkness. I was a kid who was good at a lot of things when it came to school, but when I came home, I never wanted to be there.""

Lisa J. Hession grew up in Canton, Ohio, where the Pro Football Hall of Fame is. She is the daughter of a Korean immigrant who spoke English as a second language. Hession said she has always been the "front man when it comes to talking to people about bills and things" on behalf of her mother. Hession said her dad was around but had bipolar disorder and was an alcoholic throughout her childhood. This led her to escape into school and other activities outside of the home. She moved around before settling with her husband, her dog, Jinx, and her two cats, Little Man and Mudge, in Minnesota. Hession is Scott Ryan's (*The Blue Rose* magazine and Fayetteville Mafia Press) cousin. Ryan is the one who introduced Hession to *Twin Peaks*, and she hasn't been the same since.

Tell me about the first time you watched *Twin Peaks*. What was that experience?

Lisa J. Hession: My cousin definitely introduced me to it. I was probably fourteen when we started watching *Twin Peaks*. We would sit down and watch it once a week. Of course, especially at that age, I had never seen anything like it before. I've probably seen it three or four times and seen *FWWM* more than that, but I carry it with me forever. The characters seemed so simple as I was experiencing the show, but in reality, every single one of them has this mystery of this dark past. I'd never seen complicated characters like that before, and I'm not sure if I have since—even the scenery and the feel and the world of this little town; it was just a blip in the United States. Similarly, when you're a kid you don't know where you are in the world, and knowing that even in this teeny little town there's still so much depth to it—that was a big deal for me. And the darkness. I was a kid who was good at a lot of things when it came to school, but when I came home, I never wanted to be there.

Your mom is an immigrant from Korea. One of the criticisms of *Twin Peaks* has been the portrayals of Asian characters like Josie, and also Piper Laurie, who dressed as a Japanese man. From your perspective, what do you make of this portrayal? Is it Orientalism—a white man's patronizing and stereotypical look at the East?

Lisa J. Hession: I haven't thought about that too much, but yeah, definitely that part of Josie Packard where—like you mention, that Orientalism—the fact that she's beautiful and quiet and avoids the scary and all that type of stuff. She comes from servitude. It didn't bother me because I feel like every character has a bit of that—like Podunk Pete and Ed and all those simple people. You can say there are similar qualities that are just part of the characters, and I think that's the same for Josie. Piper Laurie dressing up as the Japanese man—that was hilarious.

You wrote for "The Women of Lynch" issue of *The Blue Rose* magazine. Can you discuss the characters you wrote about?

Lisa J. Hession: I wrote a lot about *Eraserhead*, which is interesting because I didn't like *Eraserhead* at first. So I liked the challenge of rewatching it and looking through it from a different lens. Charlotte Stewart's character, Mary X—that was such a joy because I eventually got to talk to Charlotte Stewart for *The Women of Lynch* book.

It's just funny with Lynch and how he almost defines himself by the women around him. I think you can see that with Henry in *Eraserhead*. These women, even if they're passive characters, like Mary X, they strongly influence the man to the point where it changes his life forever. And then his head pops off and stuff.

Lynch's women characters include the virginal character, women of mystery, and then the answer—which the Lady in the Radiator represents—the muse, the sexy siren. I was also reading about his life and his women, and I thought, "Oh my gosh, he's such a jerk to all these women!" But also he has this curiosity about them, and I think it's just him understanding himself when he comes into it. You can't be too mad about that. There was part of me that thought, "What a jerk. All these chicks coming after him, why? Just a dopey man with his tie and his pants." People say he's sexist, or there's the *Blue Velvet* scene with violence and misogyny—I don't think it's something that he does; it comes out of art, like anything else.

Jennifer Ryan
Bookkeeper & Photographer

"People are just superexcited about the magazine, whether it's a picture in the magazine or it's something that somebody wrote or the fact that it has sparked a conversation. It restores my faith in humanity a little bit. It really makes me think maybe there are good people out in the world—that we are more similar than what we think we are."

Jennifer Ryan is the unsung hero of *The Blue Rose* magazine. She's the woman behind the man, Scott Ryan, who is the managing editor of the magazine along with John Thorne of *Wrapped in Plastic* fame. Jennifer Ryan's primary role is bookkeeper, but her other roles include taking photos, shooting promo videos, and mailing the magazine, which is a whole process for a tiny, independent business. Ryan said she never watched television fully and analytically until she was thirty-nine years old. Now she's completely immersed in the television experience. Not only does she watch it, she lives it, through the magazines and books her husband publishes. She's a project manager by day and devoted to the magazine and her husband's publishing company, Fayetteville Mafia Press (the publisher of this book), 24-7. She is also a talented quilter. She gifted me one of my most prized possessions: a handmade quilt with the iconic *Twin Peaks* chevron design on one side and cherries and coffee images on the other.

When did you first watch *Twin Peaks*?

Jennifer Ryan: It was about ten years ago when Scott and I started dating. I didn't know anything about it, because I didn't have any friends who watched it, so it was very peripheral for me. When Scott and I first started talking, he asked me if I had watched *Twin Peaks*, and I said no. And he met my sister and my brother-in-law, Josh Minton. Josh is a huge consumer of TV, and so I was surprised he hadn't seen it. So Scott said, "We're gonna watch *Twin Peaks* every week on Thursday." He had a whole list of rules about watching the show. There were definitely no phones, the kids had to be in bed at the time, and you had to sit and be engrossed. He had rules about which episode you could watch at what point in time, and the episodes that we had to have coffee and doughnuts for or coffee and pie for. We had discussions and conversations and theorizing after we had watched each episode. And then at Episode 13, he actually had us all write down who we thought the killer was. He didn't look at them, but he put them aside. When we watched Episode 14 we all had to open them up and look. It's funny, because of all the people, I was the only one who guessed who killed Laura Palmer.

How did you know?

Jennifer Ryan: I wish I could remember exactly what tipped me off. I think it was just a feeling I had about Leland. He had just a little bit of odd behavior—an almost obsession—with Laura. I thought, "That is just not normal!" Something just didn't sit right with me. I thought, "Oh, I'm gonna write this and I'll totally be wrong—there's no way it's her dad." That was kind of crazy. That was the first time we watched it, and it was a fun experience to watch it with Scott, who knew what was coming and could make it a good viewing experience for us. It was a ton of fun, because the rest of us had no idea what it was, so we totally went for that ride, and it was a frickin' fantastic ride!

What was your reaction to *FWWM*? It is definitely a David Lynch film, whereas Season 1 and Season 2 are Mark Frost/David Lynch and a bunch of other people thrown in.

Jennifer Ryan: It was just such a sad horror movie, and it was so dark. I usually am not drawn to those types of things, because I had already gone down the path of Season 1 and Season 2. My heart was so heavy after I finished watching it. I thought, "Wow, I really cannot believe she just went through all of that." It made me appreciate that Laura made a sacrifice. In my eyes she sacrificed herself and defeated BOB so that BOB would not exist and try to reach out, latch on, to anyone else. That's what she did. Because she was so young, it hit me hard, and I have to tell you, BOB is the scariest character that I have ever seen. I hadn't had a nightmare in years, but seeing BOB, there were multiple times that I actually woke up with a nightmare. He just got up under my skin.

It's tough to go back to the first time you see BOB; he's terrifying.

Jennifer Ryan: I'm the "coffee and doughnut" *Twin Peaks* watcher [those viewers who are more focused on the more light-hearted aspects], which is funny, since I'm Scott's wife. Josh chuckles about my reaction to the episode when Laura and James and Donna were in her house and BOB crawls over that couch. I literally tried to shrink back into the couch and I yelped—it just freaked me out. I'm sitting here getting chills just thinking about it, because it's such a scary scene.

I saw *FWWM* when I was a teenager. You saw it as an adult, and as a mom too. Did you have a specific reaction as a parent watching this character go through what she was going through?

Jennifer Ryan: Yes. Even putting myself back into my teenage years as a woman and being perceived as though we are the weaker sex, I was always very leery of anyone who seemed a bit too friendly and the strangers who might come up to try to talk to you. The fact that someone that you know and love and trust and is your parent could actually do that to you and put you through that, it made me look back on when the kids were much smaller and their interactions with strangers and ask, "What did I project onto them at that point in time?" My daughter right now lives in an apartment, and she's there by herself a lot. I worry about somebody breaking in and taking advantage of her because she's not with me. You always think you're safe at home, and that's not necessarily the truth. I submit Sarah Palmer knew that something was going on and that it wasn't good and that it had to do with Leland and Laura. But how scary is that, to know something is going on and not having the strength to deal with that? It's a disturbing thought.

Let's talk about your role with *The Blue Rose* magazine and the *Twin Peaks* community. You're credited as being the bookkeeper, but you do a lot of other things, including some on the creative side, for the magazine. You have shot promo videos. You're a photographer for the magazine. You've done some copyediting. You've done a lot of stuff in the background. What's it like being immersed in creating magazines for the *Twin Peaks* community? What's been your favorite experience with *The Blue Rose* magazine?

Jennifer Ryan: When we first mail the magazine out and people get it, they're so excited about getting it. Then it becomes a posting fest, if you will, on social media—"I got mine!" "Oh, I got mine!" It's just been cool to see people get excited about getting something. It's almost like you're an adult and it's Christmastime. It's like going back to when you were a kid and you were so excited about Christmas and you knew you were going to get this really cool thing, and you got it and you were superexcited about it and wanted to show everybody. People are just superexcited about the magazine, whether it's a picture in the magazine or it's something that somebody wrote or the fact that it has sparked a conversation. It restores my faith in humanity a little bit. It really makes me think maybe there are good people out in the world—that we are more similar than what we think we are.

Melanie Mullen
Producer

"I've always had this encyclopedic knowledge of actors and movies and television shows, almost a little bit like a human IMDb."

The first thing to know about Melanie Mullen is she has a comprehensive mind when it comes to filming locations. She enjoys researching where scenes are shot and sharing them with fans. She loves *Twin Peaks* and the fan community. Mullen works in television development and producing. She enjoys going to filming locations and tracking down both obvious and obscure set locations in and around Los Angeles, including those used in television shows like *Twin Peaks* and classic horror films like *Halloween*. She created Reel Experience, a company that provides guided tours of film locations in Southern California.

When did you discover you were really interested in television?

Melanie Mullen: I always had a fascination with television and film. I've always had this encyclopedic knowledge of actors and movies and television shows, almost a little bit like a human IMDb. And it was never anything that I tried to become well versed in. It was natural. I watched a movie or a show and I'd say, "Who are these people in the show? What else have they been in? Where was this filmed? I want to go there."

When did you first watch *Twin Peaks*?

Melanie Mullen: I did not see *Twin Peaks* until 2013. It was one of those shows I had known about for a long time. One of my professors in college, Bob Engels, was actually a writer on *Twin Peaks* and he cowrote *FWWM*. Just from hearing about it, it was something I knew that I would like. And then my friend Brad kept telling me how much I needed to see *Twin Peaks*. I thought, "I'm finally going to watch *Twin Peaks*!" And from the very first scene I thought to myself, "This show is going to change my life." And it very much has. I've met a lot of friends through the show. I've gone on a lot of adventures because of it. I've now been up to the filming locations many times. I've planned my own location tours of the Los Angeles filming locations. And I've just made a lot of genuinely great friends through the show.

You created a company called Reel Experience. Tell me about this company and your passion for exploring film locations.

Melanie Mullen: What I've realized through visiting film locations and meeting other people who like to do the same is there are actually a lot of us out there who enjoy that. I'm very fortunate that I was born and raised in the Los Angeles area, so filming locations have always been pretty accessible to me. My mom took me to the Michael Myers house from *Halloween* when I was twelve years old. So it's always been a passion of mine. I can't tell you why I will drive fifty miles just to go see a house. You visit a location that was used in a film that was shot thirty years ago. The film crew and cast have come and gone, but the locations still stand. To me it's a standing history of that work.

What's your favorite *Twin Peaks* film location?

Melanie Mullen: In Washington I love the falls. I love the Palmer house—the owner is amazing and is very, very kind to us, which can't be said for most people who live in a filming location. But in California my favorite *Twin Peaks* location? I love going to The Old Place, which is where they filmed the interiors of the Bookhouse. I love eating there. It's a fun spot to get brunch with friends. And as much as I dislike the character of Jacques Renault, I love visiting his cabin because it almost feels like a special treat. It's so out-of-the-way and inconvenient to get to that once you're there, it's so quiet, peaceful, and pretty. It feels like a rare treat, because it's not something you can just go to any day of the week. You have to put a big chunk of your day aside to go see it.

You've spent many years immersed in the fandom of *Twin Peaks*, whether it's hosting touring locations or going to festivals. What are your thoughts on the fan community?

Melanie Mullen: I hope that people start to focus more on the story and less on the commercialization of the content. I hope the fandom goes back to that place. The fandom has brought out some not-so-great qualities in some people, maybe even including myself. The more popular something becomes, the more people want to profit from it. If anything, before Season 3 came out, *Twin Peaks* was this kind of obscure property. Yeah, CBS owned it, but they didn't care that much about what anyone was doing to celebrate it. And now they do, because they've realized they can make a lot of money off this licensed product. I do miss the days of the *Twin Peaks* fandom when it had been gone for twenty-five years and there were only a select few who still remembered it and wanted to analyze it and talk about it and discuss different theories. Now you see it everywhere, and it's just not the same anymore.

Lindsay Hallam
Scholar

"Whenever I go to conferences it's usually the older, established, male academics. They always come in so confident, and it's almost like I wish I had that confidence. As women we have so much doubt instilled in us. Even though I have a PhD, I've been teaching for a few years, I've got the job here, this imposter syndrome really sets in."

"This is a horror film because Laura's story is one of horror, and it is a horror that is all too real for way too many people,"[1] Lindsay Hallam wrote in her book *Twin Peaks: Fire Walk With Me*, a scholarly exploration of trauma and horror. The originally much-maligned film is now getting the popular and critical credit it deserves. Hallam teaches film and criticism at the University of East London. There's no one I enjoy discussing horror films with more than her.

Tell me about your academic journey that led to the publication of your book about *Twin Peaks: Fire Walk With Me*.

Lindsay Hallam: I completed my PhD back in Australia, but the PhD was on the philosophy of the Marquis de Sade, on representations of the transgressive body in film. I always knew that I wanted to be doing something in relation to film and cinema. A lot of it has to do with finding *Twin Peaks* and David Lynch when I was in my teen years. I

---

1   Lindsay Hallm, *Twin Peaks: Fire Walk With Me* (Devil's Advocates) (London: Auteur, 2018), 121.

completed my PhD because I was interested in the idea of transgression, which probably goes back to my interest in Lynch. But I didn't really write about Lynch films and *Twin Peaks* in particular until about 2015, for a conference.

When I completed my PhD, I was teaching in Perth in Western Australia at Curtin University. I got a job over here in London at the University of East London, so I moved to London. Manchester Metropolitan University announced they were doing a conference about *Twin Peaks*, and I thought, "This is a sign that I need to start writing about it." That was the first time I wrote about *Twin Peaks*, and I wrote about it in terms of the idea of the auteur in television, because of course the idea of the auteur is very central to cinema, and what it means now in television.

Then I met John Atkinson, who does the series Devil's Advocates, and I pitched him the idea of doing *FWWM*, and a lot of the approaches that I took in *FWWM* directly relate to areas that I've been teaching. I get to teach on a third-year unit for the film course called Cinema of Affect. I do a whole term on horror and science fiction, so looking at *FWWM* as a horror film comes from that and all my other research, which is mostly on horror cinema. It's this idea of effect and how we experience films in our bodies and the deep, raw connection that we have with films, and what I feel with *FWWM*. I was teaching a unit on film history and memory and I did a lecture on trauma and traumatic memory, and a lot of readings from that, especially the book by Janet Walker on trauma cinema [*Trauma Cinema: Documenting Incest and the Holocaust*], informed another big chapter in the book. My teaching and my research are always informing each other.

I appreciate the connection you're making with horror tropes. Horror is sort of coming into its own in academia. It hasn't gotten a lot of respect for many years. Now it finally is. So what have been people's responses to the book?

Lindsay Hallam: It's been pretty good. I've managed to commit to doing a bit more with the *Twin Peaks* community through the book and through writing for *The Blue Rose* magazine. My writing about it started with that conference in 2015 and meeting other people, and then with the book people have gotten in contact with me, and then going to the UK festival as well and talking with people there. It's finding all these other people. The response has been good.

I've also been able to do some lectures here in London. I found a cinema for *Twin Peaks* days. The book had been out awhile and I hadn't done a book launch, and I thought, *Twin Peaks* Day [February 24, the day Agent Cooper enters the town of *Twin Peaks*, is celebrated by fans] is coming up, can we get a screening? So I got a screening. And then the cinema ended up doing a whole season, and I did an introduction before *Wild at Heart* and *Blue Velvet*.

It's been amazing, and it's led to other people wanting me to write other things, so it's been good. It's been nice to find all the other people, whom I've seemed to have isolated myself from all these years! There are so many of us!

You mentioned you first watched *Twin Peaks* when you were a teenager. What made you respond to the show when you first watched it?

Lindsay Hallam: It was actually the international pilot at the video library, so it has that weird, different ending that kind of solves it. But I could not stop thinking about it. I remember the television show being on, but I was just a little bit too young to see it when it was first on air. I wanted to find more, but then, when I went back to the video library, it said, "*Twin Peaks* 2," and I was like, "Oh, that's the next bit." But it was actually the second season. Obviously, it wasn't supposed to make total sense, but this wasn't making any sense. I mean, Dale Cooper was shot. So I took it back to the video library, and someone had returned the first season, and then I watched it from there. Later on I had to work to find it around the suburbs of Perth. I had to get my older brother and sister and my mom and dad to drive me around to try to find it. I think that fueled the obsession, because I had to find it and I needed to see it.

Having to work for it made me hungry to see more. It was one of the first times where there were things I didn't understand, but that made me more into it. It made me curious, because no one else I knew was into it, so I had to figure out for myself what I thought it was. When you're a teenager, of course, you're attracted to the dark side of things. I also fell in love completely with Dale Cooper.

And seeing *FWWM*—which in Australia has a rating similar to NC-17 in the US—I had to have my mom get it out for me, so again, the forbidden. Watching *FWWM* and seeing Laura Palmer and finding *The Secret Diary of Laura Palmer* in a secondhand bookstore, Laura became so important and central. I was around the same age as Laura when I read the diary. It's weird to think about; I remember watching it and thinking, "Laura's seventeen—imagine being seventeen!"

What's it like to be a woman as a professor and a writer in the world? What are some of your challenges?

Lindsay Hallam: Whenever I go to conferences, it's usually the older, established, male academics. They always come in so confident, and it's almost like I wish I had that confidence. As women we have so much doubt instilled in us. Even though I have a PhD, I've been teaching for a few years, I've got the job here, this imposter syndrome really sets in. I think it does get ingrained in us from a very young age, to always have that doubt, to never have that confidence. And when you're in academia and encounter all these supposedly intelligent people who are established, it can be very intimidating. I think one of the good things is that when you go to conferences or meetings, it's important when there isn't just a bunch of white guys talking and everybody listening. So I'm hoping that things are changing. It's still a challenge, and it's still my own challenge to speak up and to have that confidence.

I don't think you're alone in that at all. I've had those experiences, and I know many women who have had them as well. I've been to those conferences where the entire panel is older white men.

Lindsay Hallam: When you think about horror fans, it's often a bunch of guys. It's almost like they want to challenge me, like, "Do you know enough to be here?" I pride myself on the fact that I usually show that I am meant to be there, but the fact that I have to pisses me off.

My husband does not know nearly as much of *Twin Peaks* as I do; I'm the one who got him into it. But when we go to events, people will go up to him and want to talk to him, but they never ask me about the show. And he always says, "My wife is the one who writes about it; she got me to watch." It's always an interesting dynamic when we go to places and people don't already know me—they assume he's the authority because he's the guy.

Lindsay Hallam: Have you heard of Hammer horror [British cinema's Hammer Film Productions]? They're these old British horror films made in the fifties, sixties, and into the seventies. Christopher Lee is Dracula. Someone I know is editing this book about these Hammer horror films, and they're all women writers. But they're all these older guys who keep whining when all these women show up to these things and want to be heard, so she's like, "I'm going to edit this book and it's only going to be women writing about your horror films."

Jill Watson
Artist

"What I am starting to understand is that it doesn't matter what is going on in my life, it doesn't matter what I think of myself, it doesn't matter what anyone else thinks of me as long as I am open to that creative force and I'm open to letting that energy move through me."

The Snoqualmie Falls flows from above a cliff in the background. Beside it, the Salish Lodge and Spa (The Great Northern hotel) perches on the edge of the falls. Below the falls and in the foreground is Jill Watson, flanked by two fun-loving dogs and, on occasion, a few friends as well. If you're a *Twin Peaks* fan, you've probably encountered Jill, whether in person or in glimpses of her during her more-than-weekly hikes to the falls by herself, with friends, or with *Twin Peaks* folks from around the globe. For the Snoqualmie people, the falls are sacred. They believe the mists from below the falls rise to connect heaven and earth. *Twin Peaks* fans recognize the sacred in this place too, and it doesn't have to do with just the show. There is an energy here. Watson knows it. Watson was born in Alaska and was raised near the Snoqualmie Valley. She now works in radio as a producer and morning traffic and news reporter. She is also an editor for *25YL*. When she's not working or hiking the falls, she's creating. Watson drew the image of Sheryl Lee and the waterfall on the back cover of this book. Her art includes drawings and resin bowls and other household products crafted from discarded forest material. The forest has given Watson life, and in turn she gives the forest new life in her creations.

You've worked in journalism and radio. What has been your experience as a woman in journalism?

Jill Watson: In this particular industry, it's been kind of exceptional, because I've been mentored by some phenomenally strong women who broke through a lot of the barriers that were set up throughout the history of the patriarchy in the radio business. For me, the experience as a woman has been very different from the experience of many other women in this industry just because of the way I was taught to deal with obstacles in the radio industry, which is kind of a bullheaded and take-no-prisoners attitude. Now I run a newsroom, and I'm the "mama duck." I have a series of people who have to answer to me. It's interesting that my career has taken that turn, but there I am.

When did you first watch *Twin Peaks*? Did you watch it when it originally aired?

Jill Watson: I did! I think I was eleven or twelve years old when they filmed the pilot. My stepfather worked for the company that converted the old Snoqualmie Falls Lodge into the Salish Lodge, where they filmed some of the pilot, and I was there for some of that. So my family history is fairly deeply entrenched with *Twin Peaks*. I was too young when the pilot came out to watch it, but my parents had the soundtrack. I remember listening to it. I remember how strange it was and how different it was than the Top 40 music of the day or Debbie Gibson, Tiffany, Michael Jackson. I was the only person in my house who knew how to program the VCR, so I started recording the show and watching it on the sly shortly after it started airing. I remember the way it made me feel. It was very much like the music; it was so different from anything that was available—*The Facts of Life*, *Silver Spoons*, *Punky Brewster*, and whatever I had been watching up until that point. The show made me deeply uncomfortable, but it was one of the first times that I realized that kind of discomfort was fascinating, and I was hooked.

You have a connection to a friend who lived near the Palmer house while you were growing up.

Jill Watson: That's another strange coincidence in my life. So I grew up near the Snoqualmie Valley, but I went to a convent school, and that meant that I had friends all over the Seattle area. My best friend, Tara, lived in Everett, Washington. It turns out they filmed the Palmer house right next door to Tara's house. Back when they filmed it—I think I was fourteen or fifteen—we would have sleepovers and hide on the porch and watch the filming. When they told us we had to clear the streets, we'd take our skateboards and ride on our butts down the hill until we actually met some of the cast back then. So yeah, that was another crazy synchronicity regarding *Twin Peaks* in my life.

You have been producing a lot of art for the community with your exhibit in New York City [a 2019 exhibition of *Twin Peaks* art at the Stephen Romano Gallery fundraising for The Phillip C. DeMars Foundation, a nonprofit founded by Rebekah Del Rio in honor of her late son, whom she lost to cancer], your art for *The Blue Rose*

magazine, the *Twin Peaks Unwrapped* book, and art for individual fans. How did you get inspired to make this art? How did you want to portray, in a creative way, the *Twin Peaks* universe and David Lynch universe?

Jill Watson: I've never considered myself an artist. One of my degrees is in marine invertebrate zoology. I kept a lot of lab notebooks. I did a lot of nature illustrations for various species, parasites—basically, if it lives in the water and doesn't have a spine, it's in one of my lab notebooks that I've drawn. I was a very detail-oriented drawer, but I never thought of it as art. It was very much an explanation of what I was looking at through a microscope. Then, a few years back, I decided to learn Transcendental Meditation due to many of the talks that David Lynch gave. I researched it and saw the data to back up what he was saying. When I started Transcendental Meditation, this deep, deep connection started needing to express itself. It needed a way out. That coincided with the start of *Twin Peaks* Season 3. I didn't know what I was doing at all. I would take a screenshot, sometimes in my mind, of a scene or character, and I would try to draw it. I started posting some of those drawings on Facebook and in some of the *Twin Peaks* groups. People seemed to like it, so I kept going. I started doing other things, like composing music. I started making bowls, all kinds of stuff, and anything I could do to create. Then I started having private coaching sessions with Sheryl Lee. She has helped me connect in a very significant and substantial way to the creative force that is moving through me. What I am starting to understand is that it doesn't matter what is going on in my life, it doesn't matter what I think of myself, it doesn't matter what anyone else thinks of me as long as I am open to that creative force and I'm open to letting that energy move through me, that it is always there. Transcendental Meditation practitioners would call it the Unified Field. It's infinite, and it's always there, and if you are connected to that there is no limit to the creativity that can express itself through you. I feel like my years of scientific training and that kind of technical skill have contributed to the incredible creative growth that I have experienced since I started working with Sheryl. There has been such a rapid progression of quality and depth in my work since she started mentoring me. I can't express enough gratitude for that. It's astonishing what she's helped me discover regarding my capabilities.

The work you are doing is incredible. I get lost in it. You can tell it is coming from some very special, spiritual place.

Jill Watson: Thank you. It's funny, because I don't consider myself a spiritual person. I'm not religious. I've never been unless it was to impress a boy. In that case it was like, "Yes! I'll be Mormon. Absolutely!" I am a Baptist! I have converted to several religions for boys, but I have never considered myself spiritual at all until the need presented itself after a bunch of stuff happened in my life. Having Sheryl to help guide me through that helped me open myself up to those forces. It's done some amazing things for the art that's coming out of me. I don't consider myself the source of the art. I'm just the messenger.

You are working in other mediums, too. You are working with resin to make bowls and other vessels using pine cones and forest materials. What led you to create these amazing forest bowls?

Jill Watson: One of the places I have always been drawn to my entire life outside of *Twin Peaks* is an area around Snoqualmie Falls. I've been walking my dogs on the property across the river from the Salish. It's called Snoqualmie Falls Forest Theater, and it's a conservation project. You need a key card to get across the gate. I hike there with my dogs at least three times a week. It's such a powerful place. There's documentation of twenty thousand years of human history there. It's always been a sacred place to Native Americans. When you get near the falls, you can feel it. There's an energy to the land and to the mist and to the forest. One of the ways I try to honor that land is by walking it every day and by checking on the plant life, by keeping track of it by somehow noting it. When we do trail maintenance, sometimes we have to cut back bushes—sometimes trees are blown down by storms and we need to clear some of the brush away. It's always heartbreaking to lose a tree like that, because you get attached to the trees. I know it sounds crazy, but each tree in the community of trees has its own role and its own personality. I don't like to take anything out of the forest, but sometimes it is necessary. When we do trail maintenance, we end up making a large burn pile full of brush. When we have to take things out of the forest by the falls and put them in the burn pile, sometimes I will go to that burn pile with a saw and I'll take pine cones and wood or anything that calls to me or speaks to me, and I'll take it home to use in my art. I'll process wood and pine cones and sometimes cast it in resin, and sometimes I'll make a carving out of whatever it is. Sometimes I'll just put a pine cone on my mantel because I just like the pine cone. Or I'll wrap little stones in wire or make pendants or key chains or something. If there is something that speaks to me, I'll make something. The forest almost speaks to me and tells me what it wants to be. I know that sounds crazy, but it does. So I got a wood lathe and started casting bowl blanks, which are just resin and forest materials. I'll use carving tools and spin it almost like a pottery wheel on its side. It's almost in reverse. You start with a big lump and then you have to carve out whatever shape you want it to be. I started making bowls. I started making pens for some writer friends, lamps, and pretty much whatever the form and the forest dictated.

There is an energy in that place. There is an energy in the Northwest, and especially at the falls and the surrounding woods. David Lynch knew it too. He saw it. He felt it. I definitely feel it. I think the work you are doing by bringing the forest back to life is beautiful. You are taking what was in that burn pile and now it is living on in this material.

Jill Watson: I'm just giving it new life. It was already very much alive. I love sharing it with people who may not be able to come and experience that energy. There's a little bit of that energy contained in the pieces that I get to people.

You have become a kind of ambassador for *Twin Peaks* and the Northwest, including the filming locations. You've taken visitors on hikes. What's it like meeting people from all over the world who visit the real *Twin Peaks*?

Jill Watson: Overall it's been incredibly positive. There have been people from all over—some people who don't quite understand English but still understand *Twin Peaks*. They understand the waterfall, and they understand the Double R, and they understand the filming locations. It's interesting to meet people with that common love of the area that I love so much, and people who have loved it from afar and have seen it basically from David Lynch's very loving portrayal of it. I also have to give David Lynch huge credit for recognizing the energy in the area. It's such a loving portrayal of it. Watching people walk through the forest and watching the change in their posture from the parking lot through the forest and to the vista—the overlook at the falls is one of my favorite things in the world. When I take people on this hike, we get out of the car and we walk into the woods and there's a little bit of a road, and people have a little bit of small talk and they're jovial, but then we turn a corner and it's just a trail and a path. When we turn that corner people become very present and aware and they slow down. Watching their faces when they get through that forest that they've started communicating with and then watching their faces when we come to the cliff where you can see the waterfall and you can see the Salish—they are struck by how huge it is. They have become a part of the forest. When you see their faces when they see that view from the perspective of the forest, it's one of the biggest thrills and joys in my life to see people make that connection and to see the forest give that gift to them. It is one of the greatest thrills I can experience.

One of the things I talk about in my book is how there's the character of Laura Palmer and then there's Sheryl Lee. Of course there may be a piece of the characters one plays inside of the actor, but there nevertheless is a distinction between the character and actor. Can you talk about getting to know Sheryl Lee and getting past the character of Laura Palmer?

Jill Watson: Until Season 3 it never occurred to me to look into the fan base or even to go to conventions. When I first started to reach out into the community with my art, that's how I initially started talking to people—by posting pictures. I met people who encouraged me to get my nerd on and go to some of these events. I met a whole bunch of the cast and the crew. I first met Sheryl at a *FWWM* screening at the Seattle Art Museum just before Season 3 aired. There was a Q&A, and I was the last question they allowed. There was Sheryl Lee, Gary Hershberger, and Wendy Robie. I raised my hand, and I don't know what possessed me to do it, and I said, "I want to thank you," and talked briefly about fostering children and Laura Palmer's character and how the people in the town inspired me to do that. She was tearing up and kept saying, "Thank you, thank you, thank you." I didn't see her again until I decided to take The Actor's Director Workshop. I ran into her the day before the workshop in Los Angeles. We were in the same shop at the same time. There was synchronicity. I went up to her and said, "I'm really sorry to bother you. My name is Jill, and I'm taking your workshop this weekend. I don't know if you remember this, but I spoke to you briefly at a Q&A before." She shook my hand, and I said, "I'm the one who fosters." Her jaw just dropped, and she just grabbed me and hugged me and couldn't stop thanking me.

I took The Actor's Director Workshop because I've been working on screenwriting. Then I started talking to her on a fairly regular basis about creativity and accessing the creative side to myself and about how to open that channel and to let the creativity flow through me and how to be present with myself and be present with the world and not put up such a front and try to be happy all the time and not try to be the one in the room who has to lift everybody up. What I've gotten to know about Sheryl is she is all of those things. She's present. She's patient. She's kind. I've seen her with some of my friends who have endured years of abuse and trauma. They are able to talk to her because there is this energy about her. They are able to talk to her and open up to her in ways that I don't think they have ever before or since opened up to anybody. That's the start of their healing. It's this acceptance that she has for everybody who she encounters. It's a privilege to have her every once in a while climb into my brain and rearrange the furniture and make it a little bit neater and tidier. I always leave our sessions feeling more connected to that source I was talking about. She's a phenomenon.

Sezín Koehler
Writer

"It's definitely a challenge to be a woman-of-color writer. I worry sometimes my work will be a bit whitewashed, but then when I go back and read my pieces, I notice that my analyses are not like other articles. I'm one of the few people of color on the team."

In the early 2000s, Sezín Koehler was in a parked car with her friend Wendy in Los Angeles during a weekend Halloween celebration when two gang members pointed a gun at them in a robbery attempt. Koehler watched as one of the accomplices shot her friend point blank in the face. Wendy died on Koehler's shoulder. Police caught the gunmen, and Koehler spent the following two years testifying against them. Partly due to her testimony, both received life in prison without parole for murder in the first degree. Over the years, Koehler has experienced post-traumatic stress disorder (PTSD) as a result of witnessing this tragedy and reliving it in court. "That's the thing about certain traumas: all you can do is learn to live with them," Koehler wrote in a *Huffington Post* article titled "Living in the Shadow of Gun Crime." Koehler said she started publishing pieces as a "therapeutic tool" after her friend was killed. In addition to watching her friend die, Koehler struggled with trauma from her childhood and being a survivor of sexual assault. She found solace in writing, whether it was being a reporter for indigenous peoples' organizations, covering human rights issues, blogging, or writing about *Twin Peaks*. Koehler is one of a few women of color who have written about race in *Twin Peaks*. She was also mercilessly attacked on social media for writing about this topic. She's been through a lot and has come out the other side. She still loves *Twin Peaks*.

Writing is your job and your vocation and a source of healing. What does being a writer mean in your journey?

Sezín Koehler: Ever since I was little I wanted to be Stephen King—the next feminist, woman Stephen King. I've been writing since I was a kid. When I started publishing stuff after my friend was killed, I used writing as a therapeutic tool. Some of the stuff I was writing I was just writing for myself. I was still struggling with a lot of trauma I had dealt with from childhood, my friend's murder and surviving sexual assault. So I just started on blogging. I was trying to find my voice aside from my professional one. I was trying to figure myself out. My blog started getting bigger and bigger. Then I wrote an article about why I am child-free by choice, and that was my big break into *Huffington Post*. That article ended up going viral. That was a step in, but I wasn't getting paid. I could never imagine how anyone could ever make a living as a writer unless you were Stephen King. Through the *Huffington Post* I ended up connecting to the founder of *Wear Your Voice* and becoming a paid writer. Then I started writing for *Bitch* magazine, *Black Girl Nerds*, *Vice*, *Teen Vogue*. Now I'm a regular contributor to *Looper*, a news and entertainment site covering pop culture. Writing is now my job.

Twin Peaks did affect my desire to share myself and my personal experiences, because I was so badly bullied and harassed during the third season for the things that I shared. It just made me feel very unsafe talking about personal things. Right now I'm taking a break from writing about personal things. My journey was from human rights reporter to blogger to personal essayist and then the pivot into pop culture analysis. All of that was happening while I was moving around the world, marked by tension, living in strange places, dealing with the xenophobia that is everywhere. I don't feel like I belong anywhere. Even here in America it never stops. So I've been negotiating all of that. It's been nice not to have to write about that stuff anymore—stuff I was writing about for years, like microaggressions, being a South Asian American. That's how I got to this point where I am now.

You have faced racism, sexism, and xenophobia in your work. What has been your experience as a writer who is a woman of color?

Sezín Koehler: A lot of times I would want to write about a certain topic, but then the editor would say, "Well, can you bring in your own identity into this piece?" But this wouldn't be about that. Because I'm a woman of color, a lot of times white editors in particular would have this approach. Often I would just want to write about something that is happening, and who I am would have nothing to do with it. I would wonder, "Are you asking a white writer to do this?" There was almost an expectation that as a woman of color you would be expected to bring all of that personal pain into your piece. A lot of times it just wasn't appropriate. If I want to talk about the anniversary of a movie, why does my pain have to be a part of it? Then I would see white writers getting the assignments I wanted to write all the time. It was like somehow, as women of color, we are not able to write those things without putting our trauma into it. It was very odd to learn about the expectations of being a woman of color in the publishing industry. Because of that I ended up working for editors of color who are also women. They've been able to give me more opportunities.

With *Looper*, I'm working with male editors for the first time. Even though they are white men, they seem to get it. I wrote one *Twin Peaks* piece for them recently, and while another writer had pitched the majority of the topics featured in the piece, I was able to add two important points about sexual assault and how groundbreaking it was for David Lynch to tell that story, as well as how women were allowed to age on screen in Season 3. Those were two key aspects missing from the pieces, so when I took it over I included them. I could definitely tell the editors were appreciative of it, and they do give me room to insert my own agenda into the pieces whenever it is appropriate. There are a lot of pop culture sites that want the writing to remain perfectly neutral. They don't want you to talk about race or racism. They don't want you to mention issues like sexual assault. Anything that could make people uncomfortable they want you to gloss over it. I appreciate my editors at *Looper* because they accept my pitches. I was nervous about it at first, but they made me feel comfortable. But it's definitely a challenge to be a woman-of-color writer. I worry sometimes my work will be a bit whitewashed, but then when I go back and read my pieces, I notice that my analyses are not like other articles. I'm one of the few people of color on the team.

Tell me about your experience watching *Twin Peaks*. When did you first watch it? What was your reaction?

Sezín Koehler: I was a huge David Lynch fan since I was a kid. I wasn't allowed to watch him, so I would get bootlegs and sneak them into the house. I would go to my friend's house. It was so subversive. It was amazing: the surrealism and the magical realism. The first time I saw *Wild at Heart* I realized this is *The Wizard of Oz*! I didn't have anyone else to talk to about it. When I saw my first David Lynch movie, I was living in India. That's where I went to high school. I didn't see *Twin Peaks* until I was nineteen. I was doing a summer program at UCLA. They had a Hollywood Video that was incredible and had all of *Twin Peaks*. Any time I would tell people I love David Lynch, they would ask if I had seen *Twin Peaks*. But you couldn't find tapes of it anywhere. This was before streaming and before DVD. But this Hollywood Video in Westwood had all of them. I spent that summer binging *Twin Peaks*.

FWWM took me longer to understand. When I first saw it, I had not been assaulted. When I saw it again years later after the assault, my senses were affected. It wasn't my dad, but it was my boyfriend. So when I watched *FWWM* after having survived that relationship, I remember crying through the whole thing. To me *FWWM* is what changed *Twin Peaks*. When I watched *Twin Peaks* again, it was even better than it was the first time. It was the first time I had ever seen anything like that put on screen. We didn't talk about rape. We didn't talk about partner abuse. In the nineties we weren't talking about these issues openly. *Twin Peaks* was so cool because it gave us that face. I remember watching it with others, and quietly stories would come out. We would ask, "Why do you like Laura Palmer?" And someone would say, "My uncle . . ." or "My first boyfriend raped me." The first time I remember hearing stories like that was always around *Twin Peaks*. For a lot of women that is one of the biggest gifts that show gave us. We could talk about

Laura as a character, and through Laura we could talk about our own experiences and find solidarity among other women. It was like a light switch went on. The first switch went on when I saw the show. All the lights went on after *FWWM*. David Lynch already affected me deeply, but *Twin Peaks* took it to another place. That was around the time I changed my major to anthropology, and I decided I wanted to do pop culture anthropology focusing on American film.

When you've written about *Twin Peaks* these last few years, you've really interrogated it. You've talked about sexual assault, the treatment of women, and race too. You have said you got a lot of pushback from the community. Can you talk about writing about these issues and the reactions you got?

Sezín Koehler: I'm one of a few women of color who has written anything about *Twin Peaks*. I have always considered myself a resident of *Twin Peaks*, so when I wrote for *25YL* I had this experimental, almost performative writing style. When I thought about who I would be in the town of *Twin Peaks*, I thought I would be one of the few women of color. I noticed a lot of problematic things, like Michael Horse, who is a caricature of a Native American man. There are so few people of color in the show, especially since it takes place in the Pacific Northwest, where there is a large Native population. When this show was originally made, most of the writers were white. When people of color like myself are approaching something that is superwhite, we recognize how it's problematic, but we can still enjoy the show. A lot of people of color I know are Lynchian people.

When I started discussing color and *Twin Peaks*, people flipped out—especially the white dudes. The fact that I had the audacity to even try to reframe *Twin Peaks* from a gaze that wasn't a cis white male was like I had committed one of the worst crimes and I should be put to death. People were sending me messages like that. "Kill yourself!" "How dare you!" I didn't realize the violent words of attack I would receive because of it. People's reactions were so over-the-top. I wrote about other topics, such as a Brechtian analysis of *Twin Peaks*. The show lent itself to writing that was personal or about critical theory. But my personal writing is what really angered people. I don't understand why people don't want to read a different perspective. I wrote an essay critical about Naido/Diane and got backlash for it. People made memes about me. They called me Sarah Palmer, which I thought was a compliment, actually. There was racism and misogyny directed at me. I was called a social justice warrior like it's a bad thing. In the wake of that, I have to admit it's been harder for me to write about personal things. Luckily I've had more opportunities to do more journalism. And I'm grateful I did not lose all support from people in this community. Many have had my back. What's interesting is I've been approached to write about *Twin Peaks* and race since, but I don't want to talk about it. I want to talk about Laura. I don't want to be tokenized.

I'm sorry that happened to you. Everyone talks about how kind and open the *Twin Peaks* fans are, but clearly not everyone is. Even if people disagreed with it, they should not threaten you. That is terrible. And it is wrong.

Sezín Koehler: It makes me think of the episode when Sarah Palmer takes her face off and kills the guy. I wrote a piece about that, and the reactions were so over-the-top. Every guy that wrote to me was exactly the trucker. None of them could recognize themselves as the trucker. The lack of introspection was staggering. The fact that they were all coming at me the same way the trucker came at her was scary. There are so many BOBs in the community. These are people who have their families in their profile picture.

For those of us who love *Twin Peaks*, it is such a part of our DNA. Even with the troubles that I had with those in the community, I still love it so much. The town, in my mind, is my home. And Laura is the woman. She's a goddess. When I think about *Twin Peaks* and the characters, I think about the overwhelming love I have for them. This story was so important for my life. It has helped me.

Geneva Rougier
Artist

"Leland Palmer, to the people he worked with, admired him. They thought he was very smart and charismatic. If anybody knew my father back then they would have thought he was the most charming man in the world, and had no idea what was going on."

When I interviewed women for this book, I didn't set out looking for stories of trauma. I knew they were there, but I didn't want women to share their stories unless they were truly ready to. I met Geneva Rougier at the US Twin Peaks Festival in Snoqualmie, Washington, years ago. I was impressed by her artistic abilities. She brought some handcrafted wooden *Twin Peaks* necklaces and art. And I was struck by her quiet gentleness. I sensed there were some deep pools running in this person, which was not surprising, since she's an artist. What I was not prepared for was the incredibly violent and horrific story she told me about her childhood experience with domestic violence. From Shelly Johnson to Laura Palmer, the victims of domestic abuse in *Twin Peaks* are more than just fictional characters; they are art mirroring life. For Geneva and others, that art is all too real.

Tell me about yourself.

Geneva Rougier: What brought me to *Twin Peaks* and my art and Laura Palmer is all very much connected to my own history. When I was five years old, I came to America with my mother from Trinidad. Before that, my biological father came over to America first, before I was actually born, when my mom was pregnant. My mom gave birth to me in Trinidad by herself. When I was five, my father sent for us to come to America. But it was never a good situation, because, coming from a third world country, women didn't have very many rights, and he was a very abusive man. In many countries it's acceptable for a man to beat up a woman, and authorities are OK with it. So when we came to America my mom wasn't even in the country for a month before the abuse started.

In Trinidad, my mom had eight brothers and sisters, and my father had seven brothers and sisters, so we had a lot of family over there. But when she came to America she didn't have anybody. It was just her and I. He was very, very abusive to her, but because we were all alone she couldn't leave. She worked two and three jobs, and he would take her money until she finally got strong enough to put some money aside in a secret safe-account box. But all this while she had to deal with the abuse. And I did too, seeing my mom in that situation. During that time my sister was born, and throughout that time we were all in fear for our lives. I mean, he tried to kill my mom. She tried to get restraining orders, but the police can't help you from being killed. If something happens and you call the police, it takes time for them to get where you are. If you have a restraining order, they can't be every place at once. That doesn't stop somebody who is intent on trying to kill you from showing up to where you live. The police aren't going to be there to protect you. So there was a lot of fear and trauma growing up. When we finally got away, we moved around a lot. We moved to this country town—secluded—to try and be someplace he couldn't find us.

In the nineties when I was in high school and *Twin Peaks* came out, I had a good friend, my best friend, who wanted me to see *Twin Peaks*. But emotionally I wasn't ready to see it. I knew the whole gist of it, but being so close to my own situation I never wanted to see it, because it hit too close to home. I didn't see it until I was an adult. I would even stay away from watching horror movies and anything scary because I still have nightmares, to this day. I try to stay away from scary stuff that might even make me think about the things that I've gone through. My friend kept on saying, "It's just a movie. It's just a movie" about *FWWM*. And that's when I finally watched it. I could relate to the film on so many levels, including an artistic one. As a child I always used art as an escape. I wrote poetry and drew pictures to distract me from what was going on in my home life. I always used art as that vessel. So when I did finally watch *Twin Peaks*, it made me feel like I could grasp all of the wonders of it. Now that I'm an adult and a stronger person, I use that as inspiration. That's how I came about to finally accept *Twin Peaks* for what it is: as an artistic expression.

I am so sorry about what happened to you and your mom and sister. I can't imagine growing up with that terror.

Geneva Rougier: There were times he had a gun to us, and we just thought we were going to die. I remember running out of the house with no shoes on trying to find help. The straw that broke the camel's back was . . . my mom was in her car driving and he was chasing her in his car, trying to run her off the road. At that point she thought it was definitely her last day. By some miracle she saw a gas station and she pulled into it. He was maybe five or ten minutes driving behind her. She was able to pull into this gas station. There was this young man who ultimately saved her life. She pleaded with him. She said, "My husband is trying to kill me, please, please, I need help." He said, "Here is the key to the bathroom. Take the key and lock yourself in the bathroom. Nobody will be able to get in without the key." He hid her in the gas station bathroom. And when my father got there, he couldn't get to her. He finally ended up leaving. The police came and she got maybe her fifth or sixth restraining order against him. This time, because there was an actual witness, they were able to charge him. However, he fled. There were all kinds of warrants out for his arrest. He never came back. I know where he is now. I was five years old, seven years old, eleven years old, and I always thought, "He's so much bigger than me, and I wish I could fight back." But there's nothing I could do. I couldn't wait until I grew up, so I could fight back. Now, as an adult, he has had so many horrible things happen to him in his own life. He's still alive, suffering very, very badly. But it reinforced my feeling of karma, because when bad people do things, it could take a lifetime, but they do finally get what they deserve.

About eight years ago, my mom got remarried to a very loving, wonderful person. And she has gone to therapy for so, so many years. She's a religious, very forgiving person. No matter what he did to her, if you ask her she'll say, "I forgive him for what he did, and I released him through the Holy Spirit." She's one of those people. It's a painful situation, because I did call her this morning and ask her about telling this story. I didn't want to lie to you about Laura's story because it is similar to my own life. She's always very private. It was always a secret we had between us. You never tell anybody what we've gone through. But she said, you know, "I'm OK with it. You can share how you feel," because it wasn't just her experience, it was also mine. Being abused and seeing my mother abused and growing up in that way ultimately affects my artwork when it comes to *Twin Peaks*.

Thank you for sharing your story. It's such a powerful story to tell because although your story is unique, there are so many families and people who have to face domestic violence and live in fear. If you're not in it, you don't know what that's like—to be afraid of your own father, your own husband, your own boyfriend. I can't imagine going through that trauma, so thank you for sharing that. I really, really appreciate you being so candid and honest.

Geneva Rougier: I wanted to. I felt like if I said anything else to you, it wouldn't really be who I am. When you first asked to interview me, I thought, "How could I possibly even share this with you?" I knew I had to be honest with you, because then you wouldn't really know where I'm coming from when I'm doing my artwork.

Something that you said was so interesting, especially when you're a child: your love of art started because it was an escape. And it's almost like it's, even now, still a positive thing in that you're able to work through the trauma and express it. Sometimes I think that secrets can be bad for the people who keep them. They eat away at you. And if you can get that expression out in an artistic way where other people can respond to it positively, that's a powerful thing. There are a lot of people affected by *Twin Peaks* in various ways, and I've talked to many women who are doing interesting things.

Some have been a little more forthcoming with trauma and some haven't or haven't wanted to go on the record. I think your story is so powerful and many people are going to relate to it, unfortunately, because of the prevalence of domestic violence.

Geneva Rougier: It almost feels like an embarrassment for the people who are being abused. They want to hide the black eyes. They want to hide the bruises. They feel like it is almost their own fault, when it's not. A lot of times outsiders will say, "Well, why don't you just leave? Why are you putting up with this?" I can't speak for anybody else, but I know it's difficult as an immigrant having no family and being in a new country and, I mean, having to plan your escape. I'm talking about years of putting aside ten dollars, twenty dollars every week for years and years and years until you have enough. During this time you have to deal with the beatings and keeping this secret and putting on this fake smile and then dreading going home.

I can laugh at it now, but you know the scene when Leland says, "Your nails are dirty!" I can relate to that. The smallest little things would set my biological father off. David Lynch and Mark Frost and all of the other people who contributed had a vision that really portrayed that feeling—there really are people like that in the world. Leland Palmer, to the people he worked with, admired him. They thought he was very smart and charismatic. If anybody knew my father back then they would have thought he was the most charming man in the world, and had no idea what was going on.

You've been creating *Twin Peaks*-related art for a while now. What was your journey into creating *Twin Peaks* art for *The Blue Rose*?

Geneva Rougier: I had been doing a lot of cork sculptures and woodburning because I love nature. I live in the country, so I wanted to utilize materials that were in the backyard. There was always a lot of woods and leaves and stuff like that. I tried to incorporate the different symbols that had to do with *Twin Peaks* into my woodburning. When I went to the festival in Seattle, I really felt inspired. Honestly, I hadn't drawn anything for a good five years because I was just working on other

Art from Issue #2 of The Blue Rose *by Geneva Rougier*

forms of artwork, which were bringing me joy. *The Blue Rose* magazine is the reason I started drawing again after all these years. Before that I was kind of in a rut. Mentally I just didn't have the energy to do it. But when *The Blue Rose* came along, I felt inspired. I started with that picture of Laura Palmer in the heart and went there. And with each drawing I remembered who I was. I remembered my own style. It brought this feeling of wanting to create. At one point when I was at my lowest, I wrote, "I'm leaving room for creative expression to save myself from a life of depression." And that's what my art is. Now I have a portfolio full of *Twin Peaks* drawings.

What's your experience being a woman in this world?

Geneva Rougier: As a woman you have to overcompensate because it is a man's world. There are so many women who do great things who are maybe overlooked because they are female. As a woman you have to work a little bit harder to get the same type of recognition.

And also, being a woman of color—I don't think there's very many women of color in the *Twin Peaks* community. But that's fine, you know? I feel like I'm representing. I have to keep in mind, when it comes to myself, that people who are going to appreciate my stuff are going to appreciate it. And anybody who doesn't want to give me the time of day, then they're missing out.

Mary S. Reber
Actor &
Owner of the
Palmer House

"I was empathetic all my life. During the years of abuse, I was an empath without boundaries. Now I'm an empath with boundaries. I think that's where the strength comes from."

Agent Cooper/Richard (or whoever he is) arrives at the door with Carrie Page and asks, "Is Sarah Palmer here?" "Who?" replies a beautiful blonde woman in a billowy white shirt. We soon learn that the woman who answers the door at the supposed Palmer residence is named Alice Tremond. This is one of the last scenes in Season 3. We've heard this last name before. The Mrs. Tremond who mysteriously appeared next door to Harold Smith. The Mrs. Tremond who gave Laura Palmer the photo of the door in the flowered-wallpaper room. The Mrs. Tremond who also spends time with the woodsmen and the rest of the otherworldly characters. So the newly introduced character of Alice Tremond in Season 3 is an enigma connected to a past enigma, conjuring all sorts of theories about her relationship to the Palmer home and the *Twin Peaks* universe at large. This was Mary Reber's first acting role. When she opened that door to the Palmer house to greet Agent Cooper/Richard and Carrie, she opened up a whole new world for *Twin Peaks* fans. And then, she did the unexpected. Mary Reber invited fans into her home and provided them a place to process their experiences of both personal-life trauma and the joy they received from *Twin Peaks*. The Palmer home, a site of such tragedy and violence, is now a place of healing.

Talk to me about your history with *Twin Peaks*. When did you

first watch it? What was the experience?

Mary S. Reber: When it first came out, I was raising little kids. At that particular time I didn't have a lot of extra time to watch more shows on TV at night. I was already watching a couple soaps and I thought, "OK, this is just one more." I was drawn to the music, but I just couldn't watch it at the time. So my son told me, "Mom, you have to watch *Twin Peaks*; it's really cool." I remember thinking that's pretty cool that a kid would want me to watch a show from so long ago. I thought, "OK, I'm going to take a look at it." And gosh, as soon as I turned it on I was totally drawn into it. I loved the music. I loved the characters. It was just one of those things that probably sounds kind of trite, like everybody says it, but it was different. And it was moving to me. That was probably just a few years before we got this house.

Tell me about the Palmer house. I remember when this house went on the market years ago and people in the community were saying, "I hope it goes to somebody who's a fan—someone who appreciates *Twin Peaks*." Then you, a fan, became the owner.

Mary S. Reber: We were finally in a position to buy our first house. We had rented before that, with three little kids. I homeschooled, so we were on one income. This particular house just happened to be on the market. They didn't market it as the *Twin Peaks* house. The owner probably could have gotten a little bit more money for it. When we walked through the house it needed so much work. I was intrigued by it being the Palmer house, but that's not why we wanted to purchase it. It was built in 1925. It's in a nice little neighborhood in Everett. And then my ex-husband said he could actually do a lot to fix it up. So we bought the house. Then, about a month and a half later, we got the notice they were going to be filming. It was September 2014. We were gone for the afternoon and came back to a notice at the door that said they wanted to film a movie here. And we knew it was *Twin Peaks*, because obviously it's the *Twin Peaks* house and there was news about *Twin Peaks* coming back. But crazily enough, the location guy was so secret that he didn't even say what it was. He just said that they want to film something here and he needed to come over and take a look at it and there would be a director from Hollywood out on January 1, 2015. The whole thing was mysterious right from the beginning.

The sequence of events is so interesting. It's very *Twin Peaks*. You buy this house and then a month later get this filming notice. Then they actually shoot inside the home as well as the exterior. Finally, in a strange turn of events, you actually get cast in Season 3 as Alice Tremond. How did that come about?

Mary S. Reber: David Lynch showed up January 1. It was just him and Sabrina Sutherland. They were scouting out the locations. I think David is a real purist. He wanted to have the exact locations. He wanted to come out and see them for himself. From what I gather, he was wondering, "What can I use here? What's changed?" He was here three times before they filmed in October 2015. I think it was during his second visit, March or April, when I was standing in the kitchen just making sure I had doughnuts and coffee for the people who were here. He just comes in and walks up to me and he goes, "Are you an actress?" And I said, "No." And he goes, "Have you ever acted?" And I said, "No." And he goes, "Would you like to do a small part in a movie?" And with excitement and fear at the same time, I'm like, "Sure!" and he goes, "Well, it's not for sure, but we'll get back to you. And we'll make sure you get your script, and you have to go to hair and makeup. All I want you to remember is that you would be in your home, and I want you just to be natural." He was watching me as I was interacting with the people who were here. Lynch was just kind of watching. You know how David Lynch just kind of watches people? I think that's how he chooses his next person.

From what I have heard from actors, he doesn't audition actors so much as he observes and creates characters out of what he observes.

Mary S. Reber: What's funny is I always have a saying I tell people. They'll apologize to me for something and always I'll go, "Oh, that's OK." And it's funny that he incorporated that line into one of my lines at the door.

He was definitely observing!

Mary S. Reber: I know he observes people.

You get this opportunity to perform in Season 3. Then you get your script. You're not a professionally trained actor, so how did you go about preparing for this role?

Mary S. Reber: It wasn't a ton of lines, but it was enough. What threw me off a little bit is I usually don't get starstruck, but when I found out that the script said "Cooper," it's like "Oh, gee . . . I have to make sure I know these lines!" So I just practiced. I would go to the door and I'd practice. The thing is about David Lynch—I really respect him. He doesn't tell you what to do. I think he knows that people will be a little bit nervous. And that worked at the door, because that's how you are when somebody comes to your door at ten o'clock at night.

He didn't spend a lot of time with me on it. We practiced outside after we'd had our makeup and hair done in the trailers. I think he just wanted to make sure we knew our lines. He didn't have to worry about Sheryl and Kyle, but he probably was worrying about me a little bit. But the only thing he asked me to do was pause. When Kyle would say something, I'd respond, but I'd have to wait and respond, because that builds anxiety. So that's the only kind of arty direction he gave me. Then he let it just be raw and tweaked a couple things. It only took two takes, thank goodness. I was so happy about that. He goes, "That's a wrap," and I'm like, "Oh, good," because that was fun! It's funny, because I didn't know who Carrie was. So I asked one of the crew people, "Who's Carrie Page?" And they said, "We can't tell you." It was even that secret. So, I asked, "Is it . . . is it . . . Sheryl Lee?" and she goes, "Yup, Sheryl Lee." That's definitely when I started thinking, "What am I going to do? I have to make sure I know what I'm doing here!" I'm one of those people who, when I get a little bit nervous, I get scared and forget stuff. I was hoping I wasn't going to do that. They're such professionals. Meeting them in the trailer helped. And practicing out front with them helped because then I felt like I knew them a little bit. As I was standing there we did a practice take. And Sheryl looks at me and goes, "Aw, you're doing great." And then Kyle looks at me and goes, "You're doing a good job." That maximized the whole experience for me, because I was hearing from those two, so it immediately put me at ease.

What was it like meeting Sheryl Lee and acting opposite her?

Mary S. Reber: I had heard a little bit about her, just how kind and genuine she was. After watching *Twin Peaks*, I thought, "Wow, this person." I don't know what her experiences in life have been, because we're all just a kind of summation of our experiences, but she put such a face to trauma, and I respected her so much. To be able to do anything, any scene with her, was an amazing experience for me. As for Sheryl and Kyle, you didn't get that [in serious, deep voice] "we're actors" vibe from them. They were just people here to do their job. He's so good at what he does. She's so good in the movies that she's done. To be honest, I loved a lot of the actors, but if I could choose two, it would have been those two.

What was it like having your home upended with the crew installing their own props in there?

Mary S. Reber: I absolutely loved it! It was so much fun from the first day to the very last day, watching artistic people do their thing, whether it was staining the floors, staining the bushes outside or laying dead grass outside or whatever. I think it was therapeutic for me to think about something else and look at something else before the scene at the door on Friday. So it was just really cool for me to watch. I would totally do it again. We've had domestic violence in our family too, like in the show. It was therapeutic and cathartic for me to get my mind off everything and just watch this. It was a cool experience that I'll never forget, because it seemed to come at the perfect time.

I'm sorry to hear about the situation you had in your family. Several

women I've talked to for this book have talked about trauma and their own experiences, maybe not being exactly like Laura Palmer, but seeing their own story of trauma in Laura.

Mary S. Reber: I understand a different kind of trauma. Trauma's trauma, but it has different faces. Back in the day you had people either giving you bad information or no information. People either considered you a burden or a privilege. When you're a burden, people close off. When you come from church, which I did, and a church experience, people tell you, "Hey, you gotta try harder. You gotta keep going back. Maybe there's something in you that can change the situation."

What does your journey of healing look like coming back from that?

Mary S. Reber: Well, the last two years have been pretty difficult for me. I divorced last year, and then I had two years to just lean into the pain of everything that happened. And that's why I kind of closed off last year. I think during filming it was great. It was like, "Oh, this is going to take my mind off of it," but last year I was having to put my mind back into it. And until you lean into it and own it and feel every feeling . . . you can't heal. I mean, I would watch things on TV that would make me have to think about things and make me cry and make me do different things. The only time that you're going to heal is when you lean into it. I think now I feel more of a freedom. There's just more things for me to listen to, and people are more willing to listen to you and help you, and you're getting better advice these days.

Whenever I see you in person or online, you exude kindness, but you also exude this strength. Do you think that comes from your experience or was it always in you?

Mary S. Reber: Let's just say I was empathetic all my life. During the years of abuse, I was an empath without boundaries. Now, I'm an empath with boundaries. I think that's where the strength comes from.

What's it like living in the Palmer house?

I'm living here by myself. It looks a little bit like I'm being greedy. There's just one person living in this huge house. This house for me is a vehicle to allow people to come in. I've watched people, and I've learned so much. The fear of people walking through my house is just completely gone. What I'm seeing, the joy, for me it's almost selfish; it's the joy of watching people being touched. People come in, and during the walk-through they'll start telling me about their trauma. I think people who have been through trauma can sense it in each other. As they walk in the door they're leaning into their trauma, they're turning the corner, they're looking at that fan, and they start crying. A lot of people start crying. It's just crazy. It probably doesn't help to have BOB in the closet [Reber keeps a mannequin dressed as BOB in Laura Palmer's bedroom closet to amuse and terrify visitors], but at least they know he's fake, you know? It's people being able to lean into something that is hard, but it's therapeutic for them too. They walk away, and they stand outside, and they look up to the house. I just love it. I'm driven by that.

You've been an amazing host, inviting people and fans into your home. You mentioned how you set boundaries. One of the things those of us who write about the show have tried to do is not give away the addresses of private residences. Of course people can find you, but we want to respect your privacy and remind readers to respect your privacy. What do you want the fan community to know about your boundaries with your home?

Mary S. Reber: Well, let's put it this way: just the other night I had somebody walk to the door, and it was dark. And it was 7:30 p.m., and I had my blinds drawn. They were knocking on the door and ringing the doorbell and didn't stop. They kept doing it. And I looked outside, and there was a guy standing there staring at the house. Number one, I'm not going to answer my door at night. If someone needs to get ahold of me, I'm very happy to do it, but they have to make an appointment. Then there's ways I can look people up to make sure they are actually *Twin Peaks* fans. Because one time I let somebody in here and he claimed to be a *Twin Peaks* fan, and I said, "Do you want to see the fan?" and he goes, "What's the fan?" So what I'm doing now is I'm trusting my gut, whereas I didn't trust my gut before. If something is weird, I don't pass it off, I listen to it. Maybe that's why I still feel really safe here. I haven't had any bad things happen. But people will walk past the "No trespassing" sign and walk up the stairs. I actually did put something out on Twitter and Instagram. I said, "I have a sign outside. I want that to be respected." To me that's not being mean; that's being wise. This is a private residence. The lady who lived here before didn't allow people to come up. I want people who want to see the house to come in and have their experience. But then, I live here too, so I have to keep those boundaries as well. What I do now is I charge people, because I've been doing this for maybe four years. And since I like to talk, it isn't a thirty-minute visit; it goes anywhere from an hour and a half to eight hours for a visit. I figure that someone who goes and sees someplace always pays a fee, so if they come in here, just for upkeep and cleaning carpets and stuff like that, I charge per person now.

You said it gives you such joy to see the fans go through the house. When you think back to the last few years of welcoming fans into your home, what are some memories that stand out?

Mary S. Reber: Because I'm a little bit older than the normal fan base, I look at people and ask them, "When did you first watch this?" The average age is like ten to fourteen! And I think of the scene with Maddy and what happened to Laura with the incest, and knowing ten- to fourteen-year-olds watched that still floors me. And you know what? Everybody who has walked through has had some sort of trauma in their life. It comes in all different forms. It looks different on everybody. But we're all imperfect people, and everybody's had trauma. Whether you liked Season 1, 2, and 3 or whether you didn't, people are still talking about it. People are still excited about it. This is one place where they can still come to that was actually a location site. I'm just floored by how kind people are. I love people. I really do. And I love hearing about what people have been through and how they've grown and how they've healed—and how this place means that much to them. This is a really different fan base of people. Once they turn the corner and see Laura Palmer sitting on my table in that picture frame, they always grab her and say, "Oh, Laura!" It's timeless. Her picture is timeless, because her story is timeless.

When you were cast in Season 3 as Alice Tremond, you had to keep it a secret. I remember meeting you before Season 3 aired when you attended the premiere in Los Angeles in May 2017. From the very beginning we were speculating what role you would have in Season 3. Several of us thought you were Linda of Richard and Linda. Boy, were we wrong! We didn't discover what role you played until the very end.

Mary S. Reber: I didn't discover me until the very end either!

What was it like going to the premiere with the cast members to watch the new *Twin Peaks* on the big screen?

Mary S. Reber: That was really cool. I have to say that was more nerve-racking to me just because there are all these people whom you've never met before. Everybody in their own right was extremely good at what they did. It was a funny experience, unlike any other premiere, I'm assuming, because you go in there and you look at people and nobody knew who anybody was because it was still a surprise. The only people you knew were who you saw on the big screen, in Parts 1 and 2. What was cool was my house was in the very last scene of Part 2. The funniest thing I took away from that event is when I looked over at Robert Broski [a woodsman], and I thought, "How is David Lynch going to incorporate Abraham Lincoln into *Twin Peaks*?" But unless they were in the original series, you didn't know who anybody else was.

What do you take away from your experience filming *Twin Peaks*?

Mary S. Reber: There wasn't one bad experience during filming here. David Lynch was cool, because he'd walk in, and he wasn't a small talker, but you could just see and hear his wheels turning. And that was crazy for me, because I was watching that whole creative process happen right here. It was a privilege. No matter what anybody thinks about any of the series, it was just a great privilege for me to be a part of this. Because of my own trauma, I have an opportunity here. This helps give me a vehicle now, and I can help be superkind to people and watch them lean into all this. People get excited, and that gets me excited. This is just really timely that you're doing this book and covering this subject of trauma in general, because there's so much of it. What I'm realizing in talking to people is that so many have experienced trauma, and this whole series put a face to trauma itself. That's why I feel privileged.

What I think is so interesting about you and your situation and the Palmer home is you've experienced trauma in your life and you're living in a house that represents the place of trauma in the series, and yet now it's a place of healing. It's a place of healing for you, and you're welcoming in fans who are processing their own experiences, but they're also getting to laugh and enjoy the experience of visiting that home. I think that's an incredible joy you are offering.

Mary S. Reber: If I had to put a word to this whole experience it's "redemption." There's a face of trauma, and that's still part of it, but there's also a face of redemption. This house can be redeemed because there's somebody who lives here now that is letting people not just stand outside and look up, they can actually come in, and they can talk about it. It's a place of safety. I think *Twin Peaks* is not mindless TV at all. It's fragmented like a dream is fragmented. And that's David Lynch's vision, his artwork. I see some of the trauma perhaps from his life in all this. Everybody's got a story, right? But it isn't just a story of trauma; it's a story of redemption, too.

Part II:
Laura's Ghost

Laura's Ghost

`"I'm dead, yet I live."`[1] `- Laura Palmer`

One of the first images in *Twin Peaks* is of Pete Martell discovering Laura Palmer's lifeless blue body wrapped in plastic positioned like a totem on a rocky beach in the Northwest. This scene is mirrored in Season 3, Part 17 when Laura's body disappears from that same beach after Agent Cooper intervenes in the past. Toward the end of Season 3, Pete Martell does not stop and look back at the rocky beach with the giant driftwood, because there is nobody there to make him stop and notice. Instead he continues along the path and goes fishing. What happened to Laura? Theories abound. Whether Laura is on-screen or not in *Twin Peaks*, Laura's memory remains with the viewer. Her ghost perpetuates. We are haunted by that ghost.

A ghost is a phenomenon of the spirit that exists only when someone bears witness to its existence.[2] "I'm dead, yet I live," Laura Palmer, or someone who looks just like her, claims in the liminal space of the Red Room in *Twin Peaks* Season 3. Just as BOB became supernatural coding for sexual abuse, Laura Palmer's existence beyond her death in liminal and remembered spaces becomes supernatural coding for traumatic memory. Ghosts traditionally haunt people whom they had a connection to. In Season 1, Laura Palmer begins as a dead girl who

---

1 "Part 1," *Twin Peaks: The Return*. Directed by David Lynch. Written by Mark Frost and David Lynch.

2 Gina Nordini, *Haunted by History: Interpreting Traumatic Memory Through Ghosts in Film and Literature* (Denver: Regis University Theses, Spring 2016).

haunts the town of Twin Peaks not only because of the fact of her death, but also because of the violent way in which she died.

Laura Palmer becomes a memento mori, a constant symbol of loss. She haunts friends and family as they remember her life. She haunts Agent Dale Cooper, who works to resolve her murder. She haunts us, the viewers, as we bear witness to her story. In Season 3, Laura Palmer's image and the memory of her are injected throughout, including in the opening credits, the Red Room, her apparition in front of Gordon Cole, flashbacks, and, of course, the emergence of Carrie Page, who looks exactly like Laura. The ghost is a constant visual reinforcement of loss, and a relationship with the ghost of a loved one is a continuous exposure to the moment of trauma. Sarah Palmer tries, but fails, to destroy her daughter's image—that iconic photograph of the homecoming queen featured throughout the series. She cannot destroy the memory, the trauma, the guilt of what happened in her home.

This book is a ghost story in which women bear witness to Laura's ghost. While Part I of this book introduced women speaking about themselves, Part II explores how women relate to the character of Laura Palmer specifically. In the following pages, women speak about Laura Palmer. Jennifer Lynch talks about writing *The Secret Diary of Laura Palmer*, in which she fully fleshed out a character who initially, in the beginning of *Twin Peaks*, functioned as a plot point to serve the story. When *The Secret Diary of Laura Palmer* was published between Season 1 and Season 2 in 1990, young girls, including myself, devoured its contents. Thanks to Jennifer Lynch's book, we learned Laura's story wasn't about just the abuse that happened to her, but also her strength, her complexity, her will, her sexuality, her humor, her vulnerability, and her power as a burgeoning young woman.

Next, Grace Zabriskie shares an essay about Sarah Palmer, Laura's troubled mother. Zabriskie and I engage in a sort of contretemps about Sarah's culpability in Laura's abuse and death—something I continue to struggle with. Sarah had visions of pale horses and BOB, but she couldn't seem to acknowledge what was happening in front of her in her own home. Then, Sheryl Lee talks about playing Laura Palmer, the toll it took on her, and what haunts her—the realization that Laura's story of abuse is still so prevalent. Film critic and writer Willow Catelyn

Maclay shares her essay "Northern Star." Maclay wrote this piece shortly after Season 3 ended. In many ways, Maclay is Laura Palmer. She is the reason the character of Laura Palmer haunts Sheryl Lee and so many— because sexual abuse still happens to young girls.

Finally, women in the fan community discuss the legacy of Laura Palmer. They explore her tragic story but also emphasize her resilience, her strength, and her agency. Sabrina S. Sutherland said her eyes opened about Laura Palmer when she accompanied Sheryl Lee and other cast members to a *Twin Peaks* event in Australia. Sutherland said, "People would line up to see Sheryl. They all had these stories about how Laura Palmer's story was their story. And it's heartbreaking to think that there's that kind of abuse at such a young age. It's so heartbreaking that this is real; it's not something that's fictional. It really is something our society doesn't talk about. *Twin Peaks* is one of the first television shows that really had that throughout its entirety. That's the whole focus of the show. It's Laura Palmer. That is the story. Laura Palmer."

Art by Maja Ljunggren

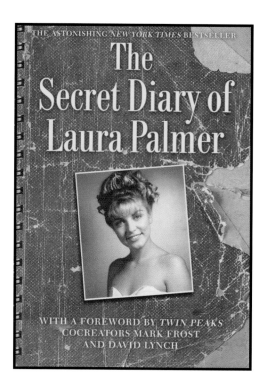

Jennifer Lynch Speaks about *The Secret Diary*

You are known in the *Twin Peaks* community as the author of *The Secret Diary of Laura Palmer*, which was published in 1990 between Seasons 1 and 2. That's not the only thing that you've done in your career—you've done so much more.

Jennifer Lynch: Oh yeah, but it is a potent thing that I have done, and certainly one that reached the most people.

Twin Peaks is important, *FWWM* is important, but *The Secret Diary* resonates with many women on a different level. I know so many young girls, myself included, who read the diary and saw themselves in this character, even if they hadn't gone through exactly what that character had been through. As young girls reading the diary, we were coming into our own sexuality. We were trying to figure things out. We were part child, part woman. Your book is so important to the *Twin Peaks* community.

Jennifer Lynch: Thank you so much! It was a privilege to write. When my father called, he asked, "Do you remember something you said to me when I picked you up from school one day?" I knew instantly that he was talking about this wish I had to be walking home and find someone else's diary and just take it with me and find out if she felt and feared and yearned for and was wondering and was curious about what I was wondering and curious about. For him to have remembered that, and for me to be what I recalled being and yet also have a shape to give it—I knew she was going to die, and so I could build on what was a very intentionally childlike voice for her birthday, as it opens, but also the voice of a girl who's writing in her diary.

It's a very different thing between what it would have been if it wasn't a diary—if it was a note or something. You know what I mean? It was very clear that her voice had to represent what I think diaries are—there's always a chance someone might find it, and so you want to be clear and you want to sound a certain way. It was a wonderful thing to be able to do, because she was the perfect specimen—she was going through things I wasn't, but I could understand them. They were relative to me because I'd had versions of them—versions of intimate family betrayals and inappropriate moments and, again, sexual awakenings—all of those textures are things people don't usually talk about with women. Even knowing that Anne Frank's diary had been edited of all the sexuality stuff was, like, wow! It was unfortunate that Laura's story was mostly abuse, but I tried to give her moments of what I thought was real, young love. And her wisdom, for the most part, was born of trauma. She was compassionate in nature from the get-go. The way she handled the trauma tended to be more self-abusive than outwardly abusive.

In 2013, at the USC retrospective of *Twin Peaks*, you said there are two specific things of yourself in *The Secret Diary*, and one was a dream with a rat gnawing its tail and another was your secret you were going to keep and not ever reveal. I appreciated that because, with women, we need to have boundaries about what we want to share and don't want to share, what's private, what's not. So you don't need to reveal that secret, but what aspects of you are in Laura? You touched on some of them, but what did you draw from your own experience?

Jennifer Lynch: Quite a bit, I think. I liked the way you responded just now to my not saying what the other thing was, because it's not, "Oh, I'm so ashamed of it" or "It's so juicy," but it comes up sometimes when people mention it—but anytime it's openly talked about, it's something everybody understands. It's all of ours. You don't need to know what was mine; it's likely the one that somehow resonates with you. And it doesn't have to be in a positive way—just "That felt very real to me."

Boundaries are weird. Because this was about her being violated by someone so close to her, and BOB or no BOB, mystically, there's still, in my mind, 70 percent of BOB that was created by Laura in an effort not to see it was her father doing this, and that he did come into her room differently. He did not come in as her father; he came in differently. So it served her not to see him. Whatever supernatural elements or just another face you give someone, you can't live and see someone doing that to you. That was Laura's experience. She was not able to process that. And so the boundaries created were about, you know, some of the boundaries I had to create. I was a kid in a more adult world. I understand having to navigate the "Is this OK that I'm feeling this?" and "When will I get to do this?" and "If I do this, then that's way more than I'm able to." Understand that people are manipulative—all of us—and you start to see her learn to get things she needs a certain way, and that's all survival mechanisms.

I was careful to play on what felt like a general experience of being a young girl coming into womanhood and a collection of betrayals with men that I was 50 percent of, but also they were betrayals of sorts. I took all that I had felt as wounds and realized they were the new scar tissue; they were the new bionic arm. However I was able to process it, those moments of terror became a superpower. And because I knew she was going to die, I could have that manifest in so many ways, because that's how the adolescent brain works too—from this to this to this to this. It was a way to really explore and feel like my questions were of a much more reasonable size because of what Laura was going through.

I was not being raped at night by someone close to me, but I had my own things. I think we all do. I know a lot of people who were assaulted whom I've spoken to, and they said the book was helpful. I asked myself and tried to answer myself in ways that would have been greatly helpful to me, and I found, if nothing else, that was the one thing that was successful—people felt affected by it. It was strangely familiar and made their lives not just OK, but human and normal and wonderful and appropriate to them. That's what we should all feel and I'd wished Laura could feel. I was sad for her that she was not going to become a young woman and be able to teach other people things. Had Laura survived, she would have been an incredible advocate.

I see that too. She was so strong at a young age. Had she survived, she would have given back.

Jennifer Lynch: Exactly! The playfulness and the terror and weirdness, the innocence, the sexuality I tried to explain as part of what was going on, but all young girls feel it. But also, she was pushing limits to see what she could get away with and what she didn't want to feel. I think that that is so common. Because she dies, I hoped it would make people want to fight to live longer.

How have the fans reacted to you when you meet them?

Jennifer Lynch: I have some of the most beautiful conversations. Those are all potent moments for me. They are shaped by two feelings. The first is a combination of a weird sort of handshake—because we usually hug, but there's a sort of spiritual handshake suddenly between myself and somebody who says, "I really needed to hear that. This was formative for me. This made what I was feeling OK. You gave me permission to be me." And I would say, "Thank you. Laura did that for me too." It's not like I have some wisdom. I just had a reason to say it out loud and a platform.

I meet a lot of people—it's not always girls—who are victims of assault and childhoods that either were directly similar or just similar enough for it all to matter to them and for them to feel OK. It's a much darker version of Mister Rogers going, "It's OK to be you." That's what I hope it did, and that's what it seems to have done. I could not be more thrilled with the chance I took with "Will they understand why her voice is this at the beginning? Will they understand the leap from this to this? Will they follow me here?" I was just trying to be as forthright as I could as Laura, and it seems to have been a good thing to do. And I'm so grateful that something that was incredibly potent for me is as potent for other people.

Art by Maja Ljunggren

Who Was Sarah Palmer to Me?
by Grace Zabriskie

Who was Sarah Palmer to me? Many things. You begin with just the gist of something. And then, I guess, it's a kind of active waiting and then paying attention to what I learn from the text to drop into facets of me. If the writing is good and comes from the writer's truth, then that itself becomes something I can trust and work with as the character is developed. You don't want to tie yourself down with too many nice, concise, declarative sentences here. It's very complex, this life. Sarah's life. From the beginning, a sense of lives before this one. They are known by Sarah on some level. Not forgotten. She lives with all the pain of this life and others, but this time she is all mother. This time nothing more important than this beautiful new child. Oh, Laura. She remembers things long forgotten. The same promises before—all broken one way or another. Protect Laura. Laura? This is not even the worst. Leland. She knows she can't protect Laura. Of course she knows Laura is already dead when she gets the phone call from Leland. She's been waiting for this call and for too many others all her entire lives.

A Contretemps between Grace Zabriskie and Courtenay Stallings
I love this. You're capturing some of the things you have touched on regarding guilt and protection and love, including fear, wrapped up in each other. Since you are a poet, you understand you can't make declaratory sentences, but you can capture a mood in a disjointed way, because that is how we think. That's how we operate. We are not always linear.

Grace Zabriskie: I guess my sense is that if you explain a little bit why it's that way, it might keep people reading past the first sentence or so. But if you don't, they might not. I don't know if I would.

You are capturing who Sarah Palmer is and what her journey is and especially her relationship with her daughter. That love and fear wrapped up in guilt.

Grace Zabriskie: It's so interesting. I realize everything I was saying was what I was doing. It almost makes me hope I never have to be her again. What is the name of that incredible piece of rock you gave me?

It's called obsidian. It's volcanic rock, and it is supposed to be a protector stone that also cultivates truth and creativity. Living your truth. Being creative. It's a dark stone, and it is supposed to absorb dark energy for you so that energy doesn't affect you.

Grace Zabriskie: What is so interesting to me about what has come out of me this morning in an attempt to give you something here is I don't believe in past lives. I don't believe in any of it. Nobody of course told me that Sarah did. She knew she'd had these lives. Nobody told me that. Then, when I decide to take her somewhere like that, which is not me at all and not any of my nooks and crannies that I am aware of for myself, then I can't help but trust it even more, because I know all those millions of synapses are doing their little magic. I shouldn't even think about it—just let her come. I want to put some more stuff about her. This is almost all just a preamble. A preamble for what is the thing. OK, keep me on the subject here. I've already said the part that interests me profoundly. Now I have to think about what might interest someone else as well.

Here is my advice to you. I think what interests you will most likely interest other people, if that makes sense.

Grace Zabriskie: It makes perfect sense. I've spent my life as a poet learning to trust that. However, it does look as though you might need something whether or not I might find it hugely interesting, in addition to what I did find interesting and I do believe someone else will. But what about the part that is really supporting the thesis of what you are doing?

This goes back to what you were exploring: on some level this mother knew something was wrong. We don't know what level that was. She loved her daughter, and she wanted to protect her daughter, as all mothers do. Where is that guilt, that protection, that love, that fear, all interacting with each other in this one woman? You said you were developing a backstory for her. Who is this woman? Where does she come from? What defines her? How does she live with the knowledge that she is somehow implicated in her daughter's death? Her daughter's abuse? That's where Sarah Palmer comes into my book. We often talk about the victim in terms of the person who was directly abused, but we don't always talk about the other family members who are involved in this and who know what was going on. This is my own take: I see them as victims as well in this. This is a tragic mother/daughter relationship. Sarah Palmer wanted to be the protector, but she failed. This book is a place for women to speak, and through speaking, find some small healing by seeing themselves in other women's experiences. Sarah has experienced

trauma—not in the same way Laura has. Sarah is also a victim. She is filled with guilt and fear.

Grace Zabriskie: I was off on a tear about this business of every time someone has been abused there has been someone else standing there watching it and saying nothing. That was my thesis of the day, which is not gone. I was kind of crazy and wild about that for a while. I do think it's a very, very important thing. I think it's underaddressed. I think it's all very well to talk about the witness having been damaged as well. I think that's true. But what about trying to say that you and I are having a little bit of a contretemps here, because I am trying to get you to see that, OK, fine, Sarah was a bit of a victim herself. However, she also stood there and watched. She heard. She knew things. She said nothing. In some ways everything that we've been talking about is me explaining more deeply why she is a victim. There's nothing to be lost, and something to be gained, by some mention of this contretemps between us.

Absolutely. And you keep pushing me on that. That is why I bring up guilt. There is guilt there because Sarah did not do anything. On some level she knew and did nothing.

Grace Zabriskie: Guilt can be anything. Guilt could be nothing more than her past lives and her failures, which has nothing to do with the fact that she did have agency. I've noted that guilt business, but it's not enough to really talk about what I'm talking about here. I'm not sure what you want to do with the book, but you have startled me loose of my own thesis.

You're giving voice to Sarah Palmer does two things. First, there might be someone out there who is reading this book who is Sarah Palmer, who had that experience of being a mother and knowing what was happening but not doing anything. Sarah didn't act with her own agency to help Laura, and it eats away at her. But there's healing in that confrontation with the self. Secondly, there are the daughters who survived abuse in the home who might read this and think,

"My mom didn't do anything even though she knew." I think there's healing in that too, because Sarah's taking responsibility. You sense her pain knowing that is not easy for her to face. Acknowledgment and bearing witness can heal.

Grace Zabriskie: What I've set up here is that she has failed in every life to do this. And she's forgotten that. She remembers a lot of things, but she's forgotten that she's failed every time to protect the child. Remembers things but has forgotten. Same promises before. All broken. One way or another. Protect Laura. This is not even the worst. Leland. She knows she can't protect Laura. Of course she already knows Laura is dead when she gets the phone call from Leland. She's been waiting for this call for too many entire lives not to know. So I'm not to make this a perfect thing. When I stopped, I realized I had pretty much finished with what I had to say that interests me. That's the problem here. So, "OK, sweetheart, you satisfied yourself. You have a nice little preface here possibly for what actually is going on, but you haven't really spit it out yet." To me, it's all there. As much as she knows. That explains everything. There's so much trauma, so much damage. They cripple the mind. She's a bit of a hamster on a wheel as opposed to someone who has meaningful agency.

I agree with you. And I think the thing that you are interested in is the thing that I am interested in. I can't speak for everybody else. That's why I said for you to say what you want, because the thing that you say is not what anybody else can say about Sarah Palmer. Nobody else played that character. Nobody else lived that character. You are the one who can best speak to that, more than anyone. People are interested in that.

Grace Zabriskie: Is there a possibility that a lack of a sense of . . . the specificity of this in terms of me trying to feel in her head could be inadequate? Does that seem right for her? Do you know what I mean? I hope not, because I sure as hell don't.

She's a mystery, too. We don't know how much she knows about

the situation. We also don't know that much about her, either. In a family where there are secrets, everybody keeps secrets. There's usually not just one. They have many. I think it's OK if there's still mystery around her. I think that's why she seems very real. All those secrets. All that guilt.

Grace Zabriskie: If you find yourself reading this, and you want it to be more specific, you can read on. None of those things are what she is about. She's about having gone through this so many times in her life and being unfortunately aware of that. There's almost a Greek thing going on here. There's her fate, and therefore Laura's fate. I think she has a sense of "Will Laura be a version of Sarah? Would Laura have been a version of Sarah had she lived? What about all the others? Where does the line come through? Does it come straight from mother to daughter? Can it be through another relative? Was my sister the one who somehow got the genes to give to the next one?" I want to say those things.

I think you are asking, "How specific should I be and how much should I go into it?" I'm open to what you want to do. I don't think you need to solve a problem or solve a mystery.

Grace Zabriskie: I'm trying to stay with Sarah and not me and, at the same time, say what all this is about. It's about me trying to fit this script into what I understand and somehow drops into my crevices and fits, and works. I don't believe in past lives, but my intuition was that this script did. The writer did. Even if he didn't know it. A good writer gives an actor a character built on truths, but the most important work happens when an actor opens her pores, her nooks and crannies, and all her synapses to pour her product of the conscious and unconscious work into those pores. The writer has done the writer's work; now the actor must create what will be the nature of the actor's work about this particular character.

Photo Courtesy of New Line Cinema

Sheryl Lee Is the One

Despite a solid career performing many different, complex roles, Sheryl Lee cannot escape the character of Laura Palmer. In 2017, Lee returned to play Laura in the Audible audiobook version of *The Secret Diary* as well as her role in Season 3. Performing Laura Palmer took a toll on Lee, who said in no other role has she been asked to do what she had to do to be Laura. But, she says, the difficult role was worth it, because she meets so many survivors who have found meaning in Laura Palmer's journey. Over the years, at festivals and conventions, survivors have relayed their very personal stories of sexual abuse to Lee while she compassionately listens and bears witness to their pain.

Between Season 1 and Season 2, Jennifer Lynch wrote *The Secret Diary of Laura Palmer*. How did Jennifer Lynch's work inform your role as Laura Palmer? So many people have told me there's this version of them in Laura's character in the book. She's intelligent, and she takes risks. She's sexual. She's finding herself. Jennifer Lynch provides this great backstory to the character.

Sheryl Lee: Oh, it was incredible—especially going into *FWWM*. I had a very well-loved and well-worn copy of it then. I circled and underlined it and constantly referred to it. I had written my own backstory for her. The trippy thing is how many similarities there were. I didn't know Jennifer was writing this until it was done. I appreciated Jennifer's work so much. When I recorded the book, I couldn't say anything about it until it was announced. Everyone kept asking, "When are you going to record that?" I'd say, "I don't know. Maybe someday!"

I hadn't read it for twenty-five years. So to go back to it and read it made me appreciate it even more in terms of her writing and her skill and knowing how young she was when she wrote it. It blew me away—the details and where she was able to go with that. It is phenomenal writing. It's so emotionally devastating and such a solid piece.

Jennifer Lynch said there are two aspects of her life she used in *The Secret Diary*—one is a dream she had about a rat, and the other she said was private and just for her. I think it's important for us to have secrets. There are the secrets that harm us, and there are the secrets that are our own that other people don't need to know. Actors, writers, artists put so much of themselves in their works. I'm always curious as to how much of Jennifer Lynch was in that character. Reading it, I saw parts of myself as a young girl—not just in the sexual abuse, but in what one goes through as a young girl: the experimentation and wanting to take risks, friendships. It is a powerful book, especially for young women.

Sheryl Lee: It was incredible, and even all the other little stuff, like the relationship with her parents and how she feels about her own body and her relationship with her pets, boys, and all the stuff that's, at that time, in one's life, is an intense time emotionally. At that age, we don't have the skills yet to know how to process, in those teenage years.

There are parts where Laura seems like she's a woman and then other parts where she's very much a child.

Sheryl Lee: Yes, which is exactly what it is like developmentally during those years. It can switch in five seconds. You want your independence, and you want your freedom, yet you still want to be held when you need to be held. You want your mom to be your mommy.

What was it like to perform the work for the audiobook and return to performing the character of Laura all these years later?

Sheryl Lee: It was strange. That was the first book I [performed as an audiobook], so I knew that creatively I was going to grow and be outside of my comfort zone, because it's a completely different skill, just like TV acting is a different skill from film acting or theater acting. I was excited about that process of trying something new. What was most important to me and the director who directed me for Audible—he was fantastic—was to stay connected to it emotionally. We made some choices that allowed for me to be in a younger state emotionally, and then to deepen through it, so there is innocence and then there is grit. I hope we were able to balance those two. There were long days of recording, and I was just there by myself with these headphones, and the director was in New York on his headphones. When you are acting, it's all about the other actor. You focus on the other actor. You listen to what they are saying. You respond to what they are doing, what they are giving you. This was just me inside Laura for this concentrated amount of time. I discovered a lot because now I am thirty years older. Certain things hit me harder or were more emotionally painful. I was again in awe of Jennifer's brilliance and the fact that she could create that when she was so young.

In _FWWM_, you have to live out those difficult last days of Laura Palmer. What was your reaction when you were asked to return as this character? How did you prepare for the film, since the movie is entirely focused on your character?

Sheryl Lee: When David first started talking about it with me it was a while before we started filming. It was an idea that he was circling. I don't remember seeing a script long beforehand. I remember having these wonderful in-depth discussions and meetings with him. I knew that it was going to be about the end of her life, those last few days, and there were certain things that were going to be explored that hadn't been in the series. So we had a lot of creative discussions. Immediately I was thrilled to have the chance to work with him again on anything, anytime, no matter what it is. I also remember feeling grateful because I had never felt finished with her: to have the opportunity to flesh her out and to get to know her better and dive deeper into who she was and explore why this happened and how this could have happened—not that we can ever fully understand anything about that. So I was grateful and intimidated. I knew from the beginning that this was a big piece of work and a big mountain to climb, and that I had to do my diligence here. I have no sense of time or how long it was when David and I started talking until we were actually filming. Of course, I saw a script at some point, but the way David directs I can look at a scene and not have any idea of what he is going to do with it.

So how do you as an actor give up that kind of control? You may think you are taking the character/scene one way, but Lynch might take it in a different direction.

Sheryl Lee: I trust his vision so much creatively, and I trust him as a person. His eye is amazing, and his emotional understanding is brilliant, so even if it doesn't make logical sense at the moment to me, I'm willing to suspend and surrender to that creative process because I trust his ability to guide me.

***FWWM* has a lot of incredibly intense scenes. What was a difficult scene for you to shoot?**

Sheryl Lee: The bar scene. That was hard because even though I'm acting, I was still a young girl in reality feeling vulnerable and exposed because of the nudity. Also, there were so many things that had to be technically right: the drugs, the drinking, etc. At that time Laura is appearing very comfortable with sexuality. No matter what I, Sheryl the actress, is going through, I have to set that aside to make sure that the character can come through.

Laura Palmer had to confront not only the evil BOB but also the fact her father was raping her and had been for a long time. How as an actor did you prepare for this and perform this? How did you as an actor or as Laura Palmer come to terms with this realization? Do you think that BOB possessed Leland? Did Leland have any role/responsibility? Did Leland have any awareness or is this all BOB taking over?

Sheryl Lee: It is such an interesting exploration, and I don't know the answer. I don't know that we need an answer. I would sit sometimes in the experience of "What if there is such a thing as actual possession and what if that is what happened to Leland?" I would sit in that place creatively and emotionally and see what that place would reveal to me. Then I would sit in the other place of "What if it really is just Leland? What if I, Laura, had to create this other character because otherwise I would kill myself if I realized it was actually my dad?" And I would sit in that place and let that reveal to me what it would reveal to me. For thirty years fans have told me what they think. There's at least half of them who think one of those things and at least half of them that think another. Then there's another group that thinks something completely different. For me, creatively, I made choices that best served where Laura was emotionally at that time that could ultimately serve the story in the best way. I don't know that I'll ever have a 100 percent, definitive answer.

One of the things I think is valuable about David Lynch's work is he doesn't provide us with definite answers, so we can think about all of the options and discuss with other people what things might mean. We can bring our own experiences into play. Lynch leaves room for that. It's interesting to hear you talk about being an actor and sitting in this place. You are allowing yourself to be open to what those answers might be at certain points but never definitively defined.

Sheryl Lee: It's different if it's something that takes place only on this plane of existence, but in that world it's different. I've had dreams in my life that were so real that I know absolutely without a doubt that it wasn't just a dream, that there was truth in it. So if I have that experience as myself, then that's what makes me suspend or stay open to these other realms of possibilities, where maybe I don't have all the answers. Things can be happening simultaneously, and maybe both things are true, or there's truth in both things.

Are there any parts of you in Laura?

Sheryl Lee: I'm going to tell you something. I had not watched *FWWM* for almost thirty years, and I watched it three nights ago. I thought I would never, ever watch it again—that I didn't have the courage to watch it again. I would feel bad because sometimes I would do these Q&A's and I could not remember. The fans remember more than I do. I didn't plan on watching it. It's coming up a lot right now in my life for obvious reasons. I knew that I was doing this with you, and honestly doing this with you meant more to me in terms of knowing and remembering what I'm talking about than other interviews I've done about it. I appreciate your angle and your perspective and your heart and your desire with this. I wanted to rise to that. Thank you for helping give me the courage to watch it again. When I shot it thirty years ago, I was in Laura. That was my perspective. That was my story. That's how I told the story. All of my focus was her. Her story is so extreme, but I can take an aspect of insecurity or feeling like I can't stand up to men...I can take lots of strings of her story and think, "I've definitely felt that," and multiply it by one hundred, whether it was self-destruction or self-worth issues or issues with men or feeling alone . . . I understood a lot of her—a lot of her pain—but the extent of it was magnified in her situation. But watching it now, I see it so differently, because now I'm a mother, and I'm turning fifty. It enrages me. This is just a movie, but how is this still happening? The statistics show it is still happening in our country. Maybe I couldn't have consciously articulated it because I was so in Laura's story, but watching it now I think, "Why didn't anybody do anything to help?" There were signs everywhere. There were symptoms of how much pain this girl was in. The other thing is how many men were involved in her destruction. Again, we're reading about it in the news right now, every day. It's incomprehensible. It's enraging. Almost every man in Laura's life contributed to her death. Why? Where is this coming from? At one point could someone have reached out and grabbed her arm and said, "I'm taking you out of this. How are you? Are you OK? What's going on? Do you need help?"

I get the sense from Laura that the right person at the right moment could have gotten her to be honest, to trust them. She's wearing a mask and lying to everybody. Are there any parts of Laura that found its way into you?

Sheryl Lee: In some ways, at certain times of my life, Laura was a bigger part of me than I was allowed to be. When people see me they don't see Sheryl. They see her. And trying to figure out how to live with that and how to serve that but also find the space where I can separate them and just be me has been a challenge since the beginning. I remember making an effort after *Twin Peaks* not to do anything like that because I had to get away from it. And I had some good opportunities to be able to do that in roles that were very different. But it doesn't matter what I do; that is all I'm known for. I'm not complaining about that, but it's a tricky thing to figure out how to navigate. She's not a living person, which makes it extra strange.

One of the other things that struck me when I saw *FWWM* again so many years later is, no wonder it got such bad press. It forces us to deal with something. Nobody was talking about incest thirty years ago. People still aren't talking about incest. They are still not talking about those men who do that to young women. The film is very, very confronting. I hadn't realized at that time how confronting it actually was. I never had a conversation with David about this. I never talked to David about the overall cultural themes. I was just telling Laura's story. I wouldn't have wanted that conversation at the time. I had to find her truth as an individual, as her own person, to be able to tell her story as honestly and authentically as I could. We'll see, since it is screening again and on Showtime. Obviously, you are having a conversation about it—thank you. I have experienced women and fans coming up to me at various times and telling me that this film helped them. I hope so. When I watch it, it is horrifying. There are images that David created that you can't get out of your mind. It's not necessarily as graphic as a lot of the films that we see now, but where your mind goes from an image that he shot. . . . When I watched it again, it's no wonder I didn't remember all that stuff. I blocked it out of my mind.

David Lynch's films seem very spiritual. Many people describe them as surreal or dark, and they are those things, but they take us to a place, and sometimes we don't want to see what's there, but by confronting what's there you can work through it. That's the reason why a lot of women have watched that film and said, "Thank you for telling that story." I've done some research on the way that sexual abuse was talked about or shown on television in the 1980s. It was discussed in those afterschool specials that were mainly instructive and/or low-budget. Then, in the early 1990s, _FWWM_ came along. People are expecting it to be coffee and cherry pie, like the television series. Then they watch it. At the core of what the story is about is sexual abuse and trauma. I think it's very difficult for people who haven't gone through that to witness it. And like you said, it's all around us. It still happens. We still have a hard time talking about it. To me it's a very spiritual film in that it's bringing to light the trauma someone goes through. It's done in a very beautiful way. It's strange to call something horrific like that beautiful, but it is. It is tapping into something.

I wanted to talk about what you said about trying to protect yourself from being only seen as Laura Palmer, which might be difficult, since _Twin Peaks_ came back.

Sheryl Lee: Just when you thought you were old enough to have that all forgotten!

So how do you protect yourself when people see you only as your character? In some ways, like you said, it can be positive, because trauma survivors see you and it can be healing.

Sheryl Lee: When it first aired, I immediately lost my anonymity. That was the biggest challenge at the time, because I had no skills to deal with it. I was so young at the time. This was my first TV role. There were times when I was scared. Literally scared. There were lots of things that if I could do again I would do differently. Looking back on that time, the hardest thing for me was I didn't know what I was allowed to say no to. You jump on this roller coaster—this thing is a hit and you have to go here and do this and be on this show and do this interview and do all these things. You feel you are meant to do everything, and that can just burn you out. Now, saying that, my heart goes out to the kids these days who are having to deal with social media on top of it. If I could do it all again, that would be the first thing that I would change. I feel like I lost my anonymity faster than I knew how to handle it. I feel like as soon as the show came out, if I could have just moved to a little cabin in the mountains for a little but still worked and had a little bit of a transition time or an adjustment time, that would have helped. I had good mentors, and I realized pretty quickly that I needed help with this and how to manage it. I spent a lot of time out of LA in my twenties because I was working on location. Once that died down, and once *FWWM* was criticized, everyone moved on to the next thing. Then it seemed like every role I did they changed my hair color. Then, all of a sudden, I had my anonymity back, because I didn't look anything like Laura anymore. I had dark black hair, or I had red hair. Then it naturally stopped. From my forties until now, I was almost never recognized, unless I went to a specific signing and they knew I was going to be there. And I became a mother. And I slowed way down on taking any acting roles at all. I started studying other things. I went through a lot of different chapters of my own personal life. I'm not sure what this chapter will be like. I don't have a clue.

You mentioned how a lot of fans come up to you and relay something very personal, including their own stories of sexual abuse. Tell me how you've come to approach that. Was it very shocking to you when this first started to happen—that people were so candid?

Sheryl Lee: When it first started happening I was still very young, but I remember being surprised in the sense that I knew what I was playing and I knew the story I was telling, but it hadn't occurred to me it could actually help somebody else. I am always just humbled that they would feel comfortable enough to share that with me. It touches me deeply. There's a part of me that feels like because I've watched the film again and because it is coming up again now and because I am fifty and I am a mother now, I'm in a different place, that I wonder if there is some way that I can serve that deeper now. I don't know if that's an organization. I don't know if that's being a voice for something. I don't know what that looks like yet, but I feel that stirring in me.

In many ways, you've served through your performance as Laura Palmer, which has allowed so many survivors to speak. And with the audiobook, more people will discover or return to Jennifer Lynch's work. When I came up with the idea for *Laura's Ghost*, I had forgotten about this poem that you wrote in 2012 [a revised version of this poem appears in the foreword of this book], and then I came back to it and realized Sheryl Lee is talking about how Laura Palmer haunts her. It is emotional. I can't imagine what it was like to go into a character that deeply and then to be recognized as that character and not being able to leave that character behind. There are a few lines I wanted to ask you about:

**"You gave my art a name
But if I did it all again
I might not do it
Quite the same"**

Could you speak to how you would not do it quite the same?

Sheryl Lee: I would have held onto me a little bit more. Part of your twenties is you figuring out who you are. Me, Sheryl, trying to figure out who I was at the same time Laura was introduced to the world was a strange feeling. The other thing is I hadn't thought about doing television or film. I was studying theater. I was going to do theater. I had a love of theater. Then, all of a sudden, my life took a very sharp right turn. I would do that again, of course. I am an introvert by nature, and I felt like because of the business, that it was expected of me to become an extrovert overnight. I tried to do that, and it hurt me greatly because it's not who I am. It took me decades to accept that about myself. I thought I had to be what everybody else wanted me to be. That is very similar to Laura. It took a long time to find who I was—not with Laura, not with the business.

We live in a world that seems to support extroverts more than introverts. I'm an introvert too. There is a book by Susan Cain called *Quiet*. The book changed my life because it provided scientific research for the reason why we need quiet and why we need to be away from people. I cannot imagine being famous and being thrust into the public eye.

Sheryl Lee: I don't know how I had the courage to do it, but something I did that I knew would help me is I would go away by myself. Sometimes I would go away by myself to Mexico. Sometimes I would go away by myself to Joshua Tree. I was fine going away alone, probably because I was an introvert. There was also something about going away alone where I could be anonymous. One of the things I love about acting is it teaches you to observe the world around you, but if you're famous you don't get to do that because you're being observed. I needed my time to be able to witness the world. I found that I had to leave LA. Some of the other actors on the show had worked before, so they at least knew part of that experience, and they had some good people around them. But I was like, "What is happening?!"

"Haunt" is an interesting word, and I'm using it in multiple ways in my book. It can be a negative or a positive expression. Ghosts can have light and dark influences. How does Laura Palmer haunt you?

Sheryl Lee: The first positive thing that comes to mind is she keeps me working with David and that group of people. In that sense she's been one of my greatest creative teachers. I've played a lot of intense roles, but I've never been asked to do anything like what I had to do for her. In that sense, truly, what she has taught me and continues to teach me every time I have to step back into her skin, even if it is for an audiobook or if it is for a poem, she's a great teacher for me in that sense, and I am deeply grateful for that. And anytime someone comes up to me and shares their personal story, that is a place where I feel like Laura haunts me in a good way. It's bad in the sense that I feel deep compassion for anyone who has to go through that. Every time I hear another person say they have been through that, my heart breaks, but in the sense of the connection of that moment, two human beings connecting and saying, "I'm hurting. I know what you are feeling. I understand. This helped me." The more of that that happens on this planet, the better off this planet is going to be. That for me is a beautiful haunting. I can't take away what happened to anybody, but I can share a moment with them from a place of deep care.

I have been judged very harshly for this work. My physical body is out there on the Internet for anyone to look at out of context, which infuriates me. Even just two days ago—I've lived where I have lived for six years, and none of my neighbors know that I act. I purposefully don't ever bring it up. If they ever ask, I just say that I work in the creative arts, which is true, or I tell them I am teaching. So my neighbor didn't know this whole time that I act, and he stopped my car as I was driving down the hill to tell me that the night before he turned on his TV and saw me. He's kind. He's a gentleman. And yet I know he'll never look at me the same. It doesn't matter that it was thirty years ago. It's a strange feeling. It's funny, because I am extremely modest as a person now and I wonder, "Is that part of it or is that actually who I always was?"

Even though *FWWM* did not originally get good reviews, critics are now beginning to acknowledge it as a work of cinematic art. People are now recognizing what an important and powerful film it is. Some art is ahead of its time. This is not just a story about drugs and teenage sex. There's a really important story here. Folks may look at you differently after they see you in the film, but hopefully they'll respect the role you played. You became Laura Palmer. That's why she is so real to everybody.

Sheryl Lee: That's because of David. The genius of David Lynch to create a character for a woman, and a young woman, that is that complex. That alone is phenomenal—that he would create a character that is that multidimensional and layered. How many times do we see roles as women that are only prop? All of his characters are so multidimensional, which is one of the greatest things about working with him. You know these are going to be complex people.

What is Laura Palmer's legacy?

Sheryl Lee: I do believe that if a person intervened she would have made it. She wanted to make it. I almost want to watch the film again and ask, "Who would it have been and which moment would it have been?" It wasn't until the very end of her life that you could feel her hope was gone. There was a survivor instinct in her. I always think of that angel at the end. For me, that was the peace that needed to happen. There needed to be peace. If anything, I would hope that the legacy is we can finally start talking about this, so that we can do something about sexual abuse, incest, sex trafficking, all of it. I feel like with Laura—don't let it be for nothing. Let's do something about this.

Northern Star

In 2017, writer and film critic Willow Catelyn Maclay reached out to me to share her essay "Northern Star," which explored her personal connection to *Twin Peaks* and the abuse she endured as a child. Willow Catelyn Maclay is Laura Palmer. Her story resonated with me because she captured what Laura Palmer means to survivors, to women. Maclay's story is about so much more than her abuse. Maclay is a survivor. She fled her home, the location of her trauma, in an attempt to leave behind the pain of her abuse. In the new home she has created for herself, she uses her writing as a catalyst to exorcise her pain. She writes about her joys and passions, including film and television, and the important role they play her in life. The following is an essay Maclay wrote in 2017 after *Twin Peaks* Season 3 aired. Following the essay, we discuss her writing and her connection to Laura Palmer.

Northern Star
by Willow Catelyn Maclay

My angel does heroin,
It could be called a home,
For someone who never heard bedtime stories,
She doesn't know happily ever after
Only a window

My angel was raped
Her best Sunday dress
burned in effigy
My angel doesn't have a saviour
Only a heavenly father
Daddy's little girl

My angel is crimson
Too unclean to ever be a lamb
Only ever a second thought
My angel waits
her gaze lingering
an image of a bedroom door
Turning,
a light shining through
Leaning, Leaning
On the Everlasting Arms
My angel screams
and I listen

— An excerpt from my journal. Written the morning after *Twin Peaks* Season 3 ended on September 4, 2017

I sit in the darkness of my bedroom, staring at posters I have plastered all over my walls, looking at the door and wondering if I'd get to sleep that night. Sometimes I'd get peace, but sometimes the door would crack open and monsters would come inside. That's how I internalized what was happening to me when I was younger, but when I grew up I had the knowledge to put it into words: incest. My father knew that I was feminine. He knew before anyone else. In an attempt to curb my own fascination with things like dresses and makeup he would come into my room, abuse me, and mutter things like "This is what happens to women. Do you want this?" Mourning the death of his son and destroying his daughter. It was an attempt to control my body. It was power and dominance. That's all rape is, but in addition to taking my body, he took my family and my home. There was no sanctuary. A wounded animal returns to its home when it knows it's about to die, but I had no such place, because my predator stalked my own bedroom. Laura Palmer is the single most important character in all of film or television for me, because she knew this feeling too.

I. The Prom Queen and the Angel

A mother (Grace Zabriskie) caught in the reverberations of a traumatic whirlpool wallows drunkenly into frame, taking a picture of the prom queen who was her daughter (Sheryl Lee) in her hand and smashing it onto the floor. Twenty-five years earlier, a father (Ray Wise) had cradled that same picture and danced with the photo, with the prom queen's face always present in his outstretched arms. The mother grips a piece of shattered glass in hand and plunges it into the image of her daughter's face repeatedly, wailing, screaming, and echoing the primal upheaval that has reshaped her entire life into a cesspool of damnation, by way of grief. The camera idles closely to her, slowly zooming, until we see the fractured image of her daughter torn to shreds. Twenty-five years earlier, that same father had raped his daughter, and she was murdered by his hand.

The image of Laura Palmer, and by extension Sheryl Lee, in the work of David Lynch is one of dissonance. She's the perfect good girl (as described by Jennifer Lynch in *The Secret Diary of Laura* Palmer) and the tormented martyr who chose to die. In *Twin Peaks: Fire Walk With Me* (1992) she was laid to rest, finally, peacefully, given an angel. Laura was saved by her decision to succumb to death with the introduction of a supernatural ring she slipped on her finger, which trapped her in a heavenly space. She was away from BOB, her father, and David Lynch. But it is happening again.

The soul of Laura Palmer has lingered through the career of David Lynch since her body was found wrapped in plastic on a cold shoreline in the sleepy town of *Twin Peaks*. She has haunted the filmmaker, much in the same way she has Special Agent Dale Cooper (Kyle MacLachlan). Cooper is a manifestation of David Lynch's obsessive need to return to *Twin Peaks* in the desperate hope of saving the girl who began as a corpse, and slowly evolved into a messianic image of grace.

Lynch has a warehouse of actors he loves to work with, all of whom have their own contextual relevance within his art, but Sheryl Lee holds a special place. She is the martyr through which David Lynch funnels his greatest streaks of empathy for humanity's unfairly damned. Nearly every woman in the work of David Lynch since *Twin Peaks* has been a manifestation of Laura Palmer in some way. In *Mulholland Dr.* (2001), Betty (Naomi Watts) is a good-hearted person attempting to help another woman in need while also trying to make it big in Hollywood, but is poisoned by the toxicity that rests within the system. In *Inland Empire* (2006), Nikki (Laura Dern) is also an actress, but her reality is unfairly ripped apart by a cursed film script that she dares to verbalize. Both of these women are in a sorority with Laura Palmer, pummeled by gendered violence, a trope that lingers in the blood of all of Lynch's motion pictures: the girl he couldn't save.

Even in the beginning of Laura Palmer's imagery in the work of America's greatest surrealist filmmaker, Lynch showed grief in the destruction of this poor girl. In the pilot of *Twin Peaks*, the melodramatic reveal of Laura's dead body is followed by near-constant images of family and friends sobbing hysterically over this girl they loved. Everyone was in grief over her death, whether they realized it or not. They were mourning her, but they were also despondent over the death of their own town. For with Laura's death, so went the soul of small-town America, but what Lynch wants us to know is that there was no soul there to begin with, and there was always horror behind closed doors. It was the case in *Blue Velvet* (1986) when doe-eyed Boy Scout Jeffrey Beaumont (Kyle Maclachlan) peeked behind the curtain of a nightmare with perverse interest, and it was the same here. There's always horror behind the suburban image of the American subconscious, but we hardly ever want to fully reckon with these things, because we want to act like fathers aren't capable of raping their own children. *Twin Peaks* is honest in pointing out the rot at the center, and the show is still dealing with the ramifications of that knowledge. At the close of the investigation back in Season 2, Cooper and FBI Agent Albert Rosenfield (Miguel Ferrer) ask who BOB might be, pondering if he's a supernatural entity and whether or not Laura's father may have been innocent at heart. Maybe BOB's just the evil that men do, but that would require us to ignore that men do evil.

One of the first images of *Twin Peaks: The Return* recontextualizes the moment from the pilot where Laura's best friend, Donna (Lara Flynn Boyle), notices an unnamed, faceless high school girl running across school grounds screaming, but now it is a slow-motion image (later again in black-and-white) with a deafening howl that foreshadows a show gripped with the pain of Laura Palmer's lingering trauma and the death that changed *Twin Peaks* forever. This is blood that stains eternal, and a horror that doesn't leave once it's nested in the body of small-town America.

Laura Palmer is the only innocent in the wake of all this tragedy. In the work of David Lynch the image of Sheryl Lee and Laura Palmer outside of *Twin Peaks* rings with angelic grace. In *Wild at Heart* (1990), Sailor (Nicolas Cage) and Lula (Laura Dern) are starstruck lovers pulled apart by circumstances completely out of their control, but throughout it all, their love persists. It's perhaps Lynch's most simplistic film in terms of plot, following a linear, if jagged, path from sweeping romantic love to heartbreak and back again, bathed in the romanticism of 1950s culture and fused onto a distinctly 1990s backdrop and flavor. Near the end of the film, after Sailor has gotten out of prison, he meets up with Lula once more, only to break her heart and tell her they can't be together, but an angel intervenes in the way of David Lynch's own Glinda the Good Witch, played by none other than Sheryl Lee. David Lynch is obsessed with *The Wizard of Oz*, going so far as to call it a "life-changing film" in Chris Rodley's career-spanning book of interviews with the filmmaker, *Lynch on Lynch*. Sheryl, as Glinda, convinces Sailor to go back to Lula, thus being a guardian angel for two potentially brokenhearted souls. In *Fire Walk With Me*, all Laura ever wanted was an angel.

The image of Sheryl Lee as a pure force and catalyst for good in *Wild at Heart* is not unlike the image of Lee in Part 8 of *Twin Peaks: The Return* where the image of homecoming queen Laura Palmer is surrounded in an orb of effervescent golden light. In the context of the nuclear horrors and origin story of BOB earlier in the episode, it creates a fulcrum where Laura is the one sacred image in the world of *Twin Peaks* and, by extension, in the work of David Lynch. She is a Joan the Maiden figure: a crystallization of Lynch's key interest in redemption through violence, and the unfairly maligned purity of a girl who does not deserve her fate but nevertheless falls in the wake of such horror.

II. There's Fire Where You're Going

David Lynch is but a single artist, and the sheer power of Laura Palmer's presence would not shake with totemic magnitude if not for the unparalleled work of Sheryl Lee in the *Twin Peaks* narrative. She has haunted the series ever since her face was revealed in the opening moments of the pilot for *Twin Peaks*. Her mere appearance was enough to rock the foundations and preconceptions of what audiences in the early nineties considered fun, kitschy, Americana. The series was never about its eccentricities. They existed on the surface as a way to lull viewers into a false sense of security. They would believe that within the center of *Twin Peaks* there too would be goodness, but at its heart *Twin Peaks* is a series about trauma, and the lingering, generational effects it can have on a personal level, and on a community. Nothing within *Twin Peaks* exists only within itself when we know that hidden beneath the plaid skirts, mugs of damn good coffee, and cherry pie there was a dead girl, and her name was Laura Palmer. Sheryl Lee would be the only catalyst in which she could come to life and give this series meaning. Ironically, when she was given a chance to finally speak, in the prequel film, *Fire Walk With Me*, her truth was ignored by audiences and critics alike. No one saw Laura Palmer. Not in *Twin Peaks*. Not in the film community. Not on planet Earth. At her funeral her former boyfriend

LAURA'S GHOST: WOMEN SPEAK ABOUT TWIN PEAKS

Bobby Briggs (Dana Ashbrook) screamed, "She was in trouble, and no one bothered to help her. We all killed her." These words were gospel, and at the time *Fire Walk With Me* was considered the biggest failure of David Lynch's career.

What lives inside *Fire Walk With Me* is the unbridled, brutal honesty of a girl suffering at the hands of incest. When we are first introduced to Laura Palmer in *Fire Walk With Me* it is through a tracking shot. It's jolting and startling to see the image of the girl who washed up on the shore given life. No longer an object. She's living, breathing, and going to school just like everyone else, but there's something subtly off about the way she carries herself, as if her body is functioning on autopilot while her mind races away somewhere else. She trudges more than walks, and her awkward, if sweet, interactions with a fresh-faced Donna Hayward, now played by Moira Kelly, create an immediate dissonance between the two characters. There is no way for viewers to see Laura Palmer without the context of the image of the dead girl, and Sheryl Lee understands that central idea in her body language—as if she too understands that her place in the world is one of temporary residence. No one lives forever, but usually we do not resign ourselves to death in the way that Laura Palmer has as a result of years of sexual abuse. She carries the grief, disgust, self-hatred, and exhaustion of someone whose body is out of her very control. There isn't a way to understand what a body is if you've never been given the opportunity to live in your own skin, without someone taking everything from you. Since the onset of puberty, Laura has been violated, and with the ongoing changes in her body she has seen a world that views her through the same lens her abuser does. The eye of David Lynch's camera lingers, letting Sheryl Lee's performance do the talking, leaning inward when necessary to create the illusion that there isn't space between the audience and Laura Palmer. It is up to us to feel empathy for her and listen to her cries. She cannot be ignored, like Bobby said she was at her funeral. We have to see her.

The true depth of Sheryl Lee's performance is the entire reason *Fire Walk With Me* resonates. In this film she casts a shadow in which every other actor in the works of David Lynch must stand. "The Girl in Trouble" being Lynch's favorite narrative pathway means that all the

228

women who live in his cinematic world are torchbearers of Laura's poor soul. Sheryl's performance is mostly realized within her facial reactions and physicality. Extreme close-ups are occasionally employed to amplify the sorrowful look deep in her eyes, or the gulp that slides down her throat before saying, "There wouldn't be any angels to save you," when talking to Donna about floating in space. Sheryl Lee plays the role with agonizing closeness, her fragile body imbued with the realization that what's happening to her will never stop. She's too far down the rabbit hole, and there's no waking up for Alice. Death becomes a constant fixture within her thought process. In *The Secret Diary of Laura Palmer*, Laura thinks about death as a release from her day-to-day violence, both self-inflicted and by others. Sheryl Lee took the textbook written by Jennifer Lynch and wrangled the soul of *Twin Peaks* away from David Lynch, Kyle MacLachlan, or Dale Cooper and fixated it firmly within this girl dying from incest. She gave Laura dexterity, life, and dreams beyond the corpse she would become. Her struggles rang true for girls like me, who experienced incest. Girls who burn brighter in the dark.

Laura chose to die. It is the only way she can grasp at any sort of agency in her own life, beyond numbing herself out on drugs and alcohol. When she eventually meets BOB/Leland in the abandoned train car, her arms are tied behind her back, further stripping her of any sort of defensive maneuvering. She wrote frequently in her diary she knew the day she'd die was coming, as BOB's attacks grew more violent and enraged. In *The Secret Diary* some fifteen pages or so have been ripped from existence. The missing pages are BOB's admittance of defeat. He's afraid, tortured by a girl growing more aware, and stronger, through her realization that to give herself and her body up meant BOB could no longer have his twisted idea of fun. Laura's decision to die grants her the ability to have a body for what could be the first time in her life. This is cosigned through visual imagery, both in *Fire Walk With Me* and the pilot for *Twin Peaks*. In *Fire Walk With Me* it's her cathartic realization that she's in a heavenly space when an angel hovers over her. The angel is a protective symbol for Laura, due to her fondness for a painting of a similar angel that hung in her bedroom. In the pilot, it's the reveal of her body, a complicated image due to her lifelessness, but upon Laura's face is an expression that isn't trapped in fear or wracked with tears, but is one of rest. A close-up of her gray, decaying face summons the rapturous crescendo of Angelo Badalamenti's score, further cementing the idea that this is a moment of peace. A smile, because it's over, but it wasn't.

III. The Three Deaths of Laura Palmer

"All the angels kneel into the Northern Lights"
-Courtney Love, "Northern Star," 1998

On October 3, 2014, David Lynch and Mark Frost simultaneously tweeted "That Gum you like is going to come back in style. #damngoodcoffee." This joint message sent film fanatics and die-hard *Twin Peaks* fans into a frenzy. Was the show coming back? Was there going to be a movie? Could all of this be real? We all desperately wanted David Lynch to return to the cult phenomenon, but we never asked ourselves what the price of that would be. We were full speed ahead, no matter the costs. The coffee, Audrey's dancing, Special Agent Dale Cooper, all of it would be not only nostalgia for the weird, but a new passion project from one of cinema's finest directors. We didn't know what we were getting ourselves into, and that was exciting. What happened was something we could have never expected, which was unsurprising in some regards, but the connotations of what David Lynch and Mark Frost had actually cooked up had deeper ramifications for the universe they had created together in the late eighties, and for the image and body of Laura Palmer.

In the tenth episode of *Twin Peaks: The Return*, there is a long scene where The Log Lady (Catherine Coulson) not so cryptically tells Deputy Hawk (Michael Horse) about Laura. She tells him that "Laura is the one" and to remember that information. It is a mission statement, if anything, on the true nature of *Twin Peaks* and the work of David Lynch as a whole. Everything traces back to her and runs through her narrative and image. She is the image over the credits. She's the body that washed up on shore. She started it all. Any connotations of Cooper's narrative or how he would get back into his body after BOB had invaded it in the series finale of the original run are smoke screens obscuring the actual mystery of *Twin Peaks*. Lynch is on record as saying he would have never solved the mystery of who killed Laura Palmer if it had been in his hands. Showtime gave him that opportunity and with it he recontextualized the very nature of many previous images in the lexicon of *Twin Peaks*, the most notable being Laura's happy ending in *Fire Walk With Me*, which is now whisked away into a temporary place of satisfaction rather than a permanence of tranquility. Dale Cooper, in his overeagerness to save Laura Palmer throughout the run of *Twin Peaks*, misunderstood the entire basis for her messages to him. Laura didn't need saving. She needed justice. She told him as much in the Red Room, but he couldn't remember who Laura's killer was. He didn't *listen*.

This continues in the most recent incarnation of David Lynch's masterwork, where Cooper, being personified through Lynch's willingness to keep the aura of Laura alive, undoes the very thing she achieved in her final moments. In Part 17 of the revival, through the show's mythology on electricity and alternate dimensions, Dale Cooper finds himself hiding in the bushes moments before Laura walks to the haunted train car where she would die. He steps out of the shadows and guides her by hand. Dale says that he wants to take Laura "home," but for an incest victim, there is no home. Home is the point of trauma. Home is the point of total loss. If your family DNA is the connective tissue that gives you life, then that is burned by fire and turned to ash when the person who helped bring you into the world fractures your very existence. Dale Cooper does not understand this, and after a momentary walk through the Douglas firs, Laura vanishes, the only thing left being an echo of a scream. Her destiny is altered and thus her image. Her body never washes up on shore. Pete Martell (Jack Nance) goes fishing, Josie Packard (Joan Chen) applies makeup, Laura never dies. This is not a moment of reconciliation and joy for anyone. It is a failure, a stripping of her agency and a true death.

The image of Sheryl Lee as Laura Palmer is further complicated by the following, final hour of Lynch's magnum opus when Cooper tries once more to bring Laura Palmer home in an alternate version of the world he used to reside in. When he comes into contact with Laura, now going by the name Carrie Page, he insists that he's an FBI agent and he needs to bring her to Twin Peaks, Washington. She's unsure of this man, but either because she recognizes Cooper's face on some level or because she needs to get out of Dodge anyway, she follows. And they travel down the darkened road of America with only headlights to guide them through the tar. Something immediately feels off in this silence, this Cooper, and this reality. The sense of dread can be felt in the abandoned buildings they drive past. This is a dead world. When they cross the bridge into Twin Peaks, there's something immediately wrong. Carrie doesn't recognize any of it, and as they get closer to her alternate-reality childhood home there is still nothing to remark upon. This doesn't change when they ring the doorbell, talk to the owners, or step away from the house. It is a failure on Cooper's part to bring her here, and while Carrie tries to console him, Cooper finally says something that unlocks the repressed memory of Carrie Page and Laura Palmer. "What year is this?" The camera sits firmly on Laura's face as she begins to crack. There's a cut back to the house, where Sarah Palmer can be heard saying "Laura?!" and then everything falls. She screams, her face stricken with complete horror. The lights go out on the world, and Laura Palmer dies again.

The essence of this final sequence is one of a lingering trauma within the heart of *Twin Peaks*. Dale never considered that this may be the most horrific place to bring a victim of incest. His thinking was never nuanced enough to look beyond his by-the-book, goody-two-shoes idealism. He never considered the girl, and neither did the *Twin Peaks* audience. *Fire Walk With Me* was famously rejected by audiences and critics alike. Laura's dead body has been made into toys, Killer BOB was made into a cute Funko Pop! figurine, and *Entertainment Weekly* never even bothered to cover *Fire Walk With Me* in its issue celebrating the *Twin Peaks* revival.

Laura Palmer was never taken seriously, and by extension, it feels like my own past trauma wasn't either. The image of her screaming face hangs over me, reminding me every day that there is no scrubbing the past out of existence, and the place of my own personal hell still exists. The posters I stared at with anxious terror are still hanging up. The TV that sometimes lit the room in a flickering haze when I heard the door creak still hangs on the wall, and my father still walks this earth.

Only the miles and distance salvage my peace of mind, but that is not permanence. It is not reassurance. It is not sanctuary.

The final image of *Twin Peaks* is Laura whispering into Dale's ear as the credits roll. It is a re-creation of the first image in the Black Lodge all the way back when Laura whispered to Dale the first time, but it is different now. Dale is frozen in horror this time, and Laura's face is obscured. She is not whispering, "My father killed me," but something different. Words we never hear, but can infer. "You killed me," and in such, Lynch damns himself, Cooper, and the audience, who never weighed the cost of what *Twin Peaks* coming back meant. Laura spoke, and this time she was heard.

"My mind and my life had been completely occupied by you. You came to me morning, noon, and night—especially night. That was your time, the darkness of midnight. You continually wove your spirit into my dream world, revealing bits and pieces of yourself, myself, and our fears and struggles. The thing I remember most about you, though, Laura, is your loneliness. That loneliness haunted me. Walking back into my empty hotel room by myself each day, left to deal with the fragmented pieces of my own life, your loneliness would still fill my room. My prayer is that you are now someplace where you are truly loved and at peaceful rest."—Much love and gratitude, Sheryl Lee[1]

A Conversation with Willow Catelyn Maclay

You have had quite a journey—from Kentucky to Canada. You're a writer and film critic. Tell me about your background and how you arrived at where you are now.

Willow Catelyn Maclay: I've had a fun cocktail of influences regarding genealogy because I'm from the American South—Kentucky, actually. I grew up in coal-mining country. I'm from Harlan County, where movies have been made that paint it like this violent area, with the documentary *Harlan County, USA* and the television show *Justified*. I

---

1   From "A Page from Sheryl Lee's Diary and Her Poem for Laura Palmer," Welcome to Twin Peaks, Jan. 24, 2013.

grew up understanding the whole notion of going to church on Sunday and having BBQs afterward. There were firearms everywhere and casual racism and all these other kinds of things that unfortunately makes the South the South. I have that upbringing in my blood. I live in [a place in] Canada now, which is completely different. That's my makeup as a person. I grew up religious, but I'm not religious anymore. Throughout all of that, I had movies. They were the thing I latched onto when I couldn't understand myself or the area I lived in. I always gravitated toward film and television. I've always been writing. I had diaries when I was younger that I wrote in constantly. That evolved into me writing about movies and writing about myself. As I got older I wanted to be a film critic, so I pursued that as a career. It's not a career that's in the best shape right now in terms of its future, with journalism being in trouble. And art coverage is going by the wayside. But it's my passion, and what I like doing. I've been writing criticism on a professional basis since 2014.

I live in Los Angeles, but I'm originally from Atlanta. I can relate to the world you come from. Most of my family didn't go to college. They are rural people who live in south Georgia. I still consider myself a Christian, but I am very wary of people in positions of power, including churches, who abuse people. I am a survivor myself. Some of the things you are describing about your own experiences resonate with me. I can imagine Canada is a very different world than Kentucky.

Willow Catelyn Maclay: I understand what you were saying about not trusting people in positions of power. My dad is a pastor. My relationship to the church was immediately very complicated. I want to believe there are people who don't exploit their positions of power, but I have a very hard time with that.

I can't even imagine somebody who is supposed to protect you like your father doing that to you, and someone who is also a religious leader. My heart breaks for you. I am just appalled by people in those positions who abuse that power.
 You mentioned your work as a writer and film critic, so what's it

like being a writer who is a woman as well as being a transgender person? You've written about having both of those identities. What has this journey been like and how have people responded to you?

Willow Catelyn Maclay: It's been a mix of internal and external ramifications. It's interesting because my transness isn't immediately visible. People don't perceive me as transgender. My transition went very, very well. So I'm not perceived as a transgender person in my day-to-day life, but I have this internal sense where I know that that is true. I can see my past in my body, basically. I carry that with me in my body language and how I write, how I think, and how I perceive the world. But in a social context I'm not necessarily perceived as transgender in Canada at least. In film criticism, I'm out and a bit tokenized. When you are an extreme minority in this position, you have to be exceptional in every way. Everyone puts that on you. You have to be great because you are carrying the weight for everyone who's not there. There's this trailblazer kind of thing attached to it. I was told I was one of the first trans people who wrote about film in *The Village Voice*. It's a heavy weight. So I carry that more internally than externally.

As a woman in film criticism and in the world—the place of a woman in the world is perceived as a cisgender woman. I deal with sexism and not being taken seriously all the time and having to work that much harder. I have to be a perfect woman too, or otherwise people might not take me seriously. That's how the two identities intersect. Women already have to deal with expectations where you have to act a certain way or dress a certain way. With trans women, there's always this danger where if you are not perfect, 100 percent, then you're not authentic. That's a double-edged sword, because if you are trying to be this perfect idea of a woman then you're reaffirming a gender stereotype, but then if you are not trying to be that, then you're not what you say you are. That weighs heavy on you as well. They both affect me but in completely different ways. It's exhausting, especially in film criticism, where there is only a handful of trans people. And then the disparity between men and women in film criticism is gigantic as well. So I am an extreme minority in a minority group of people in my position. It's a lot to put on a person. I'm a perfectionist, and I'm always trying to write the perfect essay and be "on" all the time. It's difficult.

As a woman, sometimes people expect you to write about or be interested in specific things. I work in academia, so people assume my scholarship always involves feminism or gender. Of course I'm interested in that work, but it's not the only topic I write about. For you, as a film critic who happens to be a woman and also a transgender person, do people assume that you only want to write about those topics?

Willow Catelyn Maclay: I've written for a handful of feminist publications before, and that's obviously an interest of mine. I've written for *cléo*. They are a Canadian publication in Toronto. I have written for them, and there is this expectation for me to write about transgender topics. That was hard for me to navigate. I ended up writing about more than transgender topics, but I had to prove to them that I was more than just my gender identity. I love action movies on top of loving surrealism and horror and others. And getting to write about an action movie is incredibly rare. I would love to be able to do that, but I am never asked to do it. I don't know if editors realize they are reaffirming these stereotypes, but they absolutely do. I'm usually brought in to write about transness and trauma. These are two things I am familiar with, but I can write about anything if given the chance. I've not been given a ton of chances to prove myself in different genres of film.

That is an important point. I love action movies and horror movies like you do. People are always surprised. Even in the twenty-first century people can't understand how I, a woman, do not like romantic comedies. I want to see things blow up. I can imagine how frustrating that must be as a film critic, because you want to branch out and cover these other things you are interested in and not always given the chance to write about.

Willow Catelyn Maclay: Absolutely. It happens in day-to-day life too. I bought *John Wick* on DVD one time and the cashier, a guy, thought I was buying it for my boyfriend. I was like, "I'm buying it for me!"

When did you first watch *Twin Peaks*?

Willow Catelyn Maclay: I think I was nineteen or twenty when I first watched *Twin Peaks*. I was getting into film heavily and exploring everything. After getting a lot of beginner classics, like *The Godfather*, out of the way, I discovered David Lynch. I watched *Blue Velvet*. I was initially taken with *Blue Velvet* because it was not like anything that I had seen before. He was the first director I watched who dabbled in surrealism and horror and entangling them together in this nightmare picture of American id. He was separate from everything else I was watching at the time. A few years after watching *Blue Velvet* I had seen a couple more of his films, like *Mulholland Dr.* and *Wild at Heart*, but I hadn't gotten around to *Twin Peaks* yet because it was a television show. It would take me a lot longer to get through. I was very bad at watching television. If I lose interest I will drop a show immediately. I bought the Gold Box for *Twin Peaks* with the expectation I would love all of it and go through it immediately. I watched the pilot, and I was obsessed with it to the point where I did not continue with the show. I watched the pilot a dozen times. I thought to myself, "I can't possibly go forward with this show because it can't live up to the pilot." To this day I still think the pilot is the best part of the show. That's not a knock on *Twin Peaks*. I think it's the greatest piece of art ever made. I just think the pilot is that good. It became my favorite film to some degree. A few years afterward I still hadn't gone any further into *Twin Peaks*, but I continued to watch the pilot. I got into a relationship with a person who eventually became my husband. He's also a cinephile. He's also heavily into David Lynch and horror films. That's one thing we have in common. He suggested we watch *Twin Peaks* together. That's how I got through the rest of the show—I went through it with him. Much to my surprise, the rest of the show is as good as the pilot. I was obsessed.

I finished the show, and there was this movie waiting. I didn't know what to expect from the movie. I knew it was going to be about Laura Palmer. I knew what happened to Laura Palmer. I did not think it would become part of me. Laura, up until that point, didn't have a body or a voice. She didn't have a perspective. Laura was this character who everyone talked about. She was a character everyone knew in the past tense. We saw her through other characters' perceptions. Our image of her was a corpse. And that's all we knew of her. But *FWWM* was unlike any other thing I had seen before. It completely destroyed me in a way that I found reassuring. At that point, I had not begun to grapple with what had happened to me in the past. I'm still working my way through all of that. The movie was very important to me in realizing this happened and she could be OK, so I could be OK. She had to die in order to find her peace, which is not my situation. But the fact that she was given peace in that final image in the movie is probably the single most important image in my entire life in terms of film and television.

I want to talk about the piece that you wrote, "Northern Star." In 2017, you reached out to me and shared it. When I read it I was blown away by your experience of abuse that you put so eloquently into words. You came right out in the very beginning and said, "This is what happened to me." That's so difficult to do. I've never publicly talked about what happened to me. You came right out and said, "I am Laura Palmer. This is my story. And these are all the reasons why she resonates with me." What prompted you, at that point in time, to write this and share it?

Willow Catelyn Maclay: It was 2015, I think, when I first told my husband what happened to me. That was the first time I had ever told anybody what had happened to me. I slowly got more comfortable talking about it. Talking about it gave me some control over it. I can say what happened and have my perception of it and move forward with my life by unleashing it out into the world by telling my story. I had always wanted to write something about *FWWM*. I knew I was going to talk about what happened because I've always written from a personal place.

The piece that initially got my foot in the door with a lot of film critics was this essay that I wrote on Jonathan Glazer's *Under the Skin*. I wrote about it from the perspective of a trans woman because she was a trans woman in my eyes. I wasn't talking about the movie necessarily, I was more talking about myself. So I always wanted to do something with *FWWM* and with my past. In 2015 I tried to write something and failed. I put the idea on the back burner and thought, "I'm not ready for this."

But then *Twin Peaks* came back. It was a special experience. I was horrified by what might actually be in the show because I knew what David Lynch was capable of doing with the Laura Palmer character. I knew that it was going to be a difficult journey for me to go through this show again not knowing what was going to happen. It was like agreeing to walk into some kind of haunted forest. That's *Twin Peaks*. I never knew what was going to happen episode to episode. I was worried I would get triggered or sent into post-traumatic stress disorder while reliving memories. That didn't happen to me while I was watching the show until we got around to Episodes 17 and 18. In Episode 17, Cooper travels back in time and pulls Laura out and creates an alternate reality. I thought at first he's going to give Laura a happy ending. But then I intellectually thought, "There's no place for Laura to have a happy ending." Her happy ending on *FWWM*—that was the ending she chose for herself. In *The Secret Diary of Laura Palmer*, she talks about wanting to die. In the film, she lets herself go and she's given an angel. I'm still very moved by that. But Episodes 17 and 18 shifted that ending and gave it a new context and gave it a new meaning. It took away her agency. It hurt. It hurt in a way that felt right for me at the time because I was struggling myself at the time and trying to keep my head above water.

Episodes 17 and 18 were a reminder for me that this is always going to be there. It's always going to be. It's always going to be a part of myself. It's a part of my story. When the images shifted and Laura became something different, I thought I would try to write the piece again. I wrote this poem the night after Episode 18 aired, which I put at the top of the essay. It's about her, but it's about me. I did my best to be as open and honest as I possibly could without hurting myself in reliving those memories. I thought by putting the essay out there and by writing about her and writing about myself it would give me some level of closure on what happened. I don't have what I would call closure, but I have what I would call a more comfortable relationship with my own body and my past and myself. I can confront it a little bit better than I used to be able to. After writing that essay, it gave me some level of strength over my past. I still don't think I'm finished writing about my past. But that will come when it comes. After finishing the essay I couldn't breathe. I almost had to be taken to the hospital. That's what happened to me at the end of Episode 18 as well. I just have this intense connection with Laura Palmer, because I can see myself in her. I can see my past in her. I can see some of her in myself that walks down the same road that she did. I'm lucky to be around. There's nothing that can untangle that past from myself. The fact that I can work through this in a healthy way through her has been beneficial. Writing that essay is my love letter to her and also to *Twin Peaks*, even if some of the things I say about *Twin Peaks* in it are damning. I'm not damning *Twin Peaks* the show or the movie *FWWM*, but the world in which these monsters exist.

It took incredible courage to write that piece. You gave a lot of courage to other women by telling your story. How was your essay received?

Willow Catelyn Maclay: I recall it almost being universally positive. It blew up. It's the most popular post on my blog, *Curtsies and Hand Grenades*. Sometimes people send me emails telling me that it helps them, and that was the best part of writing it. That is what I wanted to do with this essay. I needed to speak for myself, but if me talking can help anybody in any way, then it was worth it to write it. There were a few people who also suffered from incest and who were fond of *Twin Peaks* who e-mailed me and told me that I was able to put into words what they felt while watching it. That moved me. I know I'm not the only person to experience what I went through. There's not a lot of art that will make you feel less alone if you have experienced this. It's a taboo subject that people don't like talking about. It's something that happens. People don't always believe you. It happens, but people perceive it as this unbelievable thing. Even in *Twin Peaks*, there's the scene after Leland Palmer is revealed as the killer and Albert is asking Dale if he thought Leland really did it. He talks about what's more unbelievable—that a supernatural entity possessed her or that incest would happen? So if my essay helped anybody, then that's great in and of itself. When most men talked about the essay they talked about my theory regarding Cooper, but when most women talked about it they talked about sexual assault. I found that gender binary in the perception of my piece odd. It was fascinating that they couldn't understand what this essay was really about. I wasn't trying to debunk anything in *Twin Peaks*. I was just talking about what I saw and what I felt. Women for the most part understood that. Men didn't, and that messed with my head a little bit. The most comforting thing that happened with me writing that essay was other incest survivors who e-mailed me and told me that it helped them.

Incest, childhood sexual abuse, and sexual assault: we don't talk about these subjects the way we should. It makes people uncomfortable, but the prevalence of it is astounding. I believe it is important to shine a light on abuse. *Twin Peaks* did that. *FWWM* certainly took a hard look at abuse with Laura Palmer's story, as did Jennifer Lynch's book. And you sharing your own story about your own experience of abuse is really, really powerful and courageous. Something else you wrote about in that essay that stood out to me are the toys surrounding *Twin Peaks*: the Funko products—Sheryl Lee wrapped in plastic and BOB. Of course people like to look at the lighter side of *Twin Peaks*, but for many survivors these toys don't make sense. Tell me about your thoughts on this phenomenon—this person who committed this terrible and very real act of violence is now a toy and his victim is a toy.

Willow Catelyn Maclay: I've always found the perception of *Twin Peaks* versus what *Twin Peaks* actually is fascinating. Many people who talk about *Twin Peaks* bring up the cherry pie and the Americana, which of course is fun, and it's part of *Twin Peaks*, but they don't talk about what's at the center of *Twin Peaks*. The center of *Twin Peaks* is Laura Palmer. She is the catalyst for everything. It's her story. Even when she's not there it's her story. Everyone is always reacting to the aftershocks of what happened to her. I think David Lynch knows this too. Otherwise he would not have included The Log Lady repeating "Laura is the one." A lot of people are grappling with what happened to her and what she went through. That's what *Twin Peaks* is, but people have a hard time understanding that. That's true of the real world as well as *Twin Peaks*.

No one ever really took her seriously in the show. No one took her seriously in real life as a character. You can go to a *FWWM* screening at the cinema and people will laugh during uncomfortable scenes and sometimes make an ironic joke of it. People will have Laura wrapped in plastic up on the stage. And Funko Pop! sells BOB toys now. I don't think people grapple with what these images actually represent. David Lynch's work is surreal and can be vague, but he is not vague about this. BOB is evil. I think the fact that they make toys out of him reaffirms my belief that people don't actually take that seriously. BOB is a character, but what he represents is something that a lot of people experience. Seeing those products in stores is destabilizing for me. I know they are going to make merchandise out of everything they can make money off of. The perception that they make toys out of characters like BOB, and they make Leland when he's possessed by BOB, is unfortunate.

Making Dale Cooper toys is fine. Making toys of The Log Lady is fine. These characters are more benign. These are characters one can relate to. But who is buying BOB and putting him up on their shelf? I'm not saying if someone does that then they are a bad person. I'm just saying ask yourself what that means and what that means for some people. I'm uncomfortable with it. I think the *Twin Peaks* fan base would be better if they asked themselves that question. What are they actually endorsing? *Twin Peaks* is certainly everything that people love *Twin Peaks* for. It's everything quirky about it that people say it is, but it's also this other thing. I think everyone involved in *Twin Peaks* from a creative standpoint knows that, and I think that the people who work on *Twin Peaks* love it, and they love the fan base. The fans for the most part are very, very warm. I've made regular friends through *Twin Peaks*. But I think the fans should consider the full depth of what *Twin Peaks* is instead of just the good parts.

On your blog, you have a list of top tens. I was looking at your top tens from last year and you have the movie *The Tale* listed, with Laura Dern, that deals with childhood sexual abuse in a very raw way that's not just behind closed doors. It shows the manipulation. I am not always easily triggered, and a friend warned me about watching it. It was difficult for me to watch. But I thought it was important because

it explicitly shows how predators work to manipulate children and the adults around them. What are your thoughts on this film? Why was it on your top-ten list?

Willow Catelyn Maclay: It was on my critic's list for a lot of the reasons you brought up. It was very honest. It was very raw. It was very no bullshit. It was very forthright in showing how this happens and how you can bury it and how it can shift in your memory into something that is almost innocent. I put it on the list because I was taken with how it used techniques to represent memory. I have bad memory problems. My entire childhood is spotty. I have a lot of gaps. A lot of stuff is buried for a reason, and I'll probably never remember it. Some of it is clearer to me. What *The Tale* did well was show how memory can manipulate itself in your place of safety until it reveals what was really there. A lot of people, including in the media, don't understand how memory works when you experience trauma and sexual assault. People say, "Why didn't you speak up sooner?" or "Why didn't you talk about this sooner?" or anything like that. *The Tale* pinpoints why. It is very specific.

Everyone who experiences sexual assault handles it differently. And *The Tale* is the director's [Jennifer Fox] own story about sexual assault. I can't imagine how difficult it must have been to make that movie. In order to do that—I think it showed a great level of willpower on her part to say what needed to be said. I was really taken with her strength, and I was really taken by what she did with the movie in presenting it as how it actually is and being honest with it. I don't think I've seen a movie that does what that movie does by putting you in her shoes and seeing how she perceives her own memory and how she handles her own past, especially handling childhood sexual assault, which is like stepping on land mines trying to navigate what happened to you and how you question yourself a lot. You say to yourself, "How could this have really happened? Maybe I'm just thinking of it wrong." But then you think, "Why do certain images and certain sounds and certain smells and certain touches and things like that ruin me?" There is something physically wrong in how my brain perceives certain things, and that started somewhere. *The Tale* fundamentally understands this. I thought Laura Dern was incredible in that movie in showing the full realization of what happened in a way that wasn't exploitative. I really appreciate what that movie did. Even if you compare it to something like *FWWM*, rather than approaching this subject with surrealism, science fiction, or horror, she is very matter-of-fact with it. I don't necessarily think that we need movies about incest all the time, but if the right person approaches this subject with the right level of sensitivity and understanding and willfulness to center the person who is experiencing it in an empathetic way, then I think there is a place for these kinds of movies occasionally.

It is a difficult watch, but I thought, "This film is doing something I haven't seen done before." For people who do not understand the trauma of sexual abuse, they can benefit from watching the film to understand how sexual predators operate. Regarding the issue of memory, survivors often disassociate or not remember as a means of survival. Finding that space to confront what happened can be an important process too. Laura Dern did an incredible job playing that role. When I saw that film listed on your blog, I wanted to ask you about it. Thank you for sharing. Finally, for you, what is Laura Palmer's legacy?

Willow Catelyn Maclay: Laura doesn't only just represent Laura. Like a lot of images and people in *Twin Peaks*, she represents something greater. She's a metaphorical image for this tragic figure, which David Lynch comes back to again and again. They categorized her as a "woman in trouble," and she was in trouble, but the circumstances of her trouble were not of her own doing. Laura Palmer as a metaphorical image represents every woman who has gone through sexual assault. I would ask people to listen to her and see her image for what it is and take her seriously. I don't think that we ever have. *FWWM* was dismissed by critics. It took years upon years to finally accept that it was a good movie. Sheryl Lee's career disappeared after that. All of this is because people did not listen to Laura Palmer. This goes back to her funeral when Bobby is screeching at everybody that she was in trouble and no one listened. And it's all their fault. They all killed her. I would just beg people to listen to women when they talk about sexual assault. We don't make this stuff up. There's no benefit to us to talk about this. There are only risks. And it is extremely difficult to talk about this. There are instances in our past when we've been taken advantage of or abused or worse. I would appreciate it if, when considering *Twin Peaks*, people would latch onto the image of Laura and to listen to her and to accept her and understand that she is not merely just an image unto herself but for women at large.

Photo Courtesy of New Line Cinema

Women in the Fan Community
Speak about Laura Palmer

"I don't have to have experienced what Laura did to know her pain, all I really know is there is something terrifyingly wonderful about the power of feminine wiles and something horribly dark when those wiles go astray,"[1] Mya McBriar wrote in her essay "Laura Walked With Me" on her *Twin Peaks Fanatic* site. Laura Palmer's journey resonates with many women because they did experience trauma. But not all *Twin Peaks* fans have to be survivors to relate to Laura's life. Laura Palmer was complex. Part child. Part woman. All too knowing for her age. She was a doer. She was a dreamer. She was a giver. She was a manipulator. She was an addict. She was a lover. She was a daughter. She was transcendent. Now she's a ghost who haunts every single one of us.

---

1   Mya McBriar, "Laura Walked With Me," *Twin Peaks Fanatic*, May 10, 2016.

From a homecoming queen to a golden orb, Laura Palmer evolved from a flesh-and-blood girl to a floating archetype. But what do we do with Carrie Page's character in Season 3? Carrie Page, whether she is Laura Palmer or someone else entirely (depending on your interpretation), confronts the ghost of Laura's past (and perhaps her own, if they are indeed connected) when Cooper/Richard brings her to the Palmer house. Who is Carrie Page? Is she Laura confronting her own ghost? Is Carrie actually Laura but in some alternative existence?

In the following pages, the women in the fan community grapple with Laura Palmer's legacy and confront Laura's ghost. Jennifer Lynch said when she was a girl she wanted to read another girl's diary because she wanted to know if she felt the same way she did. She wanted to know she was not alone. When I set out to interview women in the *Twin Peaks* fan community, I wanted to know how they felt about Laura Palmer. Perhaps they felt the same way I do. Perhaps by sharing our stories we'll feel a little less alone. Perhaps by speaking, women will remember that Laura Palmer, despite her circumstances, had agency, and they do, too.

<u>Women Speak about</u> The Secret Diary of Laura Palmer

Mary Hütter: *The Secret Diary* was like my version of *Go Ask Alice* [1971]. It made me feel better about myself, because as a fourteen-year-old girl going through puberty and having to deal with sex things and having feelings I didn't understand and growing up in a really religious household . . . I felt fucked up. I thought, "Is there something wrong with me?" With Laura, I realize now I related to that whole virgin/whore thing Laura had. It's placed on all women. You're supposed to be both. I remember being very confused. And then I read the diary, and I felt like I was normal. Everything in there was way more fucked up, but I felt like she's totally fucked up but maybe I'm not as messed up as I think I might have been. And so I felt better about myself. I felt like I was Laura at the time, but I definitely wasn't her. I wasn't doing drugs, I wasn't having sex at all. I didn't lose my virginity until I was nineteen. I didn't do drugs or even smoke. So I wasn't her at all, but I felt like I was her. I wasn't abused by my father at all or abused at all, but I did have father issues, because my father died when I was young. The fact that I felt like I understood her so much made me more like Audrey. I only realized that when I was in my thirties. Audrey understood Laura, but she wasn't doing any of the things that Laura was doing. But she wanted to.

Cheryl Lee Latter: *The Secret Diary* made *Twin Peaks* more real and less of a soap opera. Without the diary, Season 1 and 2 wouldn't have meant so much in Laura's sense until *FWWM* because I didn't know her at all. The parts I didn't like in Laura because I saw them in myself were the dark of things. When I was younger I kept my depression and my anxiety to myself. I was battling demons other people didn't know about. Suicidal feelings. Breakdowns. When I was sixteen I had quite a breakdown. I watched *FWWM* every night for six months straight. That's what got me through it—purely because of that little angel of hope in the end. I thought for all the girls like Laura who go through all these horrible things, there's always hope at the end. I'm so happy that scene happened because if it hadn't, I think a lot of us would have felt differently about that film. It was so heavy and so painful and so hard to watch and to feel like she was barreling toward this unbearable end with no redemption in it whatsoever. It gave me hope when I was at the absolute lowest of my depression and my suicide attempts. That got me through being a teenager, knowing Laura and all the girls like Laura can get through their stories.

I actually started to write a diary myself when I was fourteen, and to me that was incredible therapy. And I still keep a journal. I think every night about the girls who haven't got the life I've got and the privilege that I have. I'll wake up in the morning and live my life, whereas they're going to have a horrendous night and bad things are happening to them. They might be out on the streets; they might be getting kidnapped. I think about all these horrendous things. I remember when I was sixteen going to sleep at night and praying to God, "Don't let me wake up, but give this life to someone who will appreciate it. Let that girl have this life and let her have a chance." And it was Laura I was thinking of and all the girls Laura represents. "Just let one of them have my life, and they might do something better with it." There are lost girls out there who, no matter how much they fight, they don't necessarily survive. Very often that fight is secret. It's private, and people don't even know that it's happening. And then you have to be extra strong—have to put this exterior on as well, which can be a lot of work. To see someone like Laura, who everyone thought was perfect, with this most privileged, wonderful life, and actually her fight was completely private—that's what makes her a character who sticks with you.

Rosie Stewart: I read *The Secret Diary* when I was about fifteen or so. I absolutely love that book. It spoke to me. It's one of those books that sort of comes to you at the right age and makes you feel better about yourself. There are certain books, particularly as a young woman, that affect you, like Judy Blume. These books come with a very obvious ministering, trying to make girls going through a difficult time in their life feel less weird about themselves, less alone, and less isolated. Obviously Laura's *Secret Diary* is a very extreme version of a Judy Blume book. But it made me feel OK about having a sexuality. It made me feel OK about having issues around substance abuse. Laura Palmer is a woman who is sort of weird, smart, and completely different from the other people around her. I always liked that about her. I always thought that was so cool.

Women Speak about Watching Twin Peaks *as Young Girls*
Jill Watson: When I was a teenager I thought Laura was so cool and she just happened to die because bad things happen sometimes. It was a scary movie. I didn't really understand anything. When I watched it more recently, I realized she was very much a victim and she was, by necessity, manipulative. She was a fully fleshed-out character. Then you read the diary and you see the death of her innocence. What absolutely killed me was she was screaming for help and none of the characters in this small town heard. It's almost as if the purpose of its smallness is to show how ridiculous it is and how self-involved everyone in this town is that they weren't able to see what was going on with this girl. And nobody could step outside of themselves to help her at all, not even the beloved characters like The Log Lady and Major Briggs. Major Briggs, arguably, was fighting larger forces and fighting evil in his own way, but she was in his house, and he saw that look on her face. He still kept reading the Bible in *The Missing Pieces*. You just want to shake him. It's the same with the character of The Log Lady, who saw what

was happening, but she didn't do anything. She didn't say anything to anybody else. She stood there crying while they were being killed. That to me is the tragedy of *Twin Peaks*.

Milly Moo: I connected with Laura Palmer when I was thirteen. That's the age when you're discovering yourself and your sexuality. You're starting to notice that there is a bit of dysfunction in the world. I've never suffered abuse like Laura has, but I related to her in the way that people viewed her and through what she'd been through and realizing the world isn't always a safe place.

Joyce Picker: I did identify with Maddy more than Laura when the show was going on. I can definitely see myself as more of a wallflower cousin who is curious. Donna started becoming more like Laura because she was curious. Maybe I should be more adventurous in my life. I don't want to be killed for it, but you know, maybe I should not be the good girl anymore. Laura gave those two permission to go there. Maddy, unfortunately, didn't have much time, but Donna, even when Laura was still alive, had a couple of moments where she thought, "I'm going to join in. I'm going to be like Laura." It never suited her, because she didn't know the abuse behind it.

Lindsey Bowden: When I was a teenager I had a lot of angst. I didn't think I was very attractive. I thought I was fat. I used to lock myself away a lot. I identified with the mixed emotions and the two personalities that were within Laura Palmer. I was one of those kids who wanted to be an adult already. I wanted to be where I was going. I identified with that dark, self-destructive side—not that I am self-destructive. I'm not. I'm very happy to have a cup of tea. But at fourteen years old, when *Twin Peaks* first came out, I identified with that struggle Laura had within herself.

Mya McBriar: When I was a young girl and I first saw Laura, there was a power to the fact that she was a dead girl yet everyone was fascinated with her. All the men loved her, and all the women wanted to be her. But she had this terrible dark secret that led to the end of her life. That mystery was fascinating to me as a kid. The series alludes to so much of what happened with Laura, but the movie shows it to you. It doesn't pull any punches. That was the thing that got me feeling such a connection to her—not because I had lived her life by any means, but I felt so bad for her. It tuned me into those darker things that go on with girls when they're going through dark periods in their life. I had a period where I hung out with a couple of troubled girls. Because I had this sensitivity to Laura Palmer, I started seeing how in real life there were shades of that in certain people. When people were very hurt or really bad things were happening to them, they would act out in the most terrible of ways.

Women Speak about Fire Walk With Me

Lindsay Hallam: The diary and *FWWM* are so raw. There's nothing hidden. They say she's full of secrets, but we get to know them. I don't know how you could watch it and not feel something for Laura and what she goes through. It might not be that we experience the exact same thing as her, but any kind of trauma or darkness that we feel and grapple with, we see it in her.

Mary Czerwinski: When I really sat down and watched *FWWM* and got into Lynch's other work, those were impressionable years where I was developing my femininity. I do consider myself bisexual, and so to see my very first cinematic depiction of that in a way that was just sort of normalized—I know it was in an abnormal situation, but you take away the fact that they're high school girls and what the context is—it was just sort of accepted. I had never seen that before. I mean, we're talking early nineties. I was still coming to terms with what that meant at the time. To see anything of that sort was so incredibly rare.

Amy T. Zielinski: She grew on me the older I got. I could not relate to her when I was younger. When *FWWM* came out, I remember making a friend of mine who had not seen any of *Twin Peaks* go with me to see it. My friend was a very innocent sort of girl, and she was like, "What the hell—what did you bring me to?" It's a difficult film, but it's a film that grows on you with time. When I saw it as a teenager I didn't fully understand what was going on and what Lynch was trying to get at. But the more you look under the hood of all of it, it's so complicated.

Maja Ljunggren: One of the scenes in *FWWM* that captured me the most was the Pink Room with Laura and Donna. Donna gets drugged and Laura tries to save Donna from the bad things that could happen. To me that was almost a situation every girl has ended up in. You have a friend, you're out somewhere you shouldn't be, and you see that that friend is in trouble. That changed my feelings toward Laura. At that moment she's seen as every school girl at that age.

Joyce Picker: She was such a mystery. People in this small town might have thought they knew her, but they didn't know her at all. Even before the movie *FWWM* we knew who she was, because of what they revealed in the show. But in the movie you get to see not only did she do these great things—Meal on Wheels, help Johnny Horne, try to teach Josie English—she was involved with orgies. This teenager, this girl from high school, she was involved in orgies. She worked at a whorehouse for her father's friend. And apparently everybody knew her, and everybody was a suspect. Many people loved her, though, no matter how torn apart a human being she was. People really cared about her.

Lisa Hession: With *FWWM* you see Laura going through all these different pieces of her life, and she only reveals certain pieces to people. I don't know that she reveals herself as a whole to anyone. That was most striking to me, because it was something I always felt. My mom, this funny little Korean lady, is all about appearances, so we might have this crazy home life—I was the one in the cute little dress and pigtails and perfect hair and everything. I was portraying this narrative about who we were as a family. It's very similar to how Laura was. It's crazy how she is beautiful—she shined into your soul—but she carries this incredible darkness with her. Segmenting herself among all these people really was survival to her, and that struck me more than I even knew at that time.

Francine "The Lucid Dream": I was just completely enamored with the mystery of Laura. She was someone I aspired to be, at least the public image of her: the grade A student and homecoming queen, this bright, shining star that everyone in her town loved. But I was also fascinated with her darker side and how she was able to live this double life and fulfill these darker fantasies of her own even though they stemmed from something very horrible in her life. It was her battle with these horrible things she was dealing with, and it was her response to something terrible. But I thought it was badass that she was able to complete all the things that a teenager tries to do: keep the parents happy, be a grade A student, but then still be able to be her own person, even though it led to her ultimate demise. *The Secret Diary* sucked me into Laura Palmer's character even more. It was the first time we had a chance to see her as a real person. We later saw that in *FWWM*, which shocked audiences. Frankly I was not a fan of the movie when I first saw it, because it was such a subversion of what we had come to know of *Twin Peaks* on TV. But I think it was necessary to really understand her. Even though the mystery of Laura Palmer was so seductive in the show, I feel like to really understand the story and the underbelly of it you had to know who she actually was as a person, so you got to know her through the book and through *FWWM*.

Cheryl Lee Latter: Until I watched *FWWM*, I didn't care about Laura. I didn't feel like we really got to know her through the show, especially the first season. We only got snippets of the nice Laura, so I thought, with James and the locket. OK, nice girl. I thought she was a bit flimsy. It was only as time went on and I got to see the person behind the beautiful facade that she becomes such a real person whom a lot of women can relate to, with her day-to-day struggles—that expectation to be good at everything, to be perfect, to be so pure inside because she was so beautiful on the outside, when actually she felt completely the opposite.

Women Speak about Laura's Story

Anita Rehn: When we start to learn about Laura Palmer, there is an immediate connection. The way she presents the homecoming queen, Meals on Wheels, you know, this beautiful light, but someone with secrets and pain and suffering and turmoil that you don't see at all. I identified with that immediately. It's become even more complex as I've gotten older, watched my girls grow, met younger people, and heard people's stuff. Laura keeps taking on more and more life. What an amazing character, because the first thing we see of her is her dead body. Then she just continues to grow a bigger life.

Rosie Stewart: So often it would be easy to say, "Oh, what have we learned from the story of Laura Palmer? Well, don't take drugs, don't engage in casual sex." But that's never Laura's story, because her story never fully applies to you. You can't really draw lessons from it like that. The thing I always take from it is that it's a story of resistance and defiance. That's the lesson I learned from Laura.

Joyce Picker: In the end, by choosing death rather than being with BOB forever, Laura chose the right thing. She chose to save herself so she wouldn't have to deal with BOB anymore and her inner pain. She discovered this person she trusted, her parent, was the one abusing her all these years, and she didn't see it was him. She played fast. She played hard. A lot of people, unfortunately, are victims of sexual abuse, and that might contribute to playing fast and playing hard. Laura tried every damn thing to overcome her pain and put on that pretty high school girl face, put on that baby voice, so people would think she's innocent, even though she lost her innocence a long time ago.

Sezín Koehler: It took society a long time to catch up to David Lynch's vision. He's always been ahead of everyone. It's still one of the most groundbreaking pieces of cinema that's ever existed. The women who love *Twin Peaks* always knew that movie was awesome. We knew that movie was for us. It was a love letter to all of us survivors. But there are just more men in the community, and they are more vocal. Most of the critics were men as well. Most of the critics are men now! The disparity is still huge. And a lot of men have committed sexual assault who didn't realize they had committed sexual assault. That's also a very disturbing thing that has been coming out. I read an article where a woman interviewed thousands of male students in college. It turns out they were presented with many different scenarios regarding sex, some of which were consensual and some that weren't. The majority of them admitted having done nonconsensual acts toward women on multiple occasions. They didn't even think about it as being rape. A consciousness is developing very slowly. The men who watched *FWWM*—maybe they saw the nudity scenes and found that titilating or disturbing, but they didn't see themselves implicated in Laura's story. Whereas now I think they would. There are men who want to be better. They are able to look at that story and be like, "Holy shit. Look what men do to their daughters. Look what they do to women in their orbit. Look at how they destroy lives." The violence and sexual abuse in the home travels so far outward. They are a part of a system that allows this to happen and allows Leland Palmer to get away with it. In my opinion, he did get away with it.

Laura Stewart: With Laura, it's such a sad story, because so many women can relate to her story. Women who shared a similar story found each other through a TV show. I don't think there's another show or film that's ever had that sort of impact, that can bring people together and allow us all to speak about our experiences so openly. We all quite openly express ourselves in our writing and in our art or whatever our creative outlet might be. Even just talking to each other on the Internet and saying, "Yeah, this stuff has happened to me too. I feel you." I think talking about it in front of men has made them more empathetic as well. There's always going to be those jokes about "How did Laura find the time to do ten jobs while she was in school and doing Meals on Wheels and while she was sleeping with half the town?" But now lots of women speak up and say, "Well, no, actually I behaved like that, because the same thing happened to me." It has made men more understanding of Laura and women in general. The thing with Laura is it's not just women who are impacted by her story. A few of my male friends also have shared their stories of trauma. One close friend attempted to take his own life. Thankfully he failed. He told me he thought about Laura Palmer in those darkest moments, and she saved him, which is incredible. If an on-screen persona makes that much of an impact in your life, that's very impressive. I wouldn't have done anything that I'm doing right now if it wasn't for her story. I probably would never have been a writer.

Mary S. Reber: When I meet people who have gone through stuff, I consider it a privilege for me. You're sitting in there with them, next to them, in their deepest, darkest pain. They're allowing you to bow in and become part of that life they've lived. And that causes them to lean in and heal a little bit. That's what I see nowadays, but back in the day when *Twin Peaks* was on and Laura went through what she went through, people saw her, but nobody leaned into her and gave her the respect and the privilege of knowing her. Everybody just passed her off.

Cheryl Lee Latter: The important thing about Laura is the dual facets of her personality. *Twin Peaks* to me is about good and evil. That sounds basic, but it's angels and devils, heaven and hell. Laura represents both. When she has the moment with Harold Smith with the black teeth, that's her letting her bad side out, letting her demons take over, giving up on the good part of herself. It's not necessarily that her angels went away—she kind of let them go, because she gave up on them. I always have this image of the good Laura in her bedroom and the doppelgänger out there in the Red Room in the woods somewhere—and they actually feel each other there. If you see the picture—the Chalfont picture—when she's looking and sees herself coming out, you see the Red Room curtains behind that Laura. I didn't notice until recently, but clearly that's the doppelgänger looking back at her.

Mary Czerwinski: The way the series is bookended—it starts with a waterfall and it ends with Laura in the ending credits. Laura in many ways is symbolic to the waterfall. The waterfall is symbolic of Laura. It's this tremendous falling of emotions, this descent into darkness, but yet water is goodness, water is pure, water is a lot of things. Water is feminine if you look at history and religious iconography. It is very virginal. Water is of the womb as giving of life. And if you look at everything in *Twin Peaks* as a circle, it begins and ends with Laura and this feminine water energy.

Melissa Reynolds: In *Twin Peaks* they made her such a real, palpable presence through the way everybody reacted to her death. That makes the audience care for her before we ever see her alive. I felt such a connection to her even though she was dead. It's great to see a woman who has so many different sides, to see a woman in film portrayed as somebody having so many different layers to her. I want to talk about the scene in *FWWM* where Laura's talking to James in the woods. Sheryl Lee goes through every version of Laura in the space of about three minutes. You see the innocent, sweet Laura, then you see the BOB side of Laura, and then you see the really damaged side of Laura. It just totally blew my mind. Her performance in that scene taught me so much about acting. Laura Palmer was a woman who sacrificed herself to stop evil from spreading. She could have easily been corrupted by BOB, but she chose to die instead to stop that evil from getting out into the world that night, which proves that she was at heart a wholly good person. Tragic as her death was, that's an incredible legacy to leave behind. True goodness.

Marya E. Gates: One of my favorite San Francisco experiences was when I went to this triple feature at the Roxie Theater, where they showed *Laura* [the Otto Preminger film], the *Twin Peaks* pilot, and *FWWM*. The first film was a connection to Laura Palmer in the way it influenced *Twin Peaks*—not just with the name, but there are a bunch of parallels between the works. *Laura* is one of my favorite noir films. I've watched it so many times. The first time I saw it I did not notice some of these parallels. After I watched the triple feature I couldn't unsee it. The thing that is so fascinating about the two is the film is about a woman, Laura, who is probably dead. Toward the end of the film you find out who Laura really was. She is not this fantasy everyone had of her. She is not who people want her to be. She is herself. In *Twin Peaks*, Laura Palmer is already dead from the beginning, but Cooper is trying to learn about her from all of these other people. He has an idea of who she was. Everyone else has an idea of who she was, but no one actually really knew her. Everyone who thought they knew her didn't really know her. Then you get to *FWWM*. What I think is compelling about it is for two seasons you are getting these unreliable ideas of who she was and then Lynch finally gives you who she was. It's not anything like the Laura you have come to know. That's why a lot of people, upon first watching *FWWM*, hate it. I was so jarred by it the first time I saw it. When I was doing a David Lynch filmography, I didn't watch that one until after I watched the show, because I didn't want it to spoil anything. I hated it. Part of it was the change in the actor who played Donna Hayward. When I rewatched it during the triple feature I realized it was brilliant. I can't believe I didn't realize how brilliant this is and how it is the three-act structure of Laura: the show, the book and the movie. You get these three perspectives. *FWWM* is the final chapter of Laura, where you find out who she is. It is fascinating, because everybody is perceived differently to everybody. The only person who really knows you is you. With Laura Palmer, you finally get to know the real her when she gets a film from her perspective.

Mary Hütter: Laura was a strong character and someone to look up to. I was challenged by that a few years ago by a friend of mine who said, "No, she's a really weak character. She was doing drugs and giving in to all these things." I was so taken aback by that, because I've never seen Laura in that way. I've always seen her as a very strong person. Her legacy is subjective. There are so many people who have different views on why they love *Twin Peaks*. For some people it's this whole sexualized thing of Laura, but I don't think that's true for everyone. She represents how women are viewed and treated in society. Laura Palmer represents women as a whole. We see her from everyone's point of view in the series. Then when we read her secret diary we see she was someone completely different. No one ever really knew her—except maybe Audrey. Laura is relevant for me because she spoke to me and showcased what I was feeling. A lot of times, mostly with the diary, I felt like we got to hear a real girl speak for herself.

Melanie Mullen: Laura Palmer is a fighter. She's such a fighter, in fact, that she gave her own life so that this evil entity could not take over her body. She would rather die than let him do that. To me she represents strength. She shouldn't be defined by the things she did while she was alive, because a lot of those things were just outlets for what was happening to her. Those things made her feel like she somehow did have control over her body when it was being overtaken.

Gabrielle Norte: Laura Palmer is a force to be reckoned with. In the original series she is a victim, and that's how I saw her for the longest time. Then I saw *FWWM* and then I saw *The Return* and actually met Sheryl Lee and saw how important Laura Palmer then became with all of these other pieces mixed in, because now she wasn't just a corpse. She was an actual human being with some real complex issues and challenges that a lot of women deal with, like sexual assault. These things aren't being talked about, yet she dealt with all of it. She's powerful. People might miss that point and just see her as a troubled person, but I see her as a complex being, like all women are and all people are. She is a force.

Mary Czerwinski: Laura's ghost is this incredible symbol for young girls. I've carried her with me in ways I don't even realize. All the characters I write and play have this duality. They also can't excise this side of themselves of what people want them to be versus who they truly are. So they're always battling with the true side and then the side of expectation. I never realized it until recently, but I write characters like that, that have a lot of depth. My female characters always have something darker—I don't want to say trauma—but they have a lot of depth to them. I like writing female characters that can be assholes. There aren't enough female antiheroes in TV and in film. And so in the plays and short films I've written, I try to make my characters be well-rounded but also sometimes be unlikable and also likable at the same time. There's an aspect to all of us where we long to be a jerk, but we're too afraid to be. As women I feel like we're always so accommodating that we sacrifice ourselves in the process. And I feel like Laura sacrificed a huge amount of herself to make sure her friends didn't have to live that life. I admire that about her. In some ways, she's a martyr. But at the same time, she still gets to be free in the end.

Lisa J. Hession: The scene in *FWWM* with Donna and Laura—the one-shot of just her getting closer and closer and she talks about burning up—that is my favorite moment of Laura throughout the story. When she talks about that fire, she loves it and can't escape it at the same time. The sadness that you feel for her and her being so trapped—that's something that we all can relate to. Women especially. Going back to the idea of holding on to this shell so we can continue going.

Maja Ljunggren: After *FWWM*, she got a lot more depth, and that made people look at not just women but children who have been exploited by their family in one way or another. When the series and the film came out, people weren't talking about those things at all. It opened up a lot of eyes for a lot of people. This was actually happening for her and could actually be happening right now in my neighborhood—a manifestation of the pain and the problems that could lead to. It took a lot of guts, I think, to write that in a movie and in a series at that point in time. Today you can see a lot of series talking about difficult stuff, but you didn't back then. That was a real no-no. That's a reason why *Twin Peaks* is so powerful: it makes people talk about stuff we didn't talk about before.

Laura Stewart: Laura's story kicked the doors open on a lot of what was happening in millions of houses across the world—not just in America, everywhere. We were always taught not to talk to strangers, don't walk in the park at night alone, always go out together, make sure you've got your phone with you, all these different things. But what can prevent that person in your own home, your own relative, from doing these things to you? In my case it was a friend's father—a man I trusted. You never expect these things to happen to you. You don't have a choice. And yet the blame is often put back on the victim. All these young girls who are assaulted by men could never have prevented their attacks. And why should women have to try and prevent being raped? Why shouldn't girls go out dressed nicely and look pretty if they want to? Why can't they go out with their friends at night and go to a park or a friend's house like a boy can without the fear of that kind of thing happening to them? So that's Laura's legacy for me. It showed people what was happening in houses across the world—that the victim is not to blame at all. Even if she was sexually promiscuous, if she was a drug user, whatever, she hadn't done anything wrong. She didn't deserve it. What was done to her was purely because a man couldn't restrain himself. In light of movements such as Me Too, this is what happens to women across the world.

Sezín Koehler: *FWWM* opened up new room to discuss these things so that they don't happen again. These social changes take a long time, because the patriarchy is so entrenched. And we have a president where many women have accused him of sexual assault. One of them is a thirteen-year-old girl. When I read about that, the first thing I thought was "This is Laura Palmer." Thirteen-year-old kids are really small. The older I get the more I realize how young thirteen-year-olds are. Without *Twin Peaks* and *FWWM*, it would have taken a lot longer for these discussions to happen. *Twin Peaks* gave people permission to talk about these things. As much as I have issues with certain things in the show, I will never, ever deny the social and cultural power of *Twin Peaks* and especially what it did for women and sexual-assault survivors. A lot of women I know in the *Twin Peaks* community identified with Laura.

Geneva Rougier: There was the way that people viewed Laura, as opposed to what she was feeling on the inside. I could relate to that because for so many years my family had to act like everything was OK. My father would beat up my mom, and then she'd drop me off at school. The teacher would ask me what's wrong, and I would say, "Oh, nothing's wrong. Everything is fine." I couldn't possibly even tell any of my friends. I couldn't tell my teacher. It was this huge secret. People would view me as this talkative child who liked to draw, thinking I was probably happy. But they didn't know when I went home that if anything set off my father he would break a plate on your head or grab you and almost break your arm. With Laura, people viewed her as this cryptic, caring, smart girl. But she's really tormented. She struggled, and she acted out in dangerous ways. And I could relate to that also. When you fear for your life, and you're still surviving, any other danger seems minuscule. With Laura, she was having to deal with the horrible thing that was happening at night, but it was OK for her to sneak out and be in dangerous situations at a bar when she was so young, because I'm sure that wasn't as scary as what she was going through in her personal life. I've done the same thing. I've acted out and put myself in dangerous situations where I felt no fear. Because when you feel the ultimate fear, everything else seems minuscule. Being terrified is internal, it's state of mind, but it makes you feel invincible to a point. How could this possibly hurt me, because when I go home I might die?

Rosie Stewart: I absolutely love Laura. She's such a superhero, you know? I identify quite strongly with her. I certainly felt that as a teenager. My childhood girlfriend and I would both talk about how we were just like Laura Palmer. You can identify with her because you've not come from the happiest home, which I didn't, or you've had issues as a teenager that are similar to hers. But she always remains slightly out of reach, which is what I love about her. *Twin Peaks* is a supernatural mystery show, so there's part of Laura's experience that you can't grasp on to. And I really like that about her—the fact that she was struggling with a demon means that you can never really reduce her story. It never becomes a cautionary tale.

Mary Czerwinski: I always used to look at her as this cautionary tale of "Oh, it's a good thing you didn't continue down this path, because you could have become her." But I like thinking of her as a fighter now. I like thinking of her as someone who ultimately fought off the evil. All of the men in the situations of possession, whether it was Leland and BOB or Windom Earle, there is an annihilation of the soul there. This is a complete possession at some point, but Laura is able to fight that off—and even if on the outside the alternative is death. That seems like such a horrible, tragic thing, but it actually means she has license over her world. As somebody who was molested, as somebody who was victimized from such a young age, she had all the power in her world stripped from her. In that moment where she takes the ring, she is in essence taking back control over her life and her destiny. She is given license as a woman to determine her fate. She chooses death, but death equals freedom, and the light comes back to her. You see that in the final moments, where she is crying, but it is tears of joy. There is white light on her. Laura Palmer is a beacon of hope.

Mya McBriar: Laura had all these horrible things happen to her, but at the same time she became a hero at the end because she was the one who was able to resist BOB. She was eventually freed of her pain. So I think that inspired that blog piece I wrote about Laura Palmer. But I was really hesitant to write that. I toiled over it for months, thinking, "Should I post this?" I try to do stuff that's more on the lighter side, but I felt like

I wanted to try to write something that was different. It was cathartic. If you put yourself out there in any way, there's always a risk of somebody not liking it or not understanding or getting a judgment of you. The Laura story, particularly if you strip away the paranormal stuff, is about a girl getting molested by her father. And I knew girls that had pretty messed-up things happen to them. This goes on a lot. I think that David Lynch is somebody who, in his dark way, does like to shine a light on this mistreatment of women. *Twin Peaks* was always ahead of its time. They didn't talk about these issues back in 1990. There's a timeless feel to *Twin Peaks*. There's something special about the character of Laura Palmer and that so many people relate to it because it was so sad and tragic and yet strangely relatable. I'll forever be haunted by it.

Maja Ljunggren: In a way Laura Palmer was what started the whole thing. She was the beginning, but she was also part of the end—which probably was a new beginning. The whole thing comes full circle. The ending of Season 3 is brilliant. I loved that it led us to another mystery. I had no idea what I wanted to happen. I had seen enough Lynch movies to know you should go into it with an open mind. If you expect something to happen, that's not going to happen. I just loved how open it was and how you can continue to dream about it. That's what I love about *Twin Peaks*—everybody has their own ideas about what happened. My art is usually that—this is what I think happened outside the world we actually see. That's why I create.

Anita Rehn: One of the countless things that draws me to Laura Palmer, and continues to, is her ability to just keep striving for more and not giving up on happiness and peace. Despite her being constantly defined by everyone around her, including Agent Cooper, she keeps moving forward, or trying to move forward, into the light. I'm conflicted, because on the one hand it breaks my heart—I'm not sure if she's ever going to find that peace—but it also gives me hope. If she doesn't find it, it's certainly not going to be because of her lack of trying. Laura will survive, no matter what.

Women Speak about Twin Peaks: The Return

Sezín Koehler: I have mixed feelings about Season 3, because *Twin Peaks* was one of those stories where every time I would watch it I would think, "Maybe this time Laura's not going to be dead." I wanted her story to end differently. I didn't want her to wash up all blue and wrapped in plastic. I wanted her to survive. So the moment when her body was erased in Season 3 I stood up and started bawling. It was absolutely stunning. But I didn't understand what happened afterwards. I felt like it went off the rails. Time travel stories are not my favorite. David Lynch doesn't necessarily like to have explanations, so maybe he didn't want anyone to know what did happen.

Cheryl Lee Latter: At the end of *FWWM*, I think Laura's angel was her being able to move on to the White Lodge because she faced her demons. She faced her shadow self. She didn't run away like Cooper did. She fought through it. Her reward was to move on to the White Lodge. When I saw her in Season 3 taking off her face, that's what the light was for, showing Cooper, "I got through it. I'm here. Here's all the power of good within me now." I think she's there to help him, but what happened next I don't know.

Jill Watson: There are several things that Laura Palmer is a catalyst for. I think her complexity is not always apparent in Season 3, since she mostly appears in the Red Room (if that is even her). The parts that we know it is her are the flashbacks and when Gordon Cole sees her in the doorway. I don't know why he sees her there. It could be the timeline crossing streams. Agent Cooper sees her in the woods and says, "We are going home." He sees her as this damsel who needs saving, but in this weird and defining way. How is taking her back to the Palmer house going to save her?

Mya McBriar: As for the part Laura Palmer played in Season 3, I have always loved the very first Log Lady intro, the one for the pilot episode, where she says, "The one leading to the many is Laura Palmer. Laura is the one." I think that line is so pivotal to the role Laura Palmer played in Season 3. Part 8 showed us that Laura was "the one." I viewed the

Fireman's golden orb of Laura as a direct link to what The Log Lady said and The Log Lady's connection to all things otherworldly in *Twin Peaks*. It was all very meta.

Cheryl Lee Latter: Even when we see the Fireman and Señorita Dido, and she kisses the globe and off it goes—I don't see that as Laura being brought into the world, but as being representative of all good. They're up there in their little heaven and they're sending all their little good onto the world. Lots of hope from Pandora's box—sending out the good things to counteract all the demons coming out of The Experiment. That's what Laura is. I don't see her as a real girl, and that's not to dismiss what that character went through and what people relate to in that character, but she's more of a representation of, as Lynch likes to see, that beautiful, perfect facade with all that dark stuff going on in the background.

Lisa J. Hession: Season 3 was so disjointed. There were parts of it that were so beautiful. But I can't even begin to think about it. What I can say is it was really nice to see Laura Palmer within the orb and in the Carrie Page scene, but I don't know what the hell it all meant. Even after I read some of the pieces in preparing to write for "The Women of Lynch," I thought, "That selfish little bastard, Lynch. Give us what you can! We do it all for you!"

Mary Czerwinski: You can change her name, but Sheryl Lee in this universe is always Laura Palmer, because Laura Palmer is the one. She has a pure feminine soul sent to combat "the evil that men do." Laura Palmer is essentially a martyr and a hero. Interestingly enough, there is a patron saint of abuse victims and incest survivors named Saint Laura Vicuña. She died at the age of twelve. She was almost the same age as Laura in the first entry in *The Secret Diary*. Laura Vicuña was recognized as a saint in 1988, just one year before the pilot for *Twin Peaks* was filmed, and Laura Palmer would become America's most famous fictional dead girl. Like Palmer, Vicuña was abused by a father figure, in this case her mother's common-law husband. She ultimately died from disease and fending off this man's affections. Her final words were basically that she gives her life for her mother's salvation. Dale Cooper had the best intentions, but couldn't see outside himself enough to let go, so he's forced to be a prisoner of the temporal loop of *The Return*. He repeats his hero complex because of his guilt [over the death Caroline] and is stuck in the lodge for eternity. Laura is freedom personified, because she saves her own soul from the corruption of evil. The abuse ended with her. She is an angel for others who would have been harmed by the evil men do. By sacrificing herself she stops the cycle of abuse. She is free. Her burden is lifted. Ironically, the name Carrie means "freeman" and "strong." Coincidence? I think not.

Melanie Mullen: Laura seems to have gotten out of the Black Lodge or the Red Room or whatever place that is. But she seems to be a different person now. She doesn't know who Laura Palmer is or who Leland and Sarah Palmer are, but when she gets to that house something happens to her that reawakens her.

Sezín Koehler: Bringing Carrie Page/Laura Palmer back to such a site of horrific trauma was never going to be a good idea. Have they never watched *Friday the 13th* movies?! "Oh, I was attacked by a guy in the woods! Let's go back there!" Then everyone gets killed by him again. That's a site of trauma, and you don't have to go back there. It's not a requirement of your healing to go back to places.

Marya E. Gates: I really enjoyed Sheryl's return in *The Return*. I think if you take all the episodes, the movie, and Jennifer's book and put them all together you have an incredible body of work that explores the insidious nature of abuse, how it can cycle through families, and how even when you've cleansed yourself of it through therapy it is always a part of you. That's why I think the ending of *The Return* is so brilliant.

Mary Hütter: In Season 3, Laura's agency was taken away, and I am having a hard time with it. Her strength reached its apex when she allowed herself to be killed instead of letting BOB possess her. This was her choice. She stood up for herself. When Cooper took her out of that reality/time stream/whatever, he took away that choice that she'd made.

I'm glad many people loved Season 3. I wish I were one of them. I've had almost twenty-nine years to ponder Seasons 1 and 2 and only two years for Season 3, so my theories aren't completely formed yet. The feeling I'm left with after viewing it, though, is heartbreak and disillusionment. Loss of hope. Loss of beautiful mystery. I didn't expect or want a closed ending. I actually feel like we got way too much of one, because the mysteries were solved. There were too many questions answered. We learned exactly where evil came from—and evil came from a woman. "The evil that men do" became the fault of Mother, Judy [Joudy]. In the original series, Laura was raped and tortured by the evil spirit of BOB, who possessed Leland Palmer. Now Sarah Palmer is also possessed. In the end, the woman is to blame. Fin.

Lindsay Hallam: In Season 3, you see Laura Palmer at the beginning of the opening credits. The opening credits have all those overhead views and those angelic overhead perspectives that also appear throughout *FWWM*. I don't know if Laura Palmer has become that angelic presence—her picture in the orb. It's hard to know. Cooper has all the best intentions, but he denies her the reunion with the angels that she gets in *FWWM*. He's taking something from her. When he finds Carrie Page, he takes her back to Laura Palmer's home. I think it's because he wants to take her back to her mother, but why would you take someone back to the home where they were abused? Season 3 did end up being more about Cooper and his fallibility. He is the white knight, the seeker—but he gets it wrong. He thinks he's doing the right thing, but he's not.

Laura Stewart: Season 3 is Cooper's story and not Laura's. He wanted to save her and didn't. I don't like the fact that her agency was taken away from her—if that is what happened at the end when Laura was swept into a different life, where she ran away from home, she took on a new persona and she still didn't have a great life, and she ended up with some asshole. I don't like that story that was given to her, even though it is probably a very likely one—a very honest one. It feels a bit like "be careful what you wish for," because it didn't turn out better with her surviving either. She still has to live through that trauma. She didn't get to make the choice, because a stranger wanted to save her life. It wasn't to her benefit to save her. Did it make him feel better? Possibly. I can't imagine that's what Lynch and Frost were going for either, especially after making such a big thing of *FWWM* being so important to Season 3, which it was. The end of *FWWM* is the true ending. She's in the lodge, and her angel comes for her.

Mya McBriar: Since Season 3 ended I've had time to process the season as a whole. At first I didn't like the idea of Carrie Page, because I only wanted Laura Palmer. Now I feel like Carrie was just Laura stashed away in another timeline or dimension. Carrie is to Laura what Richard was to Dale—just a different variation of the same person. I imagine that Carrie's life had shades of Laura's: the dead body in her living room, the horse on her mantle, etc. It seemed like darkness followed Carrie in the same way it did Laura, but it manifested itself in different ways. Learning more about Carrie's life would be very interesting.

Joyce Picker: I don't write the theoretical "What is Laura?" articles and "Who is Laura?" articles. "Is she this child of perfection or is she the child of two demons?" It was very hard to reconcile my feelings about her with Season 3. It was good to see her, and she is a bright spot in the lodge. And she literally has a bright spot under the mask of her face. But the Carrie Page stuff—I can't make heads or tails of that. After Part 17, when I saw Cooper trying to save Laura over and over again in this loop, I thought, "Does that negate the whole series?" I actually started crying because I thought, "You can't! That means she's still alive, and she's still being abused, and everything we've seen was not real." So when Cooper found Carrie Page, she was obviously Laura. We didn't know for sure until she came back to the Palmer house and the memories came back. Apparently she's taken on an identity that wasn't hers. She completely blocked out her trauma. But Carrie's not right either, because there's a dead body in her house.

Cheryl Lee Latter: The whole Carrie thing is beyond me. I haven't yet gotten to the point of processing Parts 17 and 18. Laura was saved, and in trying to save her Cooper just dragged her back out of salvation and back into the world and back into the pain. It feels like the real world is the hell. And once you get through that with the strength of facing those demons and come out the other side of it, what you're rewarded with are the good things and heaven. She got all that. She battled. Her soul was pure, and yet he dragged her back down into reality. And I do believe the end of eighteen is him wiping both of them out of existence. I believe they are nowhere. The fact that she had that beautiful white light in her meant she was there to help him. For whatever reason, he didn't listen.

Melanie Mullen: Carrie Page is Laura Palmer. I believe she emerged the way Cooper did as Dougie. There was a doppelgänger out there living another life who started living a different identity. And maybe, through that, she forgot who Laura Palmer was. And maybe by going back to that house she realized that it had gone full circle, and she was being connected to Laura Palmer again. Just as Cooper regained his cognizance through different things he saw, once she saw that house, that was her moment like when Cooper stuck a fork in the outlet. For her, that was what the house did to her. So that is what brings the true Laura Palmer back. I'm still confused as to how that could be, because she is dead. And I maintain that she is dead.

Mya McBriar: I think Lynch/Frost used the undoing of Laura's death as a representation of us, the fans. We wanted more *Twin Peaks*, but were we truly ready to shed the old and embrace the new? I was upset when Laura's body disappeared from the beach in Season 3, not because I wished her dead but because I didn't want the original story to change. However, now I think it's important to accept the changes, and in the undoing of Laura's death, us, the fans, were forced to embrace the new whether we liked it or not. And that's very true of real life, isn't it?

Jennifer Ryan: I struggle with Season 3 because I liked the world of *Twin Peaks* that was created in Season 1 and Season 2. So many of us don't really know what to make of it. I don't think that Laura Palmer is an actual character in Season 3. I view her more as a kind of ghost. There are elements of her, and there is the memory of Laura Palmer. There's always evil in the world, and people out there fighting that evil. That requires sacrifice. That requires perseverance. I don't think Carrie Page is Laura Palmer. We watched Laura Palmer die. We went to her funeral. I think the memory of Laura Palmer is there, and the themes she made known to us are there, but I don't think that Laura Palmer is a physical character within Season 3.

Sezín Koehler: When Carrie Page goes back to the house, I couldn't believe Cooper had gone through all that trouble to save her and now he was retraumatizing her. If Carrie Page is part of, or is the same soul as, Laura Palmer, why would he do that to her? Honestly, I started to think about it too much. I feel like it undermines a lot of the good work the show did. The first two seasons and *FWWM* ended perfectly. I almost feel like it was disrespectful to Laura. I know that's kind of silly to say, because the character doesn't really exist. It was almost as if they were saying her life was going to be horrible regardless. I didn't like that message. I always wished Laura didn't end up on that beach. I wish she had escaped and changed her name and dyed her hair and nobody ever heard from her again. I wish she could be free without being killed. But instead it looks like she's still mired in all of that trauma. Season 3 had a lot to do with reincarnation, and Vedic mythology was brought into it. When you're reincarnated into another body and you visit a place where something happened to your soul, it has a physical impact on you.

Mary Hütter: How does Carrie Page fit in? I'm not really sure. I hate everything about Episode 18, if I'm honest. I may rewatch Season 3 someday, but I'm not sure if I'll watch Episode 18 again. In this alternate reality of Episode 18, I think maybe we see a version of Laura Palmer had she lived. A version of Dale is still trying to help and save her, but he fails. He always will fail is the message. Conversely, I've been living with the belief that he didn't fail for all of these years. Through her own actions, with possibly the help of Cooper's sacrifice, Laura gets her angel at the end of *FWWM*. Carrie Page is a slap in the face of that ending.

Joyce Picker: As somebody who loves the show and was confused by it,

Photo Courtesy of Showtime

Agent Cooper and Carrie Page show up at the Palmer house in Part 18.

I see Laura as the woman/little girl we saw in *FWWM*. That's the Laura I know. The Carrie Page thing is a mystery. Is Carrie Page the missing page? I don't know. I give up, but I still love it.

Gabrielle Norte: Watching *The Return*, I was extremely excited to see Sheryl Lee on screen again as Carrie Page. She is such a Lynchian character. There is a lot to consider about her role in Season 3. With this theme of rebirth, or reincarnation, we see this reevaluation of the Laura Palmer character and just how important she is to the entire story. Saving Carrie Page's introduction until the end gave me even more of an appreciation for Laura Palmer and how she is essentially the heart of *Twin Peaks*. We miss her presence as a key player. Lynch reminds us of her power by delaying Sheryl Lee's appearance in Season 3. Carrie Page is a fascinating character that fits beautifully mixed in with the mysteries of *Twin Peaks*.

Amy T. Zielinski: I think something they may have been hinting at in the third season with her mother is that abuse can often lead to other abuse. People who have been abused become the abuser. That's not always the case, but if that person never sought help or treatment, more than likely that's what they know and that's what they then do. They were showing with her mother, maybe, that it wasn't just Leland. If one parent is doing the abuse, is the other parent that unknowing? How many times does the other one look away and not deal with it and just turn off? Sarah looked like she was being drugged half the time, so she didn't know what was going on. But she probably did and just couldn't deal with it. I think that's a story that's probably pretty prevalent.

Milly Moo: I suspect there's a part of the story that hasn't quite been finished off with Laura—and Sarah as well. I think there's much more to tell. I wouldn't have loved it as much if Laura wasn't there. I suppose what we're led to believe is that Cooper traveled through time and that Laura was now missing and not dead. And Cooper had to find her and return her to her mother. But she was a different person—clearly still a person going through abuse and trauma, though she had escaped her fate lying on that beach. But she hadn't escaped the trauma that her life was intended to go through.

Melissa Reynolds: I always saw Laura as a guide for Cooper in Season 3. Even though she's not physically in it a lot, her presence is there. She's like Cooper's guardian angel guiding him to his final place, wherever his final place might be. She's the one standing over him in the Red Room at the end. I'd visualised Season 3 was going to end the opposite of *FWWM*, with Laura standing over Cooper. She's there to guide Cooper on his path to death, like he did for her.

Rosie Stewart: In her sad home and hopeless life, Carrie feels like a dead end. The key thing about Laura for me was that her experience was never quite reducible to our own. She was always out of our reach. When we meet her in the final scenes of *Twin Peaks*, Carrie embodies this with grim finality. You can try to pull Laura back into the world, but it won't quite be her. But Carrie's screams at the end, as she catches the ghost of Laura Palmer, tell us that it's not quite not her either. I like to think there is a sliver of hope here. Wherever, whoever, and whenever they are, our hero and heroine are together now, equally out of reach, journeying somewhere in time and space.

Sezín Koehler: That ending. I had nightmares about that scream afterwards. What really bothered me about the third season is I felt like Laura was disrespected by how it ended. She was such a crucial figure to the story and to us, and making her ending so ambiguous felt like an injustice to her memory. She originally died with agency. At the end of the third season, I don't think she had agency anymore. It's like Cooper just took everything. I don't know why he thought he had the right to do that. Carrie Page looks so miserable, so haunted. It's sad that her story shifted and things did not get better for her. I suppose that is true to life. People are talking a lot about how men who are accused of sexual assault have their lives ruined and their careers ruined, but a *New York Times* journalist interviewed a bunch of people who had been accused of rape and found that it was actually the women's lives who were ruined and not the men's lives. We have this persistent idea in the patriarchy that accusations ruin men's lives. They don't. They ruin women's lives. Maybe Season 3 should be seen in the context of that, which is bleak.

Jill Watson: In the fan community Laura has been a catalyst for a lot of healing for people who have been through trauma, sexual abuse, rape, incest. People have identified with that particular part of her story. They are able to see that they are not the only ones whom this happened to. That is the start to a healing journey for a lot of people. That's a magical and beautiful thing.

Women Speak about Sheryl Lee

Mary Hütter: For a show that aired just a month before the Me Too movement broke big, these messages, from two older white men, feel dated and gross. What I've come to realize is Laura Palmer is iconic and magical because of David Lynch and Mark Frost. Laura Palmer is real and inspirational because of Jennifer Lynch and Sheryl Lee. Mark and David wrote Laura to be the Virgin/Whore Mary icon of the late twentieth century. She is the female figure who smiles down at us as the Madonna from her homecoming photo. She was brought to life for us as a living, breathing, confused, scared, strong, beautiful, real woman to look up to by the words of Jennifer Lynch and performance by Sheryl Lee. Two women who do not get enough credit for the world and inspiration they helped to create.

Joyce Picker: Laura is an iconic character, one of the most iconic in TV history. Every *Twin Peaks* fan holds that character in their hearts. We feel for her. As people who love the show, we mourn for her too, but we know why we had to mourn for her. Sheryl Lee's performances as Laura, Maddy, and Carrie are all so powerful. You can't neglect them. When they're on TV, you can't take your eyes off them. She's the best screamer in the world. God bless Sheryl Lee. She knows how to scream anybody awake. She's got the best scream.

Lindsay Hallam: A lot has been talked about how so many films and television shows revolve around the young girl dying. That still happens all the time on television. Laura Palmer was the one time where she wasn't just the dead girl that sets off the story. Maybe that's what's so important about her. That is part of a legacy that you can trace back to Laura Palmer and is linked to Sheryl Lee's performance. She wasn't just a vessel of Lynch's vision. She took ownership of her character, and it's reported widely the input she had into the film.

Mary S. Reber: I'm going to give Sheryl Lee some kudos here. I loved how she portrayed a person who could have so many different faces: Meals on Wheels, the good girl, and then the promiscuous girl. That's definitely a fragmented person who hasn't leaned into their pain or been able to feel anything. She did such a good job portraying trauma. I don't know what she's been through in her life, but I'm glad somebody was able to do that, and do it so well. And she's such a gracious, empathetic person and gives so much of her time to people when they come and see her. She is just so good.

Laura Stewart: In Sheryl Lee's portrayal, she becomes Laura in a sense, because she's such an empathetic, warm, and beautiful person. She seems to understand women's trauma so much that she embodies that golden glory of Laura Palmer.

Anita Rehn: I think I'm not of the majority, but I'm not a big fan of some of the burlesque things with *Twin Peaks*, specifically Laura. I just thought Laura used her sexuality to gain some more control over her environment. That was her choice to do that. She had things being taken away from her. She was being abused. But then she took power back by gaining strength through that, and I think so much of that gets lost when she's presented in that way. Here's a character something unimaginably horrible happened to, and I know that we all celebrate it, like there's this image of her dead that is an iconic image. But I don't feel like it's ours to sexualize. It bothers me. I asked Sheryl Lee about it once. I was trying to approach it in a way that I wasn't coming straight out and saying, "How do you feel about some of the fan art?" She said that most of the time she was honored, she loved it, loved all the expressions and stuff, but there are sometimes when she didn't. And I feel like she's referring to those times. She said specifically there's memes or loops of her in the Pink Room, and it just feels like you're missing the point of what's happening here. She knows that women who have gone through trauma or abuse identify with her. I think that she feels protective of that.

Jennifer Ryan: I think there's Laura Palmer the person and there's Sheryl Lee the actor. Both are phenomenal people. Laura was so alone and couldn't talk to anyone because she didn't want to let anyone in. But she knew she had to persevere. When I look at her, I think of perseverance. When I look at Sheryl Lee as a person after spending a couple of days with her and watching her interact with fans, she makes sure that you know you're not alone, that there's at least one other person out there, even if it's only for a few minutes, who cares about you and doesn't want you to feel that loneliness that we all feel.

Milly Moo: I can't say enough about Sheryl Lee's performance. I have worked with kids who've experienced trauma, and can say she absolutely nailed it. She's always been the center of *Twin Peaks*. Laura is the one. I got to meet Sheryl Lee when the cast came to Australia—a Conversation with the Stars tour. I'd actually made a Laura doll. If I do say so myself, it was probably the most beautiful one I'd ever made, more so because I knew who I was giving it to and that it had to be perfect. At some point the line to meet Sheryl parts, and I see I'm about to meet her. I don't know how to describe how I felt about that. I wanted to laugh and cry at the same time. That was a weird feeling. I said to her, "My name's Milly, and I make these dolls, and I'd love to give this to you." I hugged her. She was wearing this long velvet coat dress. It was just beautiful and felt soft and warm. Once I was face to face, it didn't feel awkward. So we had a photo taken, and she insisted that the doll be in the photo. And as I walked away, she grabbed me by the arm and said, "This is the most beautiful present that anybody's ever given me." That was lovely. People who had experienced sexual abuse were in line to meet her. They said, "I connected with Laura on this level." It hit me quite hard how often Sheryl Lee has to deal with those kinds of disclosures and how difficult that must be. But she just oozes empathy and understanding. What a burden to have to carry. I'm sure she's very grateful for that role and working with David Lynch and that David Lynch thought well enough of her to cast her over and over and over. But it really hit me that it is quite a burden to carry when it's just a story you acted out. It's not necessarily your story.

Jill Watson: For me personally, her legacy made quite a huge change in my life. About thirteen years ago I had some pretty extreme violence and loss in my life. I didn't know what to do. I didn't know where to turn. And I was ill for a while, so I did a rewatch of *Twin Peaks* and *FWWM*. And I got angry. I was so angry at that town for not doing anything to help this girl, and not because nobody was helping me. I had incredible help and support. But I felt this overwhelming need to correct that mistake. I was so mad at these people in the town, but I thought, "What am I doing to help anybody?" The answer was nothing. I wasn't doing anything, so I looked into what it would take to help kids like Laura on a one-on-one basis. So I got a license to foster. I started taking in mostly teenagers. I've had all ages in my home, but mostly teenagers and mostly girls and mostly victims of abuse. I like to think of that as the legacy that the Laura Palmer character put in my head. Not all of the endings have been happy for those girls. But I know that if it weren't for the character of Laura Palmer, these girls would never know what it feels like to be safe, which they were in my home. They wouldn't know what it was like to be loved, which they absolutely were and still are. I attribute that connection that I have with those girls to the rage that Laura Palmer instilled in me. Laura's legacy is that we all need to take better care of each other.

Part III: Conclusion

The Legacy of Laura Palmer

"It is in our house now."[1] - The Fireman

The Fireman tells Agent Cooper, "It is in our house now" in a series of clues at the beginning of *Twin Peaks* Season 3. While folks can debate just exactly what "it" is, "it" apparently is not good. And "it" exists "in our house." David Lynch's use of home in his art explores ideas of nostalgia, childhood, and the importance of place in the subconscious. "These are issues Lynch is close to and partially explain why his work deals so often with violence, sexuality, and the potential for something sinister to be discovered in one's backyard," according to he Pennsylvania Academy of the Fine Art's 2014 exhibition *The Unified Field.*[2] The duality of home as a place of both nostalgia and violence is at the heart of *Twin Peaks.*

When Cooper first arrives at the Las Vegas house of Dougie Cooper, Janey-E greets him and says, "I'm so glad you're home, Dougie." But Cooper (and Dougie, too, for that matter) is far from his adopted home of Twin Peaks. Home/Twin Peaks is both a place Cooper wants to return to and a state of mind where the viewer wants to return to but cannot. The town of Twin Peaks is not the same home that Cooper or the viewers remember: it's been twenty-five years, and something is off.

It is the Palmer house that most potently subverts the concept of the home as a place of comfort and domicility. It is the original site of

---

1   David Lynch and Mark Frost, "Part 1," *Twin Peaks: The Return*, directed by David Lynch, written by Mark Frost and David Lynch (May 21, 2017).

2   David Lynch, "The Unified Field," The Pennsylvania Academic of the Fine Arts, Sept. 13, 2014.

horror and violence against Laura Palmer. In Season 3, Sarah Palmer still lives in this home of past tragedy, accompanied by her grief and fear and rage, mixing Bloody Marys and madness in her kitchen, which is inhabited by a malevolent spirit. Home is the original place of horror.

When *Twin Peaks* Season 3 premiered on Showtime in 2017, no one knew what to expect. Season 3 was groundbreaking. It was challenging. Martha Nochimson called it a Homeric epic. "The 2017 series does not just repeat Lynch's original challenge to formulaic storytelling. It performs modernist magic in its expansion of the possible connotation of the word 'sequel,' which has historically had deeply, formulaic linear implications. . . . Lynch uses his return to *Twin Peaks* to invite us to simultaneously stand back from and engage with a Cooper who blindly and increasingly perpetuates evil. And he does it in the form of an epic,"[3] Nochimson argued.

Sheryl Lee played multiple roles in Season 3, including Laura Palmer, in a flashback/time travel/Möbius strip in which Cooper returns to the past to rescue her. She plays Carrie Page, a woman who looks exactly like Laura Palmer and who is living in Odessa, Texas, with a murdered man slouching on her couch. And she plays a woman who looks exactly like Laura Palmer in the Red Room. There is no confirmation of who this entity is.

When Carrie Page emits that iconic scream at the end of Season 3, Sheryl Lee said, she traveled back in her mind to Laura's experience and the possibility of the nightmare happening again. She said she imagined what women go through: "There are still women who need to scream who are not allowed to scream. The statistics [regarding violence against women] are going up, not down. That is the scream. There are technical things that you have to learn to do with your voice; otherwise you will ruin your voice. The emotion part of it is really trusting and surrendering, and knowing you are going to hurt. By nature as humans we don't want to hurt. We try to make ourselves feel better. As an actor, when you have to approve something like that, you have to talk yourself into not flinching away from that. When he says 'action,' you have to

---

3   Martha Nochimson, "Coda: The Return of David Lynch" *Television Rewired: The Rise of the Auteur Series* (Austin: University of Texas Press, 2019), 237-238

dive off the cliff. That is easier with directors like David, because you know he will guide you, but it really feels like free-falling."

Twin Peaks: The Return *as Subversive Fairy Tale*

What do we make of Carrie Page, and how does she relate to Laura Palmer? Ever since Season 3 concluded, people have been grappling with how to interpret what happened and what it meant. There are many modes of interpreting *Twin Peaks*, including exploring it as a psychological phenomenon. *Twin Peaks* scholar John Thorne argued the first thirty minutes of *FWWM* was Special Agent Dale Cooper's dream.[4] Martha Nochimson explored the role of the subconscious in Lynch's art.[5] And Tim Kreider wrote how *Twin Peaks* is an imaginary narrative created by someone, who may or may not be Dale Cooper, who fashioned the fantasy that is Season 3 to forget the fact that he is actually Laura Palmer's killer.[6]

Although these theories of dreams and fantasies are not without merit, I decided to approach Season 3 as a subversive fairy tale, in which the traditional happy ending is upended to allow for a larger truth.[7] The events and characters, although sometimes fantastical in their interdimensionality and otherworldliness, are rooted in reality, and therefore what happens has great consequences for them from the audience's perspective. The stakes are high.

Twin Peaks: The Return contains several conventions of the fairy tale, including supernatural beings and the hero's quest, as well as common generic archetypes such as the princess (Laura Palmer) and the seeker (Dale Cooper). The show at first appears to follow the fairy tale tradition of the happy ending, as Laura Palmer is rescued on the night of her murder and Dale Cooper/Dougie Jones is united with his nuclear

4   John Thorne, *The Essential Wrapped in Plastic: Pathways to Twin Peaks* (Dallas: John Thorne, 2016).

5   Martha Nochimson, *The Passion of David Lynch: Wild at Heart in Hollywood* (Austin: The University of Texas Press, 2007) and Martha Nochimson, *David Lynch Swerves: Uncertainty from Lost Highway to Inland Empire* (Austin: The University of Texas Press, 2013).

6   Tim Kreider, "But Who is the Dreamer? *Twin Peaks: The Return*," http://politicsslashletters.org/dreamer-twin-peaks-return/ (accessed Oct. 28, 2018).

7   Courtenay Stallings, *"Twin Peaks: The Return* As Subversive Fairy Tale," *Supernatural Studies* (Winter 2019.): 98-116.

family, Janey-E Jones and Sonny Jim. However, I argue *Twin Peaks: The Return* challenges fairy tale conventions and offers an alternative to the manufactured happy ending in the Season 3 finale when Laura Palmer/Carrie Page confronts the original home of Laura Palmer's trauma. The story provides the possibility of a radical cultural transformation in which the happy ending is replaced with an ending in which a sexual abuse victim comes home to acknowledge the reality of the trauma she experienced, forcing the audience to confront it too.

David Lynch and Mark Frost are reinventing the story of *Twin Peaks* for the twenty-first century, just as fairy tales are repurposed to confront contemporary troubles. In *The Return*, the cocreators are presenting a story that is darker and more unconventional than the original series, yet comes closer to the truth in the way that it looks at trauma directly, similar to what Lynch did in *FWWM* but inverting the story of the seeker and the princess by stripping away whatever agency Laura had won by triumphing over BOB. In the end, Cooper/Richard discovers that Laura's trauma did not disappear, but lived on in Carrie Page. Page approaches the literal threshold of Laura Palmer's home when she arrives at the door of the Palmer house and crosses the figurative threshold when she confronts her past as symbolized by the troubled home of Laura Palmer. She is awakened by that confrontation, but this is not Disney's Sleeping Beauty being awakened by a prince. Instead, it is the story of a lost and traumatized woman who is roused by a dark memory when she hears her mother call out her name.

Scholar Jack Zipes argued how subversive fairy tales can disrupt the normative structure and affirmative discourse of the traditional happy ending. Fairy tales are socially symbolic artifacts that "enable us to intercede in civilizing processes that deny the ethical fulfillment of the meaning of humanity. They speak out against passivity and exploitation. They conceive worlds of contestation in which the art of subversion ultimately reveals stunning truths that we try to avoid. . . . They pervade and invade our lives by telling us truths without telling us how to live those truths."[8] David Lynch says he loves the film *The Wizard of Oz*

---

8 Jack, Zipes, *Fairy Tales and the Art of Subversion* (New York: Routledge, 2012), xiii.

because "there's a certain amount of fear in the picture, as well as things to dream about. So, it seems truthful in a way."[9] *The Return*, when considered as a fairy tale in which the fantastical, interdimensional beings of Laura Palmer and Carrie Page confront the very real trauma of their lives, raises the stakes of what happens. While *Twin Peaks* Season 3 includes all sorts of fantastical concepts like interdimensionality and supernatural beings, the fear and trauma is overpoweringly truthful, thus allowing for a radical cultural transformation for the audience that experiences it.

This was my theory about Season 3, which I laid out in much more detail in an academic journal,[10] but I am still grappling with how Laura Palmer fits in. And I am not alone. When I asked the women what they thought of Season 3 and how Laura Palmer/Carrie Page factored into the story, they struggled with their own interpretations as well. The great thing about Season 3, as nonformulaic art, is how it challenges us. In *Catching the Big Fish*, David Lynch says, "I like the saying: 'The world is as you are.' And I think films are as you are. That's why, although the frames of a film are always the same—the same number, in the same sequence, with the same sounds—every screening is different. The difference is sometimes subtle but it's there. It depends on the audience. There is a circle that goes from the audience to the film and back. Each person is looking and thinking and feeling and coming up with his or her own sense of things. And it's probably different from what I fell in love with."[11] Interpretations of *Twin Peaks* depend on each viewer. And the viewer changes as time goes on, and so the interpretation will change. Those of us who watched *Twin Peaks* when it originally aired in 1990 were different people all these years later when we watched Season 3. We have changed. The world has changed.

---

9   Chris Rodley, *Lynch on Lynch* (New York: Farrar, Straus and Giroux, 2005), 194.

10   Courtenay Stallings, "*Twin Peaks: The Return* As Subversive Fairy Tale," *Supernatural Studies* (Winter 2019.): 98-116.

11   David Lynch, *Catching the Big Fish: Meditation, Consciousness, and Creativity* (New York: Penguin, 2007), 21.

Confronting Abuse in the 1990s and Today

Five months after *FWWM* premiered at the Cannes Film Festival in 1992, Sinéad O'Connor stood on stage at Studio 8H in NBC's headquarters at 30 Rockefeller Plaza and, in front of a live studio audience, held up a photo of Pope John Paul II while singing an a capella, altered version of Bob Marley's "War." When she got to the word "evil" in the lyrics, she ripped apart the pope's image, much to the horror of the audience and executive producer Lorne Michaels. O'Connor, still clutching the torn fragments of the pope's face, told the audience to "fight the enemy" before finally tossing the remnants to the ground. O'Connor was calling attention to the childhood abuse that was taking place in the Catholic Church. But no one listened.

Ten years before *The Boston Globe*'s Spotlight team investigated the widespread abuse and cover-up by members of the Catholic Church in 2002, Sinéad O'Connor was shining a light on childhood sexual abuse when few others were. O'Connor said she was inspired by Bob Geldof, an outspoken activist and singer with the Irish rock band The Boomtown Rats who grew up in the same neighborhood as O'Connor. Geldof has said that O'Connor is "a troubled soul, and it ekes pain and an attempt to find an understanding through her voice and through her music. The pain gives rise to a great anger, which may not be understood at all. [People] don't quite understand the intensity or how a personal pain translates into a sort of empathetic rage. The point is, you don't have to. You can just listen to one of her songs."[12]

Much of Sinéad O'Connor's pain comes from childhood abuse. She's recounted how her mother violently beat her and verbally abused her when she was growing up. "What happened to me is a direct result of what happened to my mother and what happened to her in her house and in school,"[13] O'Connor has said. A cycle of familial pain exists in abusive homes. O'Connor wanted to put a stop to it. After her mother died in a car accident in 1985, O'Connor took down the photo of the pope that was on the wall of her mother's home, which had also hung

---

12   Geoff Edgers, "Sinéad O'Connor is still in one piece," *The Washington Post*, March 18, 2020.

13   Tara Murtha, "What She Hasn't Got: An Apology For Sinéad O'Connor," *Refinery29*, Sept. 16, 2018.

there during her childhood. That image of the pope bore witness to O'Connor's abuse. No one protected O'Connor from the violence in her own home—not even the church.

For me, Sinéad O'Connor is forever connected to *FWWM*. Both were misunderstood and reviled in 1992. Both confronted sexual abuse directly. All these years later, after Spotlight and others shed light on systemic childhood abuse, as well as the resurgence of the Me Too movement, people are beginning to understand the significance of speaking out against sexual abuse. They are beginning to listen. In 1992, it was not only revolutionary to do so, but speaking out about the topic could get you booed. It could get you ostracized. It could kill your career.

Sexual harassment survivor and activist Tarana Burke began the Me Too movement on MySpace in 2006 to raise awareness of the pervasiveness of sexual assault against women. The movement experienced a resurgence in 2017 when people began using the Me Too hashtag in relation to the allegations against Miramax cofounder Harvey Weinstein, whom more than eighty women have accused of rape, sexual assault, and sexual abuse. Women from all over began to share their stories to show that sexual abuse happens every single day. The movement went viral when women told their own stories of sexual assault, sexual abuse, and harassment.

In 2016, at the beginning of this project, the resurgence of the Me Too movement hadn't happened yet, but there was something in the zeitgeist suggesting that women were tired of keeping quiet, tired of not being believed, and tired of the abuse. In January 2014, Ronan Farrow, the brother of Dylan Farrow, who had accused her father, Woody Allen, of molesting her as a child, spoke out against Allen and his alleged abuse on Twitter as the famous director was being presented with a lifetime achievement award at the Golden Globes. When Ronan Farrow spoke up, I saw his act as courageous, because he was being an ally to his sister and speaking up on a very public platform. His stance inspired me to tweet a message of support: "As far as I'm concerned, @RonanFarrow is standing up for all sexual abuse survivors tonight. Thank you." Farrow retweeted my support. I received some backlash, but not nearly as much as he, his mother [actress Mia Farrow], and Dylan did.

Less than one month later, Dylan Farrow wrote an open letter in *The New York Times* about her father's alleged abuse. Farrow wrote, "Woody Allen is a living testament to the way our society fails the survivors of sexual assault and abuse. So imagine your seven-year-old daughter being led into an attic by Woody Allen. Imagine she spends a lifetime stricken with nausea at the mention of his name. Imagine a world that celebrates her tormentor."[14] Farrow, in her own words, asked the world to bear witness to her experience. Five years later, Little, Brown and Company published Ronan Farrow's book *Catch and Kill: Lies, Spies, and a Conspiracy to Protect Predators*, in which he tells the story of Harvey Weinstein's years of abuse and cover-ups and Weinstein's conspiracy to silence the women he had abused through legal threats, intimidation, and pressure on NBC executives to squash any negative stories. We need more folks to believe women like Dylan Farrow. We need more male allies like Ronan Farrow. We need more stories about complex women like Laura Palmer. And we desperately need more stories about women who survive.

The Legacy of Laura: Finding Justice for Amie Harwick

When I decided to write *Laura's Ghost*, I had no idea we were about to experience a national awakening to the pervasiveness of abuse against women. Perhaps these conversations will lead to healing, to justice. My fear is that nothing will change. While I was finishing a draft of this book, I learned that Amie Harwick, a member of the *Twin Peaks* fan community, was discovered strangled to death beneath the third-floor window of her home on Valentine's Day. Shortly afterward, her ex-boyfriend was arrested. Her death was ruled a homicide. Harwick was a well-known licensed doctor in psychotherapy and sex therapy living in Los Angeles. Harwick was strikingly beautiful, brilliant, curious, caring, and drawn to darkness, according to her friends.[15] She suffered years of abuse and stalking before the same abuser allegedly murdered her in cold blood. Amie Harwick did not have to die. She did everything

---

14 Dylan Farrow, "An Open Letter to the New York Times," *The New York Times*, Feb. 1, 2014.

15 E.J. Dickson, "Inside the Bright Life of a Murdered Hollywood Sex Therapist," *Rolling Stone*, March 10, 2020.

she could to protect herself from her stalker, including filing multiple restraining orders. But the system failed her. After her death, her friend created the petition Justice 4 Amie, calling on lawmakers to change the laws to require mandatory in-person, long-term counseling for domestic violence perpetrators; provide accommodations so that victims do not have to testify in close proximity to their abusers; and establish a registry to warn others about abusers.

I couldn't finish this book without mentioning Amie. I didn't know her personally, but many in the *Twin Peaks* fan community did. If she were still here, I would ask her what Laura Palmer meant to her. I wonder if Amie saw herself in Laura Palmer. Like Laura's life, Amie's incredible life was cut short. Since I can't speak with Amie, I reached out to one of her good friends, Samantha Weisberg, who is an avid *Twin Peaks* fan and a writer, performer, and professor. I asked Samantha to write about her friend. The following is Weisberg's memory of Amie Harwick's life. She also describes Amie's death based on details from the Los Angeles Police Department records. At the time this essay was written, Amie's ex-boyfriend, Gareth Pursehouse, has pleaded innocent and has not yet gone to trial.

Samantha Weisberg (left) and Amie Harwick (right) together in 2017 at the Twin Peaks Festival. Photo courtesy of Samantha Weisberg

Taken
by Samantha Weisberg

She had to have been an angel or some sort of human simulation sent to Earth from an extraterrestrial dimension to help heal the damaged and spread love to those who felt unworthy and alone. Perhaps she was a bodhisattva, nirmanakaya, Melchizedek, or starseed. I've never known a human to be more compassionate than Amie was.

Amie would invite me to gatherings: tea parties, movie nights, and birthday parties—all of which would include the attendance of smart, interesting, and talented women. She was the only person in the entire universe who could get me up and out of bed to join her on an adventure. Only Amie would get on stage with me during a Jackson Browne performance and sing backup vocals to "Take It Easy." She is also the only other person I've met who would sing Tori Amos and Pantera during the same car ride. She was magical. She connected people. She stood for empowerment and celebrated women. She linked us together.

The first time I met Amie Nicole Harwick was at a birthday party. I ran into her in the kitchen. She introduced herself to me and told me I was beautiful.

On our first lady date, we met at a coffee shop. One major thing we had in common was our obsession with *Twin Peaks*. She gushed to me about her crush on Audrey Horne and how Coop was hot and nerdy. We both agreed that BOB was the greatest villain of all time. We related to Laura's secrets. We connected over abandonment issues and emotional dysregulation. We bonded over emotionally unavailable ex-boyfriends while sipping peppermint tea. We congratulated each other over both having gone to grad school and being single, independent women living in LA. I graded papers at the coffee table while she edited videos for her psychotherapy YouTube channel. Amie had her master's in clinical psychology from Pepperdine University and a PhD from the Institute for the Advanced Study of Human Sexuality. It is quite rare to find a stunning woman who is also, more importantly, incredibly intelligent . . . but there she was, sitting across from me.

On more serious nights, topics of the past would come up: ex-boyfriends, restraining orders, domestic abuse, stalkers. We ventured down dark paths and shared extremely personal information with each other. She had had multiple stalkers and was constantly in fear of running into them. We had both been in our fair share of abusive relationships. We were able to comfort one another and figure out ways for us both to never exist in that place again. One night, she told me about an altercation with an ex, Gareth. He had pushed her out of a moving vehicle onto the side of a freeway and left her stranded. This man had choked, punched, kicked, and slammed her into the ground. She had requested two restraining orders in 2011 and in 2012. She filed orders requesting he enter a fifty-two-week batterer program. In 2012, he smashed ten picture frames on her front door and then, the following day, placed roses on her porch and played music outside of her apartment. The second restraining order expired in April 2015.

I remember asking her if there was anything she could do in the present moment about the situation. She said she had already done everything she could.

One day I received a text from her.

"Can you talk? I can't text. It's serious. Can you call me?"

I called. She explained to me that she had just been to an event and something very bad had happened. She was attending the XBIZ adult entertainment industry award ceremony. While she was on the red carpet, her stalker ex-boyfriend, Gareth Pursehouse, saw her and ran up to her. He began yelling and exclaiming that she had ruined his life. He dropped down to his knees and started shaking. Amie automatically went into "therapist mode." She did not want to create a scene, so she asked Gareth to speak outside with her. She tried to calm him down. He had been hired to take photos, but as soon as he saw her, he lost control. He began reciting text messages they had sent back and forth in 2011. Amie was professional and used her methods to regulate Gareth's emotions. She told him that everything they had gone through was in the past and that they were both living very different lives now. As he lay at her feet in a fetal position, she tried to help him stay grounded by doing what she thought was right. They parted ways, but later that night she received a text from him. He wanted to see her again, but she told him that wouldn't be possible and blocked his number.

In the days after the incident, Amie installed a better camera system and beefed up security around her house. The topic of Gareth slowly faded away, and we eventually stopped talking about it as much. I know she was still terrified, but she felt that there was nothing more that she could do. She knew the police wouldn't help.

Time had passed and about a month later my boyfriend and I had just finished up a day of mining for gems in Pala, California. I didn't have service, but I noticed a missed voice mail. It was from Robert Coshland, another one of Amie's best friends. Why would he call and not text me? Why would he leave a voice mail? I was worried and tried to calm myself down. We left the mine. As soon as I had service, I called Robert back.

"Hi"

"Hi, Sam. Where are you right now?"

"I'm in the mountains in Pala. Why? What's going on?"

"I'm about to tell you some very upsetting news"

I told my boyfriend to pull over, and I started shaking.

"OK . . . I'm ready."

"Amie was murdered last night."

I reached for the door handle and fell out of the car. I crawled to a patch of dirt and wildflowers on the side of the road and screamed.

I don't remember a lot after those moments. I do remember dry heaving. I remember begging Robert to tell me it wasn't real. I remember wailing.

"Is it him? Is it that guy?"

"I am almost 100 percent positive that it is him."

I later found out that sometime during the day Gareth Pursehouse had broken into Amie Harwick's home. He had entered through the French doors of her living room by breaking the glass pane and opening the door from the outside in. He then proceeded to walk up the stairs, enter her bedroom, and quietly wait for her arrival. Hours went by. Around 1 a.m., Amie returned from her Valentine girls-night-out event. She parked her car in her garage and came in through the front gate. She unlocked the front door and walked into her house. She came up the stairs and headed into her bedroom. There was something else in the room with her—someone was sitting on her bed. She dropped her things and raced out of her bedroom, but the six-foot-four man grabbed her. The beads from her rosary fell to the floor. She fought for her life. She tried everything she could to defend herself, but he was too strong. Somehow, for a moment, she was able to break free. She ran to her balcony, threw open the door, and screamed for help. His giant hands came up from behind her, and they closed in around her throat. Still, she persisted. With clenched and bleeding fists, she punched and scratched for her life. He strangled her so tightly he crushed her strap muscle. Then, when she was unconscious, he tossed her over the balcony.

When the fire department found her, they brought her to Cedars-Sinai Medical Center. She was still unconscious when the surgeon went in to mend her internal wounds. She had sustained severe injuries of her brain, liver, and pelvis.

Amie Nicole Harwick died on February 15 at 3:26 a.m. of blunt force injuries to the head and torso. The manner of death was homicide.

I have lost people in my life, but never someone like Amie.

Her funeral took place in her hometown of Lancaster, Pennsylvania. It was an open casket, and I was grateful to see her one last time. I waited in line to view her while Tori Amos's "Cornflake Girl" played over the funeral home's speakers. She was buried in her favorite A-line midi dress with a Peter Pan collar. She was wearing her favorite silver sparkling heels. Her signature shade of red was painted across her lips. I told her that I loved her and that she looked really beautiful.

Could this have been prevented? I firmly believe it could have. Laws on restraining orders need improvement. In order for the restraining order to be effective, a safety plan needs to be put into place for the victim. Amie should have been able to contact the police after her altercation with Gareth at the award ceremony. Even though her restraining order had expired, she shouldn't have had to go back to the courthouse and begin the entire process over again. The police should have been able to protect her. If Gareth had been monitored and watched, this could have been prevented.

I want justice for Amie. I want justice for every person who has experienced living in fear of the past—terrified that one day, the monster will come back. He came back for Amie and no one could save her. My hope is that Amie Nicole Harwick's story will change the world.

I have a recurring dream of being at her house the night he killed her. In this dream, he still breaks the glass pane and comes in through the French doors in her living room. He still creeps up the stairs and climbs into her bed. Yet instead of him attacking her when she tries to run away—instead of him strangling her unconscious—I appear behind him and free her from his grasp. Both of us, together, attack this vile monster. I crash the vanity mirror over his head. Amie sprays him with aerosol hairspray and I set him on fire. This time, it is him falling over the balcony to his well-deserved death.

Amie and I embrace, and then I help her down the stairs. We are vigilant and triumphant. Goddesses praise us as they watch from above: The Morrigan, Kali, Athena, Hecate.

I wake drenched in sweat, with clenched, bleeding fists.

I wake up and she is still taken.

Victims of abuse in the United States can call the The National Domestic Violence Hotline at 1-800-799-7233 to access safety from their abusive relationships. #JusticeForAmie

---

This book is a ghost story. The trauma of the dead haunts the living.

But this book is also a story of hope.

Readers bear witness to the powerful impact Laura Palmer has had on women. Readers bear witness to how difficult it is to navigate the world as a woman. Readers bear witness to women's complexity, intelligence, creativity, and beauty. My ultimate hope is readers can bear witness to women and lift them up and believe them when they speak.

Photo by Scott Ryan

Epilogue:
Laura's Ghost and Me

"When I call out
No one can hear me
When I whisper, he thinks the message
Is for him only.
My little voice inside my throat
I always think there must be something
That I've done
Or something I can do
But no one no one comes to help,
He says
A little girl like you." [1]

---

1   Jennifer Lynch, *The Secret Diary of Laura Palmer* (New York: Gallery Books: 1990), 12

When you've survived trauma, you encounter ghosts everywhere. Some are benevolent. Some are not. I search for the benevolent ones. When I attended the Twin Peaks Festival in Snoqualmie, Washington, in 2017, I encountered a kind of ghost. The moment seemed sacred, private, my own. It seemed so profound I could not put it into words. It seemed intimately connected to this project, my book about Laura's ghost.

During a tour of the filming locations, our tour bus stopped briefly at a crossroad near Mount Si. I looked outside my window and saw, in the middle of a verdant pasture, a group of seemingly solemn horses gathered in a circle around another horse, which was lying prostrate, dying on the soft soil. We happened upon something so intimate—horses gathering and grieving over one of their own. The odd thing was, no one on the bus seemed to notice the funeral wake happening before our very eyes. But I did. I turned toward the horses and bore witness to their grief. Their grief became my own, and mine theirs. The white horse that lay prostrate was not the pale horse looming over Sarah Palmer. This was no portent of a violent death. This was a communal mourning. We took stock. We witnessed. We acknowledged.

Twin Peaks is such a cosmic story in and of itself, but the cosmic implications extend beyond those boundaries. Perhaps that's why so many of us recognize it as a spiritual story. The horses called to mind how horses play a role in *Twin Peaks*: Laura's pony in *The Secret Diary of Laura Palmer*, the white horse in Sarah Palmer's vision before violence occurs, the whinny we hear at the end of Part 8 when the Woodsman journeys into darkness, and Carrie Page's horseshoe necklace and the horse figurine sitting above her fireplace. Somehow all of these things are connected. I'm still trying to figure it all out. Maybe horses represent death like the pale rider in the Bible's Book of Revelation. But maybe they represent freedom—a way for little girls to escape.

Twin Peaks is a spiritual story, and for me it is the story of Laura Palmer. In the summer of 2016, I decided to write a book about the legacy of Laura Palmer in which women explore her ghost and the way she haunts us. There's this quote I love by Robert Moss. He wrote, "Australian Aborigines say that the big stories—the stories worth telling and retelling, the ones in which you may find the meaning of your life—

are forever stalking the right teller, sniffing and tracking like predators hunting their prey in the bush."[2] This book project has been stalking me for some time.

At the 2013 University of Southern California *Twin Peaks* retrospective, someone asked Mark Frost how he and David Lynch balanced the comedic with the serious in *Twin Peaks*. Frost quoted Joseph Campbell: "You have to embrace the joyful sorrows of life or else it will crush you."[3] This is why *Twin Peaks* resonates with fans. It embraces the joyful sorrows of life. At its core *Twin Peaks* is about a young woman full of life and possibilities whose life is cut short. She's a victim of abuse and murdered in her prime. But she never allows the devil in. Even in the end she resists BOB. Laura Palmer is a heroine. I came up with *Laura's Ghost* as an image and as an idea of how Laura Palmer both haunts and inspires women. Personally, when I saw Laura Palmer I saw myself. I wasn't the homecoming queen, but I knew how to wear a mask and keep a secret. And even though Laura never allowed BOB inside, she was damaged. Laura Palmer's story is the story of many women. It's mine, too.

I am a survivor of childhood sexual abuse. This is the first time I've talked about it in print. Most of my friends and family do not know. It's not as if I never told anyone. I told someone when I was five years old, and I was told to be quiet. I told someone when I was a teenager, and the reaction was, "That didn't happen." So I stopped telling. Until one day, many years ago, I couldn't take it anymore. I called the sheriff's station in the town where I grew up. They said the statute of limitations was up, but I went on record anyway, in case anyone else made a report. It was one of the most difficult things I have ever done, but I'm glad I did it. I did it to protect little girls. I did it to protect the little girl in me because no one else would.

Before *Twin Peaks*, people rarely explored childhood sexual abuse or incest in film and television. In 1984, there was a television film titled

---

2   Robert Moss, *Dreamgates: An Explorer's Guide to the Worlds of Soul, Imagination, and Life Beyond Death* (New York: Three Rivers Press, 1998), 144.

3   Courtenay Stallings, "USC Twin Peaks Retrospective, Jan. 27," *Red Room Podcast*, Jan. 27, 2013.

There's Something about Amelia that confronted it head-on. I'll give the show credit for addressing the topic of sexual abuse, but what the show failed to do was put the focus on the victim. Instead, it humanized the father, the abuser. In the end, the father stays married, and rather than go to prison he attends group counseling . . . with his wife by his side. There's no justice. There's no long-term protection for Amelia or any other little girls.

When *Fire Walk With Me* premiered in 1992, I witnessed the horror of what Laura Palmer's character endures, and I saw my own horror in her story. I needed to see this abuse as evil because it was. It is. When I saw Laura's story, I knew that I wasn't alone. David Lynch, Mark Frost, Jennifer Lynch, Bob Engels, Harley Peyton, Sheryl Lee, and the other storytellers gave me this gift: the gift of Laura Palmer and her story. Laura will always haunt me. She and I are intimately connected through our shared story of trauma and survival and hope. And now, especially after this book, I know that I am not alone.

RESOURCES FOR SURVIVORS

The author is donating 10% of all proceeds she personally receives to The Rape, Abuse & Incest National Network, an organization dedicated to supporting survivors. For more resources for sexual abuse and domestic violence survivors, please visit the following organizations' websites.

The Rape, Abuse & Incest National Network
www.rainn.org
Get help: (800) 656-HOPE (4673)

National Domestic Violence Hotline
www.thehotline.org
Get help: (800) 799-7233

ACKNOWLEDGMENTS

There would be no *Laura's Ghost* or Laura Palmer if David Lynch and Mark Frost did not get together in a Los Angeles diner in the 1980s and, over coffee and cherry pie, discuss creating a story that takes place in the Northwest in which a small town discovers a dead beloved homecoming queen. Thank you to Mark Frost and David Lynch for creating this iconic character who means so much to so many of us. And thank you to Jennifer Lynch, Robert Engels, Harley Peyton, and the other writers who contributed to her story.

David Lynch and Mark Frost created the character of Laura Palmer, but it was Sheryl Lee and Jennifer Lynch who breathed life into her. I cannot imagine this book without their voices in it.

Thank you, Sheryl Lee, for supporting this book when I approached you in 2016 with the concept. You have been more than gracious with your time and support. Thank you for returning again and again to explore a character who was not easy to perform, to personify, to relive. Thank you for contributing to the foreword to this book. Thank you for allowing your poems to be printed inside. You are not Laura Palmer, but you must be haunted by her ghost. She won't leave you alone and neither will we. Thank you for everything.

Jennifer Lynch provided Laura Palmer with a backstory in *The Secret Diary of Laura Palmer*, and I am grateful to her for making time in the middle of a pandemic to speak with me. Lynch is fearless and vulnerable and incredibly intelligent, just like Laura Palmer.

Grace Zabriskie invited me into her home, and I spent more than five hours with her while she answered questions about *Twin Peaks* and showed me her incredible art, even taking me into her woodshop so I could see where and how she creates her pieces. When I interviewed Zabriskie, she was still grieving over the loss of her daughter, the painter Marion Lane. I am forever grateful to Grace for sharing her home and her thoughts with me while grief still resided in both.

Sabrina S. Sutherland has been nothing but gracious and available to me throughout this process. Thank you, Sabrina, for meeting me at coffee shops in Santa Monica to talk about *Twin Peaks* over tea and cappuccino and, even more importantly, to speak about yourself and your incredible career as a female producer in Hollywood.

It took a village to write this book, and this book would not be possible without women speaking to me, opening up their hearts and minds. Thank you to all of the women who participated in this book. Thank you for being candid, vulnerable, and sharing your stories. There are so many additional women I wanted to interview, but I had to cut myself off or else this book would be more than a thousand pages. Thank you, Willow Catelyn Maclay, for sharing your personal and powerful story in this book. A special thank you to Samantha Weisberg, who wrote a thoughtful and lovely tribute to her friend Amie Harwick, who was struck down way too soon and whom we will never forget. I'm thankful Amie's name and story are immortalized in this book.

Laura's Ghost is about giving voice to women, but it's not just a book for women. It's for everyone, regardless of their gender, including men. Thank you to the men in my personal and professional life who have supported me and this book, especially Bob Canode, Scott Ryan, David Bushman, John Thorne, Brad Dukes, Pieter Dom, Andreas Halskov, Ivan Butka, Mark O'Brien, Matt Marrone, Ben Durant, Bryon Kozaczka, Joshua B. Minton, Rob E. King, Andrew Grevas, Aaron Cohen, Thor Åmli, Brad Payne, Karl Reinsch, Vinnie Guidera, Blake Morrow, Bryant A. Loney, Bob Rich, Ross Dudle, Eric Sillanpää, and David Lee Morgan, Jr.

A special thank you to Bryant A. Loney, a talented writer and copy editor, who was a tremendous help and support in bringing this book together.

Thank you to Natalie Rulon, a former student, who designed the incredible front and back covers. Thank you to Jill Watson for contributing her ethereal art to the back cover. Thank you to Amy Zielinski for taking the author's photo that appears on the back cover. The photo was taken beneath a pine tree in Franklin Canyon Park, the site of many *Twin Peaks* locations and my favorite place in all of Los Angeles.

An extra special thank you to my editors and publishers, Scott Ryan and David Bushman of Fayetteville Mafia Press, who saw the value in telling these stories. I am grateful to you for your guidance, your editorial advice, and for publishing this book.

When I decided to write *Laura's Ghost*, the first three people I told were Bob Canode, Scott Ryan, and Dr. Elizabeth Smith. These three individuals have supported my writing more than anyone else in my life.

Dr. Elizabeth Smith is my colleague, my mentor, and my friend. She graciously served as an editor of this book. I was grateful for her support from day one. I am even more grateful for her editorial advice. In a book that emphasizes the importance of women speaking, it was vital to have an editor who was a woman.

Scott Ryan, the copublisher of this book, has supported my writing for many years on multiple platforms, including *The Red Room Podcast* and *The Blue Rose* magazine. Thank you, Scott, for your support and for bringing me along on your many endeavors all these years.

The very first person I shared my idea for *Laura's Ghost* with was my husband, Bob Canode. Bob is my rock, my best friend, and my biggest supporter. He knows the struggle of being a writer because he is one himself. I'm thankful for his editorial advice, his honesty, and his unwavering support. In a world filled with BOBs, he is an Agent Cooper.

Lastly, this book is dedicated to Laura Palmer, Sheryl Lee, and women everywhere. It is the women who have survived to tell their own stories who gave me the strength to write this book. Thank you to all survivors, but especially Dylan Farrow and Roxane Gay. Thank you, Dylan Farrow, for your bravery in speaking up about your childhood abuse. Thank you,

Dr. Roxane Gay, my favorite writer, for inspiring me and for sharing your personal story of survival. I participated in one of Gay's workshops on trauma, which helped me hone a small piece of this book. Roxane Gay is a survivor and an inspiration. In Gay's book *Hunger*, she talks about not wanting to diminish the gravity of what happened to her. We can move on without being perfect. We can move forward without pretending we are unscarred. Amen.

BIBLIOGRAPHY

Anderson, Hephzibah. "The Secret Meaning of Ghost Stories." BBC. Jan. 22, 2016.

Babbel, Susanne. "Trauma: Incest." *Psychology Today.* Feb. 7, 2013.

Bushman, David and Mark Givens. "Hazel Drew: The Original Blue Rose Case." *The Blue Rose*, June 2017.

Canby, Vincent. "Review/Film: One Last Gasp for Laura Palmer." *New York Times.* Aug. 29, 1992.

Czerwinski, Mary. *Elements of Change: A Collection of Poems.* Scotts Valley: CreateSpace, 2015.

Davenport, Randi. "The Knowing Spectator of 'Twin Peaks': Culture, Feminism, and Family Violence." *Literature/Film Quarterly*, Vol. 21, no 4 (1993): 255-259.

Dickson, E.J. "Inside the Bright Life of a Murdered Hollywood Sex Therapist." *Rolling Stone*. March 10, 2020.

Dom, Pieter. "A Page from Sheryl Lee's Diary and Her Poem for Laura Palmer." Welcome to Twin Peaks. Jan. 24, 2013.

Edgers, Geoff. "Sinéad O'Connor Is Still in One Piece." *The Washington Post.* March 18, 2020.

Farrow, Dylan. "An Open Letter to the New York Times." *The New York Times.* Feb. 1, 2014.

Hallam, Lindsay. *Twin Peaks: Fire Walk With Me (Devil's Advocates)*. London: Auteur, 2018.

Kreider, Tim. "But Who Is the Dreamer? *Twin Peaks: The Return.*" http://politicsslashletters.org/dreamer-twin-peaks-return/. Accessed Oct. 28, 2018.

Lynch, David. *Catching the Big Fish: Meditation, Consciousness, and Creativity.* New York: Penguin, 2007.

Lynch, David. The Log Lady intros. "Pilot." *Twin Peaks*. Written and directed by David Lynch. April 8, 1990.

Lynch, David. "The Unified Field." The Pennsylvania Academia of the Fine Arts, Sept. 13, 2014.

Lynch, David and Kristine McKenna. *Room to Dream*. New York: Random House, 2018.

Lynch, David and Mark Frost. "Part 1." *Twin Peaks: The Return*. Directed by David Lynch. Written by Mark Frost and David Lynch. May 21, 2017.

Lynch, Jennifer. *The Secret Diary of Laura Palmer*. New York: Gallery Books: 1990.

McBriar, Mya. "Laura Walked with Me." *Twin Peaks Fanatic*. May 10, 2016.

Moss, Robert. *Dreamgates: An Explorer's Guide to the Worlds of Soul, Imagination, and Life Beyond Death*. New York: Three Rivers Press, 1998.

Murtha, Tara. "What She Hasn't Got: An Apology for Sinéad O'Connor." *Refinery29*. Sept. 16, 2018.

Nochimson, Martha. *David Lynch Swerves: Uncertainty from Lost Highway to Inland Empire*. Austin: The University of Texas Press, 2013.

Nochimson, Martha. "David Lynch: Twin Peaks." *Television Rewired: The Rise of the Auteur Series*. Austin: University of Texas Press, 2019.

Nochimson, Martha. *The Passion of David Lynch: Wild at Heart in Hollywood*. Austin: The University of Texas Press, 2007.

Nordini, Gina. *Haunted by History: Interpreting Traumatic Memory through Ghosts in Film and Literature*. Denver: Regis University Theses, Spring 2016.

The Pogues. "Haunted." Track #2 on *Sid & Nancy: Love Kills* (Motion Picture Soundtrack). 1986. Vinyl and Cassette.

Rape, Abuse & Incest National Network. www.rainn.og.

Reynolds, Melissa. "Donna Hayward." *The Blue Rose* "The Women of Lynch," August 2018.

Rodley, Chris. *Lynch on Lynch*. London: Faber and Faber, 2005.

Stallings, Courtenay. "*Twin Peaks: The Return* as Subversive Fairy Tale" *Supernatural Studies* (Winter 2019): 98-116.

Stallings, Courtenay. "USC *Twin Peaks* Series Retrospective, Jan. 27." *Red Room Podcast*. Jan. 27, 2013.

Stallings, Courtenay. "USC *Twin Peaks* Series Retrospective, May 5." *Red Room Podcast*. May 7, 2013.

Stewart, Laura. "Lula Fortune." *The Blue Rose* "The Women of Lynch," August 2018.

Thorne, John. *The Essential Wrapped in Plastic: Pathways to Twin Peaks*. Dallas: John Thorne, 2016.

Zipes, Jack. *Fairy Tales and the Art of Subversion*. New York: Routledge, 2012.

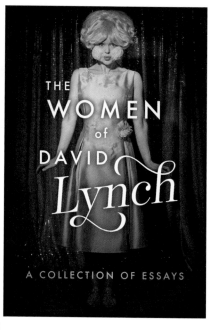

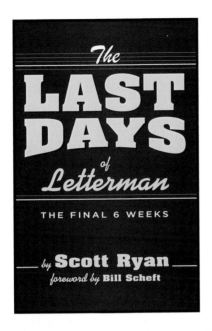

Read an inside look at the final six weeks of *Late Show with David Letterman,* all told through the words of the staff that wrote, directed, and produced those iconic last twenty-eight episodes in 2015. *The Last Days of Letterman* by Scott Ryan

ISBN: 9781949024005

Mark Frost cocreated *Twin Peaks,* wrote for *Hill Street Blues,* and has written over ten books. Learn about his life, his craft, and his career in this new book by David Bushman.

ISBN: 9781949024104

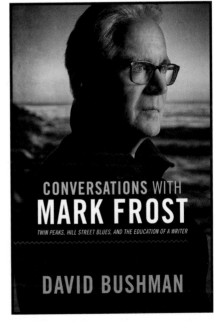

Ken Fortenberry solves one of the greatest real-life mysteries in aviation history as he searches for the killer of his father and the cause of the crash of Flight 7.

ISBN: 9781949024067

Scarlett Harris takes a deep dive into the world of female wrestling and some of the greatest characters in all of sports. This book will be released in February 2021.

ISBN: 9781949024180

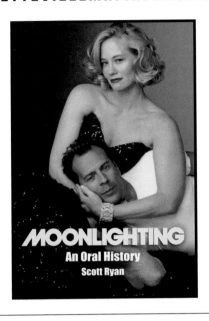